MW00440022

Out of the Shadows

Out of the Shadows

My Life Inside the Wild World of Hunter Biden

LUNDEN ROBERTS

with Josh Manning and Erin Brownback

Skyhorse Publishing

Skyhorse Publishing books may be purchased in bulk at special discounts for sales promotion, corporate gifts, fund-raising, or educational purposes. Special editions can also be created to specifications. For details, contact the Special Sales Department, Skyhorse Publishing, 307 West 36th Street, 11th Floor, New York, NY 10018 or info@skyhorsepublishing.com.

Skyhorse® and Skyhorse Publishing® are registered trademarks of Skyhorse Publishing, Inc.®, a Delaware corporation.

Visit our website at www.skyhorsepublishing.com.

Please follow our publisher Tony Lyons on Instagram @tonylyonsisuncertain.

10 9 8 7 6 5 4 3 2 1

Library of Congress Control Number: 2024940265

Cover design by David Ter-Avanesyan
Cover image courtesy of the author

Print ISBN: 978-1-5107-8229-7
Ebook ISBN: 978-1-5107-8231-0

Printed in the United States of America

To Navy Joan,

Your potential is endless, and I am beyond blessed to be your mama. If darkness ever creeps into your life, know that you will never be alone, for I will always be in your corner. Never forget you come from a place of love.

Your father and I have faced our own dark times and have climbed mountains to overcome them.

Fearless already runs through your blood. Now do it justice.
—Nikita Gill

Contents

Author's Note

For every story, there's the truth, and then there's what the media tells you. Since my daughter was born, this is the story that everyone has been asking for, as I experienced it, in my own words. I make no claim that this is the whole truth. This is the truth as I witnessed it, through my eyes. Many of the names are changed, because I respect people's privacy, and I know what it's like to have stories told about me. This is the story of my sweetly raw, sometimes passionate, sometimes chaotic relationship with Hunter Biden and how it gave me the greatest love of my life—Navy Joan.

Prologue

I read somewhere that people have these "before and after" dates etched into their memory. Dates they'll never forget and times that changed them into who they are now. I seem to have several of those dates, but one in particular seems to have impacted my life more than any other.

My life *before* Hunter Biden was that of any other young, wild, and free woman in her 20's. Living day by day, emotionally detached, making many impulsive decisions that should've been based on deliberate thought, but with no worries and lots of carelessness, I survived with plenty of crazy stories to tell. Emotional intelligence was something I lacked. As I was writing this book, I realized how unaware I'd always been of my feelings, and the process of writing allowed me to find the place in time where I was able to connect to them.

If I could speak to the Lunden from *before*, I would tell myself just how dumb and naïve I was. In fact, I'm probably lucky to be alive today, in spite of lacking the sense of concern.

I was an adrenaline junkie, solely thinking of myself and what adventure awaited me, never taking the time to debate the consequences. The small-town girl from rural Arkansas, known for being my father's daughter and a star basketball player, that's who I was. Drama never found me, but turmoil might occasionally.

My dad used to tell me I could "shit in a swinging bucket." Sometimes I found myself in the right place at the right time, like the first time I went turkey hunting and killed two turkeys with one shot. But my parents always feared I'd find myself in the opposite place.

Sometimes the situations I wind up in aren't as luck would have it, but chaos would. For example, when college basketball coaches showed interest in me in High School, my counselor had to call me in to inform me I had two social security numbers. I had somehow gotten more than one identity when I was born. I should have used one for the Lunden I was, and the other for the Lunden I'd become.

I was known as a local stellar basketball player who spent every high school night at the gym, making enough shots to become the next Kobe Bryant, while my friends went out and partied. It showed on the court. People would come from all over to watch me play, and games where I didn't score 20 points or more, my teammates and coaches would feel bad for me, knowing I had to ride home with my mother. I was her studhorse, working hard to please her, but the bear of disapproval was always on my hindquarters. She didn't tolerate anything less than my best and sometimes that could be hard. That woman always had the highest expectations for me.

I ended my basketball journey at the Division One level. It had been my dream growing up to take my talents to the top, like most athletes. But I wanted more. I felt my life was destined for something else. Only fools are satisfied, right?

Basketball may have been my first love, and I dedicated my entire childhood to it. I was never one for having boyfriends or catching feelings. In fact, a basketball would lie next to my pillow every night. I was too scared to be burned like cornbread in a skillet like most girls, but after a trip to Washington, D.C., in junior high, I soon found my second love.

From the moment I arrived, I knew I wanted to live on the east coast. A connection formed in just a few short minutes and I can remember not wanting to leave after the few days spent there. The history, the architecture, and the momentum; I was in love. It never occurred to me that someday I would live there, nor could I imagine the chaos that would follow. It was just a dream anyway.

After graduating from Arkansas State, I began working for my dad. He has created an empire in customizing guns and is world renowned for his talents in the hunting industry. He's been on several TV shows, but it's hard to be star struck by anyone when most of my dad's friends are country music stars.

Working in the office with my dad's right hand, my aunt, I became fascinated with crime shows. We would sit in the office and believe we had the crimes solved before any evidence had been taken in. Soon, I could see myself working on a case and in a big city. After falling in love with Ted Bundy while watching an interview, I knew I was a magnet for red flags.

Criminology and psychology were my two minors at Arkansas State, but my interest grew stronger. When an ad popped up on my computer one day for a CSI school located in Washington, D.C., I applied immediately. I also flew out to meet the director of the program just to assure a better chance of my acceptance. I was accepted and off to D.C., another impulsive decision that most people might take years planning for.

Soon, I was back in the city I had fantasized about living in, learning to do what I loved. This was my dream, but I never knew that dream would turn into something I could've never imagined.

A thousand miles from home, I was able to create a whole new persona. Out from under the demands of basketball, my parents, and anyone who knew me, I found myself free to reinvent who I was, who I wanted to be. Each moment felt like it was the only one that would ever matter, and I lived for each second.

And then there was the *after* Hunter Biden, the night I was invited to a place called Rosemont Seneca.

Hunter once told me that an idle mind was the devil's workshop, but when you're in a big city with so much to get into, I could see the devil setting up shop there, too.

Chapter 1

First Hit of Hunter

Every woman has that man she wants to save; for me it was Hunter Biden.

The chill November breeze hits me as I walk into the 7-Eleven in Dupont Circle, my favorite part of D.C., with its lively dining and nightlife. It's getting colder each day. The homeless people outside know me by name. I've shared my taquitos a time or two. It follows me, wherever I go—this feeling of needing to do more.

My friends joke that I'm sort of dead inside. I wouldn't totally agree. I have feelings, and when I love, I love hard. But I'm awkward in the way I show it. Avoiding feelings is my go-to. But one feeling that's impossible for me to ignore is empathy. Remember when the Grinch's heart grew three sizes? That's me when I see suffering. I transform from awkwardly dead inside, into someone who can't keep the concern stuffed inside. On cold days in the city, I've purchased more blankets at CVS to give to people on the streets than I keep in my own home. I've always believed that if you do enough good, good will come back to you.

So tonight I'm handing out a couple of hot dogs and socializing with friends while I drink my Gatorade—trying to rid myself of the lingering vodka tonic breath. My Uber is four minutes away. My phone buzzes, but it isn't Uber. It's my friend Kelsey, surprised and glad that I'm still out in the city. Assuming she needs a place to crash, I ask her what's up. She's been invited to a small after-party, and hopes I'll be her wingman. I am anything but tired, and she knows which 7-Eleven to come to. It's our clique's late stop after most nights out. I cancel my Uber.

D.C. is insane. Connections, parties, powerful people, lots of drinking, drugs, did I mention partying? It's nothing like my upbringing, and one could get lost in the sauce. I am marinating in the sauce.

As I slide into Kelsey's dark gray Chevy Malibu, I quiz her with the usual questions. "Where are we going? Who are these people? Is this a good idea?" The answer to the last question is always a no, but we laugh, because no matter how bad our ideas are, we manage to somehow survive them. Which makes for good stories. All I get is that we're going to some embassy penthouse on the waterfront, and some guy with the last name Biden who's apparently kind of important will be there.

A few minutes later we park our car off K Street and walk to a simple, cubical building of glass, lit up elegantly at night, and sitting on a deep green lawn that separates it from the waterfront. Large sculpted letters peek out at me from behind enormous plate glass windows, spelling out the words HOUSE OF SWEDEN. Strangely they make the place seem approachable, but apparently that is the last thing it's supposed to be. In that moment, I realize I've seen this embassy during summer lunches on the waterfront and day parties with friends on the yachts docked alongside the wooden walkways. The waterfront was always my favorite place to hang out during the summer months.

Kelsey pulls me to a dim parking lot on the side of the building where we get a key fob out of the glove box of an unlocked black Chevrolet truck with the entire side dented in. Things are getting pretty sketchy.

"Hold the door," she whispers as I stand in the light of the security camera on the back side of the building, and she zips the fob back to the truck and closes the door. And we're in. We have just officially invaded Sweden.

We walk up the long staircase to the penthouse, because apparently we're supposed to avoid the elevator, and I'm thankful that the vodka tonics are still keeping my anxiety from skyrocketing as I wonder what we've gotten ourselves into. Finally, we hit the landing on the fifth floor. I catch my breath, straighten my dress, and we make our entrance.

It's definitely more of a grown-up after-party, not the loud, college parties I've been to so recently. It's more mellow, with quiet music in the background. Familiar music. Could it be my home state native, Johnny Cash? I like this place, and someone here has great taste.

A large glass room with a long conference table is wrapped by a balcony and the most beautiful views of the city I've seen thus far. A yellow velour couch under the bar separates the conference room from the kitchen, with a sign above reading "Rosemont Seneca." Noted. Thank God for iPhones. I google the name and find we are at some high-end management firm. Consider us marked safe.

For once, I'm thankful Kelsey needs a smoke break. I've never been one to grab one of those cowboy killers. The smell gives me a headache, but I am not going to miss out on a chance to see this view. So I follow her out on the balcony. It's chilly, but that just adds to the moment. My breath hangs in the air, shimmering from the soft lighting. Kelsey is engaged in conversation with someone, but I can't stop admiring the view. Looking south I see the infamous Watergate building and the iconic Kennedy Center glowing off the Potomac River. I'm definitely not in Arkansas anymore. But this place is it. The elite. The top of the top.

I wander down the hall looking for the bathroom. Maybe five people are inside the apartment, counting me. They're low key, sitting on the couch, having a drink, doing a few casual drugs. No big deal. It's D.C. I pass an office that somebody nearby says belongs to John Kerry's son.

In the bathroom at the end of the hallway, the heated towel rack has my full attention until something else catches my eye. Across the hall is a half-open doorway leading to a smaller back office that is less inviting lit solely by a desk lamp.

"Fuck," I hear from the other side of the doorway.

I creep in, pushing the door open a little further to see a man sitting in an office chair leaning over a small desk, meticulously organizing a series of small glass tubes and copper strands. He looks determined. He isn't wearing after-party clothes like everyone else; instead he's sitting there in brightly colored boxer briefs with parrots all over them. I'm intrigued. He turns in his chair and catches me in his stare, his gaze intense with furrowed brows and the most beautiful blue-gray eyes I have ever seen. Then a quick and genuine, "Hey."

William Shakespeare claimed, "The eyes are the window to the soul." I understand those words more in this moment than ever before. In his eyes I see sincerity, kindness, love, and lots of hurt. I know he is more than meets the eye. He is complex, but how? He has my full attention.

I introduce myself, and his eyes never leave me. He sets down a smoky glass tube, slowly stands from his chair and greets me with a hug. I'm shocked. I wasn't aware city men even knew how to hug. I thought that was a southern thing.

When I get a closer look, I'm even more shocked by the paraphernalia on the desk. I try to act like I'm not fazed, but my eyes keep bouncing back down to stare at it without my control. His name is still ringing in my ears, "Hunter Biden." So this is the guy of some importance everyone seems to know. He acts so . . . humble.

I sink into an expensive leather chair with bronze nail head details, and he wants to know where I'm from, why I am in D.C., why did I want a degree in CSI, what my family is like, what my plans are. When he finds out I am an Arkansas native, he goes to a bookshelf in the front room and comes back with a signed picture of Johnny Cash, addressed to him.

So he's the one with the good taste in music. I never would have thought it. If he isn't asking me questions, he's making witty comments about my answers, mocking my southern accent which has a way of making us both laugh out loud, or just nodding as if he knows something about what I'm talking about but would rather listen to me than have to talk about himself. He definitely does not want the spotlight on him, and this draws me in even more.

In the first five minutes he has learned my entire life story, and the only thing I know about him is that he is suffering. I can tell he's brilliant, and he has a demon on his back. Other people pop into the bathroom for a quick fix, but Hunter's demons keep him in this dark back room so they can have him any time. I feel his pain.

I look down at the fancy chair I'm sitting in and see a small plaque label on the arm reading "Senator Barack Obama 2005–2008." This is typical D.C., even the furniture brags about its connections.

"Umm, this is President Obama's seat," I say with slow realization.

"Uh, yeah, that's his chair from the time he served in the U.S. Senate," he says, as if it's no big deal.

The wheels are turning in my head. "Wait, so you have Obama's senate chair, and your last name is Biden." Boom. "Are you kin to Joe Biden . . . like Vice President Joe Biden?" I'm looking now to see what his face can tell me. It's a slow grin, a proud acknowledgment that I could tell he had made more than a few times before. "Yes, he's my dad."

I feel like I'm in one of those videos where the narration begins with, "You're probably wondering how I got here." Back to the iPhone, I have to google this. Turns out, he is indeed Joe Biden's son.

I'm sitting in our former president's senate seat and looking into the eyes of our former vice president's son while he organizes and uses things I would never expect him to partake in. But he isn't a vice president's son. If you never asked him who his dad was, you would never know. He's just Hunter. He is his own.

With everything Hunter is using that night, it would be easy to think of him as your usual junkie. But he's not. He might be smoking crack cocaine and drinking vodka straight from a gallon Tito's bottle right in front of me, but he is not a crackhead. He is well-composed and intelligent; he listens when I speak. In my first twenty minutes with Hunter Biden, I know he is the most charming human I've ever met, even in his parrot boxer briefs. He is one of the only genuine people I've met since moving to the big city. He is someone I want to get to know better.

It feels like no more than an hour has passed when Kelsey appears in the doorway. She says hello to Hunter and lets me know it's morning. Sunlight seeps into the small office, but I'm not ready to leave . . . him. We literally talked the night away. I get up, give him a hug, and walk out. No number exchange. Hopefully Kelsey got it with the after-party details.

We sneak out the way we came in, back onto U.S. soil, without the Swedes being the wiser, and make our way to the car. Click click click, nothing. We are desperate to get to my place and crash, but a dead battery is keeping us put, right down from the House of Sweden. Kelsey calls the number for the after-party, and sure enough, Hunter answers. She tells him we're stranded, and even after a night of partying, vodka, and drugs, Hunter immediately comes down to check on us, wearing more than just briefs.

All it takes is one call from him, and minutes later a guy shows up with a new battery that fits, installs it, then drives off. Hunter has handled the costs and Kelsey doesn't owe a penny.

This is my first experience of the Hunter package—wit, charm, kindness, and a phone that could make anyone else's problems go away. I didn't realize it, but while the guy was fixing the vehicle, Hunter got my number from Kelsey.

A little over a week later, Hunter gets back in town. He's been gone since the day of the car rescue, but we've been texting on and off. It is nothing heavy or romantic, but now that he's back, we decide to get drinks at a tiny bar in Georgetown. Before meeting him, I call Rana, one of my most trusted friends and the only born-and-raised loyal Democrat from my hometown.

"How in the hell did this spark up," she asks incredulously. I fill her in on the Rosemont Seneca night, and all the while I'm talking she's googling. "Be careful," she warns. "It says here he has been discharged from the Navy for cocaine." I am not about to reveal I sat with him while he did it the other night.

"Well, I don't know about all of that, but we spent hours talking. He's such a kind person. You would really like him," I say, trying to reassure her that I am not about to get sucked into a life of hard drugs and . . . I don't know . . . dishonorable discharges? We hang up and I head straight for Georgetown.

He's wrapping some business up in the office, so I wait for him on the stairs outside the Swedish Embassy while the sun is setting over the Potomac. He approaches from behind, and before I can see him I can smell that smoky, unforgettable fragrance from the first night. It's etched into my memory. Hunter is better looking than I remembered, about six feet tall, this time clean shaven, wearing a blue pea coat, jeans, and brown Gucci loafers. He cleans up nice. He looks distinguished and vibrant.

The first words from his mouth are, again, "Hey, how are you?" But it's not your typical in-passing question. It's genuine. It's Hunter. As I'm describing my day to him, I can't help but be more curious about his. We walk a few blocks to the bar, and fortunately I'm wearing flats because I couldn't remember if he was taller than my five feet seven inches. He is.

At a corner in Georgetown, a man pulls out his phone. I hardly notice, but it bothers Hunter. He believes the guy is taking a picture of him. I hate that. How hard it must be for someone to live their life constantly in the spotlight.

He opens the door at a small café lounge, and I pick a purple couch lit by lamps on two end tables. Ordering Tito's on the rocks, Hunter compliments the waitress' bracelet, and shares with her a story about the one he's wearing. I noticed it the first night, a silver band with what to me looked like the What Would Jesus Do fish engraved in the metal around it. It obviously means something to him.

"So how do you do it," I say as we sip our drinks. "I'm sure people expect you to be an entitled asshole, but somehow you manage to relate to anyone."

My curiosity amuses him but shooting him straight makes him chuckle, I don't think he's used to people being so straightforward with him. "You just treat people the same. Be kind. It's not some huge, unbearable task."

As we talk, Hunter informs me that he is going through a divorce and the difficulties he is facing. I can't confess that I already know because I googled him again after we met. Doesn't every girl? I can see it has an effect on him. He loves his family and hates feeling like he has let anyone down.

The lounge starts flooding with Georgetown students, and our inevitable exit is near. But again, I'm not ready to leave. While we're finishing our second drink, Hunter tells me he's been staying at the Ritz-Carlton down the street with an open bar. Do I want to check it out? Hell, yeah, I do.

It's a gorgeous five-minute walk to the Ritz, where the large gold demi-lion ushers us into the palatial lobby. We pass walls of red brick, hanging chandeliers, and a marble desk looking older than America, and then an easy ride up the elevator and I find myself inside Hunter Biden's place for the night. It's a suite. The humble, down-to-earth guy I applauded for seeming so relatable to anyone at the restaurant is probably spending more on one night here than the average American makes in a month.

He tour-guides me around the rooms, acting like it's not a big deal. I take it all in, knowing that it actually is a very big deal, to me at least. D.C. is unpredictable, but I never saw myself at The Ritz-Carlton with the former vice president's son, having a drink from his open bar and seeing where the night goes.

"What do you want to drink first," he asks from the mini fridge.

There are only a few small bottles of Tito's left, so, with a little smile, I opt for Grey Goose.

We're playful and jab at each other. I like getting under his skin. "Fuck you, you fuckin' fuck," he says without anger. It's his favorite word. We laugh together.

Hanging out with Hunter feels like home away from home. I am safe and comfortable, taken care of. I don't know where things are going, but I'm open, and waiting to see. Will he be one of my best friends or something more? He's witty and smart, and he's got a lot going for himself. I enjoy his company, and there aren't a lot of people in D.C. I feel that way about.

We make our way to the fainting couch at the foot of the bed, and I kick off my flats beside his Gucci loafers. The joking is gone now. Conversation is deeper now as we lean on the bed. We talk about family and friends, people who have let us down, and ways we've been hurt. He has a lot more of those than he would like to admit.

I notice something in his eyes I hadn't noticed before. Not an emotion, but a color. I'm looking at his striking blue-gray eyes, but in one of them there is a hint of brown, like a freckle on his iris. The uniqueness is intriguing. I'm attracted to him even more.

The foreseeable lull in the conversation finally comes and he leans in ever so slightly. I move toward him, and my mouth meets his. His lips are harder than I expected. It's almost like a shield, keeping anyone from getting into the softness behind. But I don't mind; I have my own walls up.

As I sink into his kiss, I'm not thinking he's my future husband or about how in love I am. I'm just wondering where this will go. As we slip into the bed, somewhere in the back of my head a phrase I've heard before pops up—the first hit is always free.

Chapter 2

Secret Squirrel

Steam escapes the bathroom doorway as I lay in bed listening to the water running. He's showering again. I must have drifted off. I'd bet he didn't sleep at all.

He emerges, and without missing a beat, we launch into conversation like last night never ended. Either he's a morning person or sleep is a rare thing in his world. My money's on the latter. Another facet of the Hunter package: his addiction leaves no room for peace or even basic rest. It has no mercy.

At least things aren't awkward, but then again, I can't imagine awkward existing in Hunter's world. I think he could charm his way out of a black hole, let alone a little social discomfort. And in the short time I've known him, we have become friends. Or have we? Friends with . . . benefits? Anxiety hits my bloodstream like caffeine as I try to label it, us. I hate labels. They feel like cages. How can one tiny word fit something as complex as this? And why am I even thinking about this? I just met this guy.

That's it, I'm leaving. Fresh air might help me get out of my head. I pull on yesterday's clothes. The walk of shame, or rather, Uber of shame, across the city feels daunting.

"I gotta get back home."

"Can I order you up some breakfast?"

"No, thanks. I'm not hungry."

"Okay, well, I have to meet my uncle soon anyway. Can you call me later?"

"Yeah, okay." One of the first things I learned about being friends with Hunter: you don't get in touch with him; he gets in touch with you. Reaching him is nearly impossible, and reserved for when he needs you, not the other way around.

I hug him goodbye and close the door as his phone blows up with another call. He's late for his uncle, and as calm as he seems, I suspect being late is his norm.

Back in the real world, I navigate the Georgetown Ritz lobby again and step into a fresh breath of crisp D.C. morning air with a side of "What the hell have I gotten myself into?" I replay the night: the stories, the laughter, the ease. Time with Hunter melts everything else away. Lost in the moment, one might say. Did he enjoy himself too? Is it possible he likes me back? Talk about a surprise. One of many with Hunter. Maybe I kind of like this Biden guy. Would that be bad?

Despite my openness with him, Hunter has a mysterious side I haven't quite cracked. He might tell me what I want to hear, but a tiny doubt lingers in the back of my mind. How does he really feel? Silver-tongued devil, some might say. I want to figure him out the way he did me, but I have a feeling he won't be as easy.

At home, I throw on leggings and a sweatshirt and dial Kelsey.

"Wanna get brunch? I have something to tell you."

"Uh, yeah."

A good friend bails you out of jail, but a best friend sits next to you in your cell and says with a smile, "Damn, that was fun." Kelsey's in my cell. She joins in my chaos and laughs me through the trauma that might follow.

We slide our burrito bowls onto the metal table at Chipotle and I spill.

"So, I had drinks with Hunter Biden last night."

No surprise there.

"And then I went back to his suite at the Ritz."

"And . . ."

"And I just left a few hours ago."

We laugh at our knack for finding ourselves in these situations. Spending time with the former vice president's son should feel like a big deal, but with Hunter, it just feels normal. Plus, I'm not easily starstruck. My aunt calls me Mr. Bean, Rowan Atkinson's character from the British TV series, because I tend to float through life unassumingly, creating a trail of chaos in my wake.

Once, at a concert, I sat VIP backstage and asked a man sitting on a speaker where the nearest restroom was. He politely escorted me, only for the door to open into a fancy dressing room with his pictures all over the wall. He was the lead singer of the Read Southall Band. I was an idiot. But I hit the veggie tray, used the restroom, and when I came out, I thanked him and told him what a fan I was. He laughed, knowing I had no clue. But he didn't feel disrespected; that's all that mattered.

Chaos follows me everywhere. I guess Hunter and I are alike in that sense.

For the next few months we see each other, talking, texting, spending time at his office or hotel suite, or visiting the garage loft of his father's house on Chain Bridge Road that served as home base during his divorce. People ask how long we've known each other, and he always claims "a year or so." It isn't that long; it just seems that way.

I'm typically on guard in D.C., getting to know people before letting my walls down. Intentions aren't always what they seem. But with Hunter, it's different. From the first night he asked about me, I trusted him.

On March 1, my phone buzzes me awake to a tabloid headline, "Beau Biden's Widow Having an Affair with His Married Brother." Every tabloid claims that Hunter is romantically involved with his sister-in-law, Hallie. The media's having a field day with the family drama, and my heart hurts for him. I grab my phone, fingers tapping out a text: "Hey, I saw the news. Checking on you. Are you okay? If there's anything I can do, please let me know. Keep your head up." Twenty-four hours later, a quick "thank you" arrives.

A few days go by and he reaches out again. He asks if I want to meet up. Well, of course. He's staying at the Watergate Hotel and plans on ordering dinner. Kelsey and I are at my house watching *The American President*. Ironic. He says bring her and come on! So we take off.

As soon as the door opens to his suite he hugs us both, inviting us in. The Watergate suite's menu looks like a feast. I quickly order a Caesar salad I know is really good, and then pull Hunter into another hug. The tabloids have dragged him through the mud, and my gut twists seeing him like this. He pulls me aside as Kelsey decides between the seafood tower and black truffle risotto, and as I give him another hug, he squeezes out a quiet, "Thank you." I'm thinking he's just really happy we came to hang out and take his mind off things, then he adds, "You were the only person who genuinely checked on me when everything happened. Thank you for that." I act as if it's no big deal, but there's a small sting in my chest. So, it's real.

"You need to meet Hallie," he says. "You'll love her! And she'll love you! Let's all get together!" Am I really spending time with a guy who's in a seemingly open relationship with his sister-in-law? I can't believe I'm even thinking about it. That would never be okay with me. But for some reason, with Hunter, it's different. Guess I've joined the dream team.

We find a day that works for the three of us, and I head to our first rendezvous point—the Georgetown cafe where Hunter and I went on our first outing. Meeting new people gives me anxiety, and this is not your normal meetup, but Hallie gives me a warm smile that's disarming and genuine. I understand what Hunter sees in her. No envy, I think she's great. After all, we're just friends, right?

A few drinks later we head back to Rosemont Seneca, Hunter lagging behind to grab cash at an ATM. Hallie and I walk down the street like best friends. She's timid too, but we cover the awkwardness with small talk. Just as we settle into conversation, Hunter's back. "I, uh, have a small appointment," he murmurs, and ushers us up to his office.

At a big conference table, we sit and talk with Hunter through the open door to his gorgeous, glass-enclosed office. Hallie claims to have a headache and disappears into the back room. We're either getting on her nerves or boring her to death, I think, but find out she's not a huge fan of his next appointment, or vice versa.

Hunter's phone rings, "You're about to meet someone special." My anxiety spikes. I'm not sure I can handle meeting any more special people.

Too late. A knock echoes on the door and Hunter lets in an eighty-five-pound woman, near five feet, two inches, with just a couple teeth and a balding spot where her scalp shows through her short hair. Just when I thought the dream team couldn't get any dreamier.

It's Bicycles, his supplier. Hunter introduces her by her real name, not the street name everyone calls her when she's not around, and she scans me with suspicion. He leans in, whispering, "She gets protective, especially around women." Clearly she's protective, but not for the same reasons I am. He's her meal ticket. They make their supposedly secret exchange behind the glass walls of his office, and he buys his dealer a supply too, maybe so she doesn't short his supply. What a deal.

She's still shooting me daggers when I say just loud enough that we all can hear, "Look, I'm from Arkansas, so if she thinks all eighty pounds of her would like to open a can of whoop-ass on me, I'll gladly mop your office floor with her." He laughs, mocking my southern accent, but hustles her out the door. I can't figure out if he's more worried Bicycles will try to shiv me, or that I'll make good on my threat and he'll lose his supplier.

With Chinese takeout and a twenty-minute late-night drive to McLean, Hunter, Hallie and I are at Joe and Jill's place on Chain Bridge Road. It's a gorgeous brick home with big columns, and the Bidens are leasing it from a friend of the Obamas. At least that's what Hunter tells me. Everyone is someone on Chain Bridge, and I love visiting here. I always go straight downstairs to the fridge tucked off Joe's office where ice cream, Cokes, and sometimes Gatorade are stocked, then head up to Hunter's wing of the house.

But tonight we're the dream team. Hallie manages a few bites of take-out and stays long enough to show the tension between her and Hunter. He's rubbing the spot where his neck meets his shoulders and wants to call someone to give him a massage. Hallie's suspicious, but instead of arguing she heads upstairs for the night.

I stay for the night, but run home the next day to let Ada, my German shepherd, out. After showering and changing into a tan romper, I Uber back to Chain Bridge. Hallie is sitting on the front porch, smoking. I pull up a rocking chair and sit. She's out here because she and Hunter aren't getting along. I listen, and when we go back inside, for some reason they want me to mediate.

"You all just don't get along," I laugh after hearing their complaints. Hunter thinks Hallie is suspicious, always accusing him of lying and questioning anything he says. Maybe paranoia is plaguing her too. She claims he lies, and he claims she isn't understanding, and he feels used. It looks to me like her demons are darker than his. Hallie is sweet but doesn't seem very street-smart, and she needs Hunter to take care of her.

They're not supportive or encouraging of each other; they don't even act like they like being around each other. They're never affectionate in front of me, and whatever they have between them, it seems toxic. Maybe they clung to each other's sharp edges to weather a storm, but now there's wreckage all around.

Hunter storms off to his wing of the house to call a masseuse, leaving Hallie and me at the kitchen counter. "He really trusts you," she says. "That isn't something he does with most people." She claims he confides more things in me than she would ever know. I don't know why she's offering this insight or how it makes her feel. I can't imagine. There isn't any trust between them, and I know Hunter is feeling used a lot in general, when he's needing to feel love.

Hallie goes to lie down on the couch, and I visit Hunter in his wing. "Can you believe this?" he asks. "Can you believe her?"

"Yeah, Hunt, she's pretty upset."

"You're not siding with her, are you?"

"No," I assure him. "You both are just so toxic to each other." It's kind of sad to see.

I spend a lot of time at Chain Bridge with Hunter, but never again with Hallie. My closest D.C. friends, Savanah and Kelsey, visit too. We all goof around, drink, or watch things on TV or the internet. It's always a good time.

His bedroom is a snowstorm of clothes, with a fresh avalanche each time the closet opens. He gathers new things wherever he goes, so they tend to pile up. His wing above the garage has its own entry, with a spiral staircase leading to a small balcony where Hunter smokes an occasional Winston. At the bottom of the staircase, a couple of black SUVs sit to the side, protecting his privacy. It is his hideaway throughout his divorce. He stays there when Joe and Jill are out of town, or when he's not staying in a hotel suite, or renting a house in Annapolis after his divorce becomes public, and who can blame him? The place is gorgeous, with plenty of space to be alone, or have company.

Weeks morph into months, with visits, texts, calls, and FaceTimes scattered throughout. We see each other on and off when we are in town and stay in contact when one of us is traveling. One day Hunter's supposed to come over but cancels for a last-minute trip. No big deal until he reveals the trip is to China.

"Hunt, if I make a last-minute trip, it's like to 7-Eleven, or Annapolis, not on the other side of the world!"

But I'm there when he gets back.

As Hunter and I grow closer, so does his bond with my best friends. My loyalty is fierce, and I guard his secrets. I never bring anyone around him who might jeopardize his public reputation, only those who can look beyond his addiction. I want to protect him. So Kelsey, Savanah, Vanessa, and Lydia are the only girls I let in. They're my closest friends, and I know their allegiance to me will make them protect him the same way I do.

We spend a lot of time with Savanah and Kelsey, and when we're all together Hunter loosens up. It's like he can be a kid with us. Kelsey is at Northern Virginia Community College taking online classes and working part-time jobs, like waitressing, and interning at a dermatologist's office. At Chain Bridge, she does her schoolwork on Hunter's laptop. One time we're up in his wing and she says she has to head home to take a test. "Just do it here," Hunter offers. "Like I don't have internet? Log in and take your test." She logs in on his laptop, and we all take the test together.

I don't really know what Savanah does. She's sort of the Chandler Bing from the TV show *Friends* of our group, no one really knows what it is that she does. She might be in school too, but definitely online, because every time we call, she's always randomly nearby, even though she lives in Manassas. Savanah has a little hooptie but drives everyone else's car. Every time she drinks, she ends up in the hospital thinking she's dying from a hangover, so she doesn't drink. Which works out great because she is an excellent designated driver. If she opened a designated driver business, she'd make a fortune off us.

Vanessa is with us sometimes too. She's quieter than the rest of us, and doesn't give Hunter a hard time, mostly just laughing at our antics. But for the most part it is us four, Kelsey, Hunter, Savanah, and me. We spend so much time together, we have an official group name, "AMOEBA." It's a one-cell microscopic organism, but Hunter just calls it a parasite and jokingly describes us as parasites too . . . well, mostly jokingly. It's also our code word in case of emergencies. The AMOEBA pact seems to be that we take care of Hunter by keeping his secrets and helping him loosen up, and Hunter . . . well . . . just takes care of us. We do our part of keeping his secrets, and over time they grow.

One night after a dinner filled with more drinks than food, Kelsey and I decide to surprise Hunter at Chain Bridge. We Uber there, but can't remember the gate code, and instead of calling, we decide to break in. First, we try army crawling under the gate. Utter fail. Then we grab the black bars and try climbing over. But we laugh too hard to even pull ourselves off the ground. For the next five minutes the Uber sits in the drive, contemplating either calling the cops or offering us a ride back to sanity. The two most incompetent burglars in the D.C. area. But we finally slip through the gate and run up the spiral staircase to Hunter's balcony. As we knock on the door, we're surprised he doesn't answer. We know he's there; we FaceTimed earlier. Then it hits us; he's paranoid about what crazy person might have gotten to his door without going through the gate first. We double over in laughter again. After calling to him, we hear, "Are you fucking kidding me?" a couple of times. He opens the door, shaking his head. "Get it together," he orders with disgust and a hint of humor.

The break-in isn't our main reason for coming. I want to see him, and Kelsey needs some advice on work issues. He's primed, cocked, and ready. He's on high alert, and always gives the best advice.

"Okay, turn your phones off and leave them on the couch," he demands. "We need to walk like a hundred yards away so nobody hears us."

Kelsey eyes me with amusement.

"You want my advice, then put your fuckin' phones on the couch, turned off, and follow me outside, fuckers."

We comply. We don't want to agitate the demon of paranoia. Plus, as harsh as that might sound, he really isn't. Hunter jokes, and never says anything that would really make us feel bad. Even at his worst, he isn't mean. He just likes making us laugh and using his favorite word.

Phones surrendered, we walk the required hundred yards to the corner of the back lawn. Kelsey pours out her situation to him, and he takes it all in, eyes intent. Suddenly his eyes double in size as he snaps his attention to her waist. My eyes follow. Silence. Then, an unmistakable BZZZZZZ.

Hunter's face contorts. "What the actual fuck? You brought your phone? You *don't* listen. Just incompetent!" He storms off, back inside, leaving us rolling on the ground laughing.

Kelsey's work phone in her jacket pocket has given her away. She's worried she set off a panic attack. He just lectured us about breaking in through the gate. "How the hell did you make it this far in life? How do you survive without me?" Followed by that perfectly timed phone call. He thinks we need to grow up, and it's our mission to help him loosen his grip on control, even if it's just for a brief, chaotic moment.

Phones are a big deal to Hunter. He's gone through hundreds in his life. Models change, numbers change, but one constant remains: it's impossible to get ahold of Hunter unless he wants to be reached. If the paranoia is haunting him, he might even hide the phone you're trying to reach him on and buy another one to get him through the moment.

Another time Kelsey and I are out eating when we think we smell Hunter. "Is someone smoking crack cocaine?" We pinpoint the source of the aroma and suspect the guy coming back from the restroom is up to something.

"What are you doing?" we get up the nerve to ask with a smile.

"What?" he says, looking at us like we were crazy. "Nothing."

"You smell," Kelsey says, sniffing him. "Are you wearing something."

"Yeah, it's Tom Ford Tuscan Leather."

"Oh," we say simultaneously, looking like we're the crack addicts.

From then on, we realize the smoky aroma that comes with Hunter is Tom Ford Tuscan Leather, which is probably just as expensive.

Over time, I start working for Hunter off the books and doing small unofficial things. When his Porsche needs to be moved, I handle it. When an Audi or a BMW needs to go from Delaware to one of the rented houses in Annapolis, I take care of it. Whatever he needs, whether dropping off dry cleaning, going over things with his assistant, Katie Dodge, at the office, or restocking his daily Tito's gallon, he calls me.

Watching Hunter in action, wheeling and dealing with people, I can't help but think about how I could build a long-term career working with him. It might sound self-serving, but it's true. Plus, being around Hunter means living a ridiculously fun life as a bonus.

Crime and CSI school are a fascination of mine, and I love discussing high-profile cases with my sister and aunt, and crafting our own theories. But as I work for Hunter, a new side of myself comes to the surface. I enjoy helping people who need it, and Hunter needs all the help he can get.

Plenty of people start as executive assistants but end up becoming their boss's professional right hand. I want to become the Donna to Hunter's Harvey Specter, assisting him professionally, but even more so, being there for him personally, because he is a broken man.

I'm not some pure feminine hero though, swooping in to save a man. I'm having as much fun as I've ever had, reveling in the present, partying on a whole new level. The booze is good, and the drugs . . . well, I can't say I don't try and do things, but none of it ever gets its claws in me. Still, the scene is all new to me and I'm fully immersed in the moment, drinking in every second of this thrill ride, living only for the now.

Knowing I love the TV show *Scandal* and staying at the Watergate because of its political history, Hunter tells me one day about another hotel. It's a story of scandal about politicians, drugs, and prostitutes. I'm fascinated by crime, so we decide to visit. After lunch, we check in to the historic building. Our first greeting is from a weird smell that lingers throughout the old-fashioned room. A thirty-two-inch TV sitting on top of an old wooden dresser is probably the only upgrade this small room has seen in decades, and the maroon carpet looks like it's a hotel original.

"Pull the top cover off," Hunter says, messing with the bed. "Who knows what we might catch in this place."

I do, but we don't stay long. He takes one of his many showers for the day trying to rid himself of the demon on his back and is talking on the phone in the bathroom, while I sit, dressed in his light blue button-up, browsing the internet on his laptop.

"Honey, I'm out of battery," he calls. "Where's my charger?"

I rummage through the backpack that I brought for him, then the briefcase. It's not here.

"You didn't pack me a charger," he howls in disbelief. "You're the most insubordinate assistant ever."

We laugh because we know he's right.

As time goes on, I learn more about Hunter, both the good and the bad. One night I see his kindness and generosity when we come across a homeless man and his son. Their clothes are worn, and it is clear they are struggling to stay warm. Hunter doesn't hesitate; he presses a little card into the man's hand, "Show this to the people at the desk." He sends them to the nearby Ritz for a warm room, a hot shower, and all the room service they could want, all on his tab.

Other times I see the darker side. As his drug use escalates, so does his paranoia. Despite it all, he refuses to quit. One night at his Annapolis house, after his fifth shower to try to wash away the hold they have on him, I ask him if he would consider quitting. "Honey," he declares, "You can want me to quit, but at the end of the day I will not quit until I *want* to quit. This is my addiction, no one else's. I'll change when I'm ready, and hell, I'll probably outlive *you!*" He promises me he's going to get frog venom injected into his system to clear everything out so he doesn't have to go to rehab, and being gullible, I believe everything he says. But the frog venom appointment is never made, if it exists at all. He's right. He won't quit until he wants to, no matter what anyone else wants.

The sunrises on Chesapeake Bay are among my fondest memories of being in Hunter's Annapolis house. Savanah and Hunter are engrossed in TV and conversation, but I can't take my eyes off the painted sky and shimmering water, until I hear "Whole Foods." My stomach growls and I join them downstairs, finding them on Hunter's ever-present laptop scrolling through memes. Savanah reads off the infamous images of former vice president Joe Biden and former president Obama that had the social media world in a frenzy in 2017. We laugh, but Hunter doesn't find them as funny. He is proud of his dad and feels the memes are a form of mockery. It's just jokes, no harm meant. He cracks a smile at a few, probably more amused by our laughter than the jokes themselves, and claims we need to get ready and be productive for the day, even though it's Saturday. He goes upstairs to change, but Savanah and I stay in the sweats we've been lounging in.

Hunter comes back downstairs, and I can't resist bringing up Whole Foods again. We make a plan to go. "You owe me a phone," Savanah tells Hunter. Something happened to hers some time before and he loaned her one of his many, which turned out to be one of his dad's phones, complete with Joe's pictures and information still on it. She's been using the phone for months, with the same wallpaper Joe had chosen of him and Jill. I didn't know. All this time I just thought she was a loyal Democrat.

We find a Whole Foods near a Verizon Wireless store. Two birds, one stone. At Hunter's direction I'm driving Hallie's small white BMW SUV while in the back seat he organizes the materials in his backpack, and Savanah gives directions riding shotgun. "Here is good," Hunter shouts from the back. Whole Foods is two or more blocks away, with Verizon across the street from it.

He's out the door, sneaking across the street with backpack on, Dallas police cap pulled down, hands shoved in his pockets, and looking determined and incognito. We crack up, trying to figure out what the hell he's thinking, and follow ten feet behind on his secret squirrel mission.

We reach Whole Foods after trailing him at 5 mph and pick up our food and the pasta he's asked for. Back in the BMW, we see him walking across the street in our direction. He shoots out a stiff arm, head down, as if he does not want to be seen, but his antics just draw more attention as he points toward a parking spot farther down the road. I guess ours isn't good enough. We laugh, but of course follow what we think he's telling us to do.

Pulling into our new parking spot, we lose sight of him until he slow-jogs in front of the vehicle toward the driver's side. I turn around, expecting him to open the door, but he's gone. Then the passenger back door swings open. He circled the whole car. Pausing just a moment, Hunter flies headfirst into the back seat with his backpack, a bag from the cell phone store, and his ball cap hanging on for dear life. His legs fly through the air, pointing upward as he lands on his stomach. Savanah and I whip around to see the commotion. "Go!" he screams.

"Hunt, what the fuck," Savanah shouts. I'm just focused on the gas pedal.

He pops up like all is cool. "I thought I saw somebody!"

"Who? A burglar? Someone familiar? You're obviously running from them. Your ex-wife? *Who?*" I'm curious. I don't understand this secret squirrel shit.

"I don't know . . . nobody . . . What did you guys get to eat?" He's obviously over it and on to the next thing.

"Whole Foods. Here's yours." We hand him the white box of pasta he asked for.

"I don't eat Whole Foods."

"*What?*" We both flip around again.

"Oh, okay. Thanks."

I like to think I'd make a pretty good detective, but I never learn who Hunter thinks he's seen that day.

Chapter 3

On the Pole

I've always loved the CSI world and thought that was what I wanted to be. But as my life in D.C. expands, that dream begins to fade. I haven't been making it the priority I need to, so when the registrar at George Washington says there's an issue with my financial aid, I'm not upset. Honestly, I could use a break from it for a while to sort things out.

My lease is three months from being up, but I want to take my dog Ada and go home for the summer. I talk to Hunter. "Here's what you're going to do." He gets me out of any bind, and tells me I should go home, only to turn around and text, FaceTime, and call over the next couple months just to let me know I've abandoned him and need to come back.

I leave my German shepherd in Arkansas, where she's being royally spoiled by my dad, and when I get back to D.C., I'm ready to sort everything out. However, things don't always work out as planned, and my ability to take a left turn when I know I should be taking a right one kicks in. A friend of mine is a cocktail waitress at a club called Mpire, and she makes good money. "You should really come check it out," she suggests.

"It's not like it's a career path, but you make money while having a good time! It's a stepping stone." I'm curious.

Mpire exceeds my expectations—glitzy, glamorous, and nothing like what I think of as a strip club. I'm in awe, feeling like I have stars in my eyes as I take in the structure, camaraderie, and . . . well, the class. Dancers elegantly dressed in long gowns mingle with uniformed bartenders, cocktail waitresses, security, and management. My friend introduces me to Valerie, who's a doctor, but traded that career for being the owner's right hand because she makes more here. When I'm presented the opportunity to work at Mpire, I hesitate at first, both bashful and flattered, but ultimately decide, "Ah, heck! Why not?"

I've never done anything this risqué before. I'm not doing anything "wrong," and this will take financial stress off my mom and dad, who always help me out monetarily when needed. These are the thoughts running through my mind, trying to justify why this is a good idea. My intention is to have an ephemeral adventure that will tame the young, wild, and free me—and that's exactly what I do.

Working at Mpire, I discover a natural affinity with a few of the girls, who are some of the most authentic, compassionate, and true-hearted friends I've ever met. So it deeply irks me when people who've likely never set foot in a gentlemen's venue like this, stigmatize the women who work here, denouncing and criticizing them, and suggesting that they can only be duplicitous gold diggers. After all, some of the sneakiest and most dishonest people I've ever met were dressed in fancy suits and ties.

Savanah, Kelsey, and Lydia always joke with me, saying I am destined to be an NBA player's wife. With each night of fun and each new connection, the CSI dreams fade a little more, and aspirations of a glitzy, glamorous life in D.C. quickly replace them. I am young and dumb and would never recommend this lifestyle to anyone, but I can't say I don't have fun, and I definitely end up with some stories.

Hunter hasn't actually been to Mpire before, or at least, I haven't seen him there. But given my job, it's inevitable that he'll show up eventually. I wonder what it says about me that now I'm the one corrupting him. But I guess not much, since he loves gentlemen's clubs and would probably eventually sniff out Mpire on his own.

AK owns Mpire and becomes one of my favorite people on the planet. He isn't some stereotypical creepy guy who owns dancers, like the Hugh Hefner type. He's a respectable, good-looking guy who is courteous to the women and men who work for him, and he charms people with either his wit, or his gorgeous smile.

"I swear, D.C is the place where high school class secretaries from all over the world come to get further in life," he says one day to me over lunch at Daily Grill as we're looking out the window. "It's their melting pot." It's one of our first conversations, and he isn't real sure of me yet, nor I of him.

"I was my high school class secretary," I say back, not sure how he will take it. We both burst out laughing.

"Seriously?"

"Yes," I assure him, I'm telling the truth. We laugh harder and become close from that day on.

Mpire's rules are strict. No T-shirts or caps of any kind, no phones out, no pictures, and no touching any girl. I think you actually have to stand a certain distance away. And everyone who comes through the door has to scan their ID to a database to get in. It's how they keep up with who is banned and who they do or don't want coming in.

AK knows about Hunter and me, and he'll go to considerable lengths to protect his privacy. D.C. is a political city, and the Biden name holds a lot of weight. AK allows Hunter to come in and sit at his "Owner's" table a couple of times. The girls know if someone is sitting at AK's table, they are important to him or the club. And Hunter sits there, hat pulled down low. It's another privilege AK allows to preserve his anonymity, along with never making him scan his driver's license.

Over my time at Mpire, Hunter shows up a few times, Savanah and Kelsey often joining him. There's nothing sexual between them and Hunter. They are my best friends and become like little sisters to him. Even when I am not around, they hang out, have fun, then fill me in later. Kelsey and Hunter drink and party while Savanah chauffeurs.

One evening we're hanging out at Chain Bridge, and I get a call from AK. Big Spender Construction Guy is there. He's from North Carolina and fancies himself a southerner, and he likes talking with me. Tonight I'm in jeans, but AK says come in and hang out anyway.

Hunter, Kelsey, and Savanah drop me off at the club, and I sit and talk with Big Spender, and his friend Bird Man, who caws like a bird when he's drunk. Sometimes girls at clubs have a reputation for stealing from people, but he likes that he can sit with me at a table with ten thousand dollar bills on it and know I'm not touching them. We chat, and I might subtly let him know one girl is struggling to make rent, or another one is paying her law school tuition. He gives them $5,000 and buys bottles of the most expensive champagne the club has to offer.

About thirty minutes before clocking out, I call Hunter to let him know it's time to pick me up, and immediately after he answers the phone, I start laughing. He is in an absolute "cocaine and vodka state of being." I can hear Savanah laughing in the background. Just before hanging up, Hunter asks me to grab some baby powder for him. Baby powder? Okay, that's new. Maybe he's chafed his legs? Who knows, it's Hunter.

After punching out, I run by the CVS down the street, grab a giant plastic bottle that looks like it would powder a thousand babies, and go back to Mpire to wait. The security guy sees Hunter Biden's Range Rover pull up and lets them park right outside the front door.

I hop into the passenger seat looking at Savanah with her hands on the wheel, hesitating to take off. She wants to see my reaction to the back seat. I turn around and see Kelsey dressed in sweats, while Hunter is in nothing but his underwear in the back seat of his Range Rover in the middle of Dupont Circle. I throw my gray BCBG scarf at him. "Oh my gosh! Cover up! What if we get pulled over?"

He is in a good mood and laughs. "The scarf isn't big enough." Then he asks, "Did you get it?" I toss him the CVS bag. He roots around in it like he's looking for something buried deep. Then he pulls out the baby powder. "What the fuck is this?" As he holds it up, Kelsey spits out her Tito's and belly laughs. Savanah turns to see what he's holding and has to pull over because she's holding her stomach from laughing so hard. I don't get it. "You told me to stop and get baby powder." His jaw drops for a second, and then half mocking, half irritated, but also chuckling from my stupidity, he shouts, "Are you kidding me? What the fuck?"

Savanah and Kelsey can't get ahold of their laughter, and apparently, it's even funnier because I'm still lost and don't understand what's so funny. Hunter is acting like he didn't ask me to stop and get him baby powder. "No, I'm not kidding. I'm so lost." I exclaim.

He just looks at me. "Baby powder is street talk for cocaine. So you don't say it over the phone. You literally just left a nightclub where somebody had to have had coke. What the fuck am I going to do with this?" I can barely hear him over the laughing. For once, I didn't understand Hunter's shorthand. "Should I have known?" Kelsey and Savanah both burst out, "yes" simultaneously. Their stomachs are getting a better workout than at a core class.

But I think they're crazy. We've only made it to the corner of the street, so I decide to get out and walk back up to Mpire for a poll. I go into the dressing room where seven girls are looking over a new rack of elegant dresses.

"I have a quick question. If someone asks y'all to grab some baby powder before they pick you up from work, what do y'all think they want you to . . ."

Every girl in that dressing room interrupts me at the same time: "Cocaine!" Savanah and Kelsey were right. It was Hunter, and I really should have known. I feel like an idiot.

One evening I plan to stay with Hunter. He's taking his friend Devon out for some cheering up, so he says I should meet them in the city. They're getting drinks but looking for something more exciting. I suggest Mpire and arrange to meet them there with Savanah as my wingman. Kelsey is off with the only twentysomething guy in D.C. who has gout.

As we enter the foyer, we're directed upstairs to the small, private lounge on the third floor with a balcony that looks out over the second floor. From there, you can see the raised glass booths that girls would shower in for the right price. The club is one of a kind.

The lights in the lounge are cool purple, the walls are covered by black curtains, and there is a little stage about eighteen inches high with a floor-to-ceiling pole. There sit Hunter and Devon Archer on the black leather U-shaped couch. They have known each other for years and served on the board of Burisma together.

Something seems to be going on in Devon's world, and Hunter is determined to cheer him up. They've had a couple of bottles of Tito's on ice delivered, and a few girls are coming through to dance or talk, but Devon isn't interested. I don't know what Devon is upset about, but it must have been something big, because what guy says no to that?

Savanah and I join them, and it's obvious Devon looks mopey, slightly slumped on the couch, holding his drink and speaking to Hunter in a low tone. That's when Hunter decides it's time to pull out the big guns. Without warning, he hops up on the little stage, grabs the pole, and starts a dance that has us all, even Devon, falling back onto the couch with laughter. Hunter has been adamant about learning to twerk for some time now, and I guess he thinks this is the time to put all his practice into action. Who knew, at a strip club, Hunter wants to be the one on the pole.

Out on the main floor, on a mission from Hunter, I talk with a few girls I really like and trust. "Come up to the third floor. We have a small group there; it's safe and fun!" Tiffany, Jessica, and another girl jump at the chance and come back to the lounge with me.

We order whatever we want on Hunter's tab, and sit and drink while he leads the conversation, quizzing everyone on their lives. Devon and Hunter sit in the middle of the couch, with me to Hunter's left. The girls fill in around us. We drink more than we should, and during one of Hunter's intermissions, Jessica and I hop up on the little stage and start singing, dancing, and generally making fools of ourselves.

From that stage, I look out at both of these men, who look wealthy, educated, handsome, and important—exactly what you would expect a couple of businessmen in the city to look like on a casual night out. I stop my dancing to speak to a security guard who's come upstairs, when something catches my eye. A red glow in that dark room.

Hunter has pulled out his favorite pastime and is taking a hit in front of everyone. Devon isn't paying any attention to him, and I immediately scan the girls' faces to see if anyone saw it, while still entertaining the security so he won't turn around. I mostly trust the girls I've chosen to be there, but it doesn't matter. The former vice president's son smoking cocaine in public or being dragged out of a gentlemen's club for using isn't something I want to see happen. I am a lot of things for Hunter, but first and foremost, I see myself as someone who does my best to protect him from scrutiny. The best I can do is make sure the people I let near him aren't going to spread around what they've seen.

I redirect the security guard out of the room and sit next to Hunter. "You can't just whip that thing out here like a cigarette, Hunt!" I try to compose myself and not draw more attention, but I'm also trying to get my point across to him. "You've got to go to the bathroom for that!" I lead him out of the lounge, across a balcony, to a small bathroom tucked behind a sliding door that blends with the dark walls. On my way back, I spot MoMo, one of my most favorite security guards. He is slightly under seven feet tall, Moroccan, and although his hands are registered as lethal weapons, he is a big teddy bear.

"Hey, we were just told Hunter had some sort of pipe out trying to smoke crack?" One of the girls had ratted. My judgment on who to trust had been off. I know they have cameras, so denying it is no good. I can't lose the trust of AK and MoMo, but I have to protect Hunter.

"Oh no, he was just smoking marijuana," I cover for him. In D.C., marijuana is legal, and since you can smoke it from a glass pipe, nobody could prove otherwise from watching the video.

MoMo looks at me for a couple of seconds, flashes his ever-ready smile, and sort of laughs. "Oh, sure darling! Just make sure he keeps it contained." His accent is thick, but even through it, I can tell he is on to us, but doing me a favor because he likes me. It's our secret.

Hunter comes out of the bathroom, and I signal it's time to go. I trust MoMo to keep things quiet. He definitely has my back. But I hate putting him in a situation like that. And one thing we all know about AK is he does not tolerate drugs. Some nights he even calls in the drug dogs to keep his place clean. It also doesn't help that Hunter's paranoia is starting to possess me too.

We walk back to the lounge, and Hunter pours himself another drink, striking up a conversation with the girls. I sit by a seemingly lonely Devon and let him know what happened. "Yeah, it's time to go," he agrees, but getting a high Hunter out of a strip club isn't that easy. Fifteen or twenty minutes later he slips away to the bathroom again.

When he doesn't come back in his usual amount of time, I go looking for him. The bathroom door is open, so he either never made it, or just hadn't come back to the lounge. Then I hear a giggle that stops me in my steps. From across the balcony, I can see through the glass shower to the corner nook where I catch a glimpse of long red hair and olive skin, a body straddling someone laid back on a couch with their loafers kicked up on a small platform. Gucci loafers. Hunter's Gucci loafers.

"What the fuck?" I round the corner of the balcony hotter than a two-dollar pistol. I recognize her immediately once I have a clearer view. She has beautiful red hair down her back and olive-colored skin. It is Tiffany. I remember the glint of gold around her waist.

He is talking and laughing with her, as she entertains him. Then he spots me. His eyes just about jump out of his head. He can't move fast enough to get her off him, but I move faster. I shove her a little harder than expected, and out of the corner of my eye I see her body fly up against the wall and onto the couch, while never taking my gaze from Hunter. I stand him up by the collar of his blue pea coat and listen as he starts pleading.

"Honey, she asked to talk to me, and I was trying to get her off of me, but in a polite way! It's not what it seems!" Tiffany gets back on her feet and immediately apologizes. I shove my palm in her face, contemplating sending her on another flight against the wall. She knows how I feel about Hunter, but the money in her hand made her forget.

Touching is against the rules at Mpire. She could be fired, and he could be banned. I should report it, but then I'd have to answer to the physicality of what I did to her, so I just steam off, not letting go of Hunter's collar. I have already asked MoMo to have Devon and Savanah meet us at the elevator, so it is no surprise to see them standing there waiting.

Hunter knows I'm pissed, so he goes to his "go-to." If he can't avoid blame, he makes an excuse. "Honey, just listen, this is all her. She's the one who cornered me. I couldn't get her off of me. I especially wasn't going to do it the way you did. That was wrong!" I can only glare at him. I can't imagine how awkward the elevator ride must have been for Devon and Savanah, but all I can see is red.

We get to the front foyer to exit when the manager stops us to say Hunter's card didn't go through. Hunter hands me his credit card and asks me to stay and handle the bill while he takes Devon to check into the Washington D.C. Ritz-Carlton. Savanah stays with me to help settle up.

I need to cool down, so on the way back to the hotel, Savanah and I stop off at &pizza in Dupont circle. It's quick, and we're hungry. Randomly, our friend Vanessa is there. She's had the same idea. This place is open late and is a pretty popular stop. Hunter never minds when we invite friends back to his fancy suites to party, so we ask Vanessa to come hang.

Vanessa, Savanah, Hunter, Devon, and I sit sort of in a circle on the beds, desk chair, and couch, drinking and listening to Hunter's playlist. He plays "Southside of Heaven" by Ryan Bingham over and over. The lyrics seem to resonate for him, especially the parts about being lost and losing faith in his family, running like "a lost bound train / Running on cocaine and out of control."

By 3:00 a.m. the party has fizzled. Devon is passed out in his bed alone, like he's been most of the night. I feel sorry for him. I don't know why he is so down, but it is obvious he is. I sit on the desk at the foot of the other bed, while Hunter is in the computer chair with his laptop open, facing me. I never know what he is doing on it, and I don't really think about it, but it's always there.

He sits there looking at me with his fingers steepled at his nose, leaning back in the office chair trying to read my mood. He tries to make a joke about Tiffany. Savanah and Vanessa chuckle with him, but it lands flat with me. Too soon. I still have the image of him being straddled by a redhead. It might take some time before this one settles.

Chapter 4
Hmm, Not Hmm Hmm

One evening, I'm cross-legged on my bed FaceTiming my sister Randi Jo, when there is a sudden knock on my door. It's Hunter.

"Look at my socks," he says as he bursts through the door. His colorful footwear has mountains on it and the phrase, "Not all who wander are lost." "It's your favorite quote. I got them because of you."

I'm smitten that he pays attention to the details and remembers everything I say, but I can't resist, "Well could've fooled me. I thought you had wandered and gotten lost! Where have you been?"

It's been weeks since we last spoke, so his sudden appearance fills me with joy. Who knows what he's been up to, but I love that when he resurfaces, showing me his socks is priority number one. I hug him, excited.

I'm renting a basement apartment in a beautiful home in Chevy Chase, owned by a lovely young couple with two small children. D.C. life gets lonely at times. Everyone seems caught up in their own things, and a quiet apartment in the city is too solitary for me. So the laughter and playfulness of the children and couple upstairs make lonely days feel less isolating.

Hunter explains that he tried the front door first, looking for me, and was directed to my basement apartment. I wonder if my landlords recognized him. How funny. They're probably on the phone now with friends and family. "You won't believe who's in my basement. Hunter Biden." That's a conversation piece.

Hunter realizes I'm on FaceTime, grabs the phone, and chats with my sister like a best friend he's known his whole life. It's a perfect diversion from my question about where he's been. My sister entertains him , as he charms her into telling him about her recent divorce and the chaotic events going on in her life. He's definitely on something and I can smell the rubbing alcohol aroma of too much vodka, so while she talks away, I discreetly ask what he's been up to. Keeping my voice low so my sister won't hear, I cautiously inquire, "Hey, Hunt, have you been doing anything?" He looks me in the eye intently and matter-of-factly replies, "Yes, I've been doing hmm, not hmm hmm."

"What?" Randi Jo asks on the screen. "What is he talking about?"

"Oh, he means he's been doing cocaine, but not crack cocaine," I say, interpreting Hunter-Speak for her.

Alcoholics Anonymous teaches that admitting your addiction verbally is the first step toward recovery. Speaking the words out loud makes it real. Hunter, on the other hand, brushes it off casually if you bring up drugs or crack cocaine. He laughs it off, treating it more like a cigarette addiction. He downplays it, and as long as you do the same, everything is fine, and he seems happy. But he's no dummy. Deep down, he knows it's serious. He's fragile in a way, and I never want to cross that line. Mocking him or his addiction could hurt his feelings and damage his ego, making me never hear from him again. So, Hunter says hmm hmm, because saying crack cocaine would make the addiction seem more real.

Despite him claiming to have only done hmm, I don't recall ever seeing him snort a line while we've been together. He did plenty of hmm in the past, but after trying hmm hmm, he hardly ever went back. When he parties, his poisons of choice are hmm hmm and a gallon or more of Tito's.

If you are with Hunter for an entire twenty-four hours, four of them are spent with him cleaning and organizing his "stems," as he calls them. He fills glass tubes with copper strands meshed together to filter the drug and gets just the perfect filter system set to smoke through. Few people who meet me would ever suspect I know the perfect crack pipe setup. After spending so much time with Hunter, I can load anyone the Rolls-Royce of a stem to smoke crack cocaine through, with the perfect amount of copper and a soft tip to prevent lip burns. I may even have a tiny scar on my chest from a time Hunter dropped one on me while I was lying down.

As time passes and the addiction demon sinks its claws deeper into Hunter, he becomes more erratic, and the chaos around him (and me) becomes more extreme. Some moments are hilariously bizarre, while others are heartbreaking. He disappears for weeks at a time, making it harder to reach him than ever. Everyone in his life knows you can't get in touch with Hunter, Hunter will get in touch with you.

The night he shows up at my place wearing his "Not all who wander are lost" socks, Hallie tries reaching him over and over. He wants me to go with him to his Annapolis house, and I can see he shouldn't be driving since he's been drinking too much and not sleeping from doing hmm. Plus, I never turn down spending time with him. Out front is a small black Audi SUV parked on the tree-lined street. That is new. I'm used to his silver Porsche, his black truck, or the Range Rover. I wonder if my landlords are peeking out, curious about my relationship with Hunter. But the house is quiet. In small-town Arkansas, everyone feels the need to know every detail of your life, but I love that D.C. respects privacy and people have too much going on to concern themselves with you.

"You drive! I'll navigate," Hunter shouts as he walks toward the passenger side. I don't argue, but I do suggest maybe we type his address into my GPS. And it's a good thing I do. I use GPS to get everywhere, and

Hunter passes out before we even leave D.C. I have no intention of waking him. I wonder how long he's been on a binge and feel grateful that he found his way to me when he needed rest.

Thirty minutes into driving, his iPad goes off over, and over, and over again. I shake his shoulder, "Hunt, Hallie is calling you." He jolts awake and grabs the iPad, putting it to his ear like a phone. "Hello!" he shouts, still not fully awake. I can hear her muffled voice asking what he's doing as he talks loudly with his cheek pressed to the tablet.

"Hunt, she's on FaceTime, not a call."

He looks at the iPad for a second and fumbles it like a hot potato. It lands between the console and his seat. "Whew," he exclaims. "That was close."

"Hunt, you didn't hang up the phone," I laugh watching the worry on his face as he looks down in between the seat and console at an angry Hallie. It was obvious he didn't want her to know he was with me this time. He digs until finally recovering the iPad and hurries to push the end button.

Bye, Hal.

Hallie and I aren't the only other characters in the Hunter Biden "dramady." There are lots of supporting cast members—some are businesspeople like Devon Archer, some are drug dealers like Bicycles. And then there's Big Boy.

One night Hunter calls me to join the party at Rosemont Seneca. Kelsey and Savanah are already there, and once the clock strikes midnight, I ditch the birthday party I've been hanging out at and head out the door to the waterfront.

I go through the usual back-door entrance to the House of Sweden and march up to the fifth floor.

Rounding the corner I notice several things. First, there's Savannah already asleep on the couch. I've never met anyone who can go to sleep as fast and stay asleep as long as that girl can, and she does it all the time. If you walk into a room with Savannah already inside, there's at least a 75 percent chance she's going to be peacefully snoozing. If there's a raging party in the room, the chances of her sleeping climb to as high as 90 percent.

I see Kelsey giving me a look like she knows I'm fixing to have a reaction to something, and she wants to be front and center to see that reaction. Scanning past Kelsey I finally see an absolutely massive man "cooking" in the kitchen.

The man is at least seven feet tall with a hulking four-hundred-pound frame and dressed in an oversized-tall T-shirt. He's definitely a Michael Oher type who shops the big and tall. His black sweatpants look as if he's worn them every day for the last year, stained down to his ankles and his once white, dingy tennis shoes. He greets me with a smile and reeks of . . . kindness?

Kelsey motions for me to come to the bathroom with her. So I follow, wondering just who the mysterious kitchen cooker could be.

"You won't believe this," she whispers as we push our way through the bathroom door. There's still water on the floor and in the bathtub from Hunter. He occasionally soaks in the tub when his neck and shoulders start aching.

"Oh God, what?" I ask as I automatically go into "clean up for Hunter" mode and let the water out of the tub.

"I was sitting in Hunt's office earlier, telling him how I wanted these new shoes, but I didn't buy them because they were too expensive. He gives me a mini sermon on how I shouldn't ever let lack of money stop me from anything I want, then he got in his wallet and handed me ten $20 bills."

"Okay? And? What won't I believe about that?" I say, laughing. That definitely sounds like Hunter.

"Well, listen. Hunter gave me $200, and I put it in my sock for safe-keeping. A couple of minutes later Hunter tells Big Country to run and grab him some cigarettes. Big Country tells Hunter he doesn't have any cash, so Hunter offers him some of the money in my sock!"

"Wait, so is that Big Country out there?"

"Yeah, and he's got my money."

"Your . . . sock money?"

"Yes. He took $30 from my sock."

"The sock that is on your foot right now?"

"Yes!"

We both laugh at the seemingly random big guy who walks up and took $30 cash from Kelsey's foot and shoved the rest back in her sock.

"Who is this guy anyway?" I ask.

"I told you—Big Country. Apparently he's Hunter's friend/bodyguard."

"How the hell do I not know about this guy?"

"I don't know. From what Hunt said earlier tonight Big Country does shady work," she says, not knowing if Hunter was joking or being serious.

"Hmm . . . weird. With him in the kitchen with the pans and all, I thought he was maybe some kind of personal chef Hunt's trying out or something."

"Well, kind of. He's cooking hmm hmm."

"What? Cooking it? That's what he's doing in there?"

"Well, he's doing something, testing it or something for him. I don't know. He's like melting it or something in a skillet with a spoon. How the hell am I supposed to know what all that means?"

"Well, that makes sense, I guess." I say, finally comprehending what was actually going on.

For the rest of my time with Hunter, Big Country drifts in and out of stories. Sometimes Hunter would send him to pick me up from my apartment so I didn't have to Uber or drive my car into the city.

That was all well and good because he seemed like a gentle giant. He was always very respectful to Savanah, Kelsey, and I. We felt safe around

him but definitely became a little skeptical one day while in the kitchen
of Rosemont.

Hunter was in one of his more playful moods and wanted to show
Kelsey and I how well he could perform yoga poses. It's obviously a laugh-
able moment that we always take too far, because Kelsey and I both join
him trying to do the same pose. We are balancing on one foot with the
other foot in some crooked position, trying to keep our balance, when
we tumble over like a row of dominos. It doesn't help that we've been in
the Tito's bottle. We sit on the floor laughing when we look up to see Big
Boy laughing with us.

"You wanna try a yoga pose?" I ask.

"Nah . . . Nah, I'm gonna leave that to you three," he replies laughing
as he focuses on the skillet in front of him.

"Big Country, you know you can come off as scary," Kelsey volunteers
as the booze tickles either her bravery or her carelessness. Hunter gives
Kelsey the "shut up" look.

"How so?" he asks.

"You're kind of mysterious. I bet you've killed people."

"Who says I haven't?" he shoots back with a grin.

Kelsey and I both tune in and sober up a little bit. We've talked about
this in private before. We've had this theory that Big Country is a hit man.
I'm starting to think our theory was spot on.

"You have?" she asks.

"I'm not saying I have. I'm not saying I haven't. But if I had, would
I tell you?" He turns to look at the two of us sitting on the floor gazing
up at him with stunned faces. His eyes flash from those of a warm gentle
giant to those of a stone-cold killer.

By this time Hunter has left the kitchen and walked back into his
office. Either he's avoiding the conversation because he knew where it was
heading, or he was bored with it.

"Well, this is fun, where's Hunter?" I ask, trying to seem nonchalant and failing completely. I grab Kelsey's arm and motion for her to follow me into the office. Big Country lumbers back to his skillet.

"Hunt, is Big Country a killer?" I ask after tracking him to his office.

"What? He is not going to hurt you," Hunter laughs.

"Um, that's not what I asked . . . and are you sure he won't?"

"Have you wronged him?" he asks, laughing while leaning back in his office chair. "He's a teddy bear, just don't get on his bad side."

Hunt's mysterious grin makes me question a lot about this guy in the kitchen. I know Hunter would never harm a fly, but he wouldn't need to if he's got Big Boy on his side.

"Have you ever been on his bad side? Better yet, have you ever had him handle someone that was on your bad side?"

Hunter laughs again. "No, of course not."

What Hunter said didn't matter. From that day forward our theories about Big County turn into facts as far as we're concerned. Savanah, Kelsey, and I joke lots of times that one day Hunter will decide we all know too much and will send Big Country to give us a "special" ride home.

As the date of my birthday gets close, Hunter suggests a girls' weekend, promising to cover all expenses, but finding the right time proves difficult. We decide to postpone until after my visits home in the spring and summer. One September day I remind him. I just want a few close friends in a luxurious hotel with an open bar, room service, movies, and our own private party. By 2:00 p.m. he has the presidential suite of the Rosewood Hotel rented for the night, with all the room service we could want.

Savanah agrees immediately, while Kelsey can only join us for a portion of the night. She's dating a guy who has gout, and he wants her to spend less time with us and more time tending to him.

The suite is beyond stunning, with hardwood floors, crystal chandeliers, and classic furniture in white and gold damask. The earth tone leathers and leaf motifs on cream backgrounds are refreshingly elegant. The entryway boasts mirrored pedestals with modern sculptures and a beautiful marble floor in brown, gold, and cream concentric circles. A huge black bathtub with a TV above it can fit eight people and is big enough to host a party all its own.

I lounge with Hunter on the cream couch, getting on his nerves by using the remote to open and close the curtains, wanting him to capture the perfect snap. This place is fancier than our usual rooms. I'm like Julia Roberts in *Pretty Woman*, and he is Richard Gere, amused at my excitement.

When Savanah arrives, Hunter realizes he's left his laptop at Rosemont Seneca. He doesn't leave it anywhere, even his office, and needs to head back to work to get it. But I want him to stay for girls' night and offer to get his laptop for him. That works; he has calls to make and heads down to the lobby bar.

Savanah gets her things together, and I grab Hunter's backpack and head downstairs. We see Hunter across the lobby, and just as his eyes meet ours, the oversized purse Savanah is inexplicably lugging over her arm opens up, one handle falling toward the floor, and a roll of toilet paper bounces out and makes a beeline across the marble as she chases it. "Are you fucking kidding me?" Hunter's face reads. Twenty-five feet later, Savanah catches the wayward roll as Hunter reaches us, walking hard and determined.

"What are you doing?" he scowls.

"Well, the hotel gave us an extra supply of toilet paper and shampoo, and I was taking it to my car so I didn't have to buy it at home," Savanah explains, looking like it should be obvious.

"You haven't even stayed here one night, and you are taking toilet paper to your car?" He's incredulous. "And you didn't just take the wrapped ones, you had to take the one from the holder?"

"I liked the way they folded the end of it," Savanah says, making sure it's securely stuffed in her bag.

"Unbelievable."

And we're out, leaving Hunter to marvel in amusement at how dumb we are.

Savanah drops off her contraband, and we walk the few blocks to Rosemont Seneca, laughing as I suggest she should have a drink or two tonight. She's going to have to fight off her hypochondriac tendency to end up in the ER with a hangover.

We sit outside the door of the Swedish Embassy for what feels like an hour before Hunter calls the security guard to let us in. With the laptop in our possession, we put it in his backpack and head back to Rosewood, meeting up with Kelsey on the way.

Just before the hotel entrance, a guy walks straight past us, hands jammed in his jacket pockets and hat pulled down low. Savanah and I are engrossed in describing the beautiful suite to Kelsey, when a confused look comes over her face. "Is that . . . ?" she asks, pointing to the man. Savanah and I turn to see a very incognito, mysterious Hunter walking right past us. He obviously sees us but is doing some secret squirrel shit. We head to the room, chalking it up to Hunter's normal suspicious crap, and pay it no mind.

Back upstairs, we explore everything, thoroughly nosing around the entire place, and taking videos as if we're on *MTV Cribs*. We're enjoying the complimentary chilled champagne on the bed and entertaining ourselves with the automatic window treatments again when Hunter walks back through the door. We don't ask where he's been. He probably would divert to something else.

"You have to stay and drink with us," Kelsey pleads with Hunter. We are AMOEBA. Everyone loves to have Hunter around.

"Okay, fine. I'll stay for a while. Kelsey, you get the music. Savanah, you order room service. Lunden, you fix us a drink."

I speak up. "I have the best taste in music, and you give the DJ job to Kelsey?! What the hell, Hunt!"

"Fine," he replies. "Lunden, you get the music going. Kelsey, you order room service, and Savanah you handle the drinks!"

"*What*? You want the one person who doesn't drink to mix drinks?" Savanah exclaims.

"*Fuck it*! There are three of you and three jobs. Fuckin' *figure it out*," he shouts. We are on his last nerve, per usual, but we all laugh. We love getting under his skin, plus we know that "fuck" is just his favorite word. He wears a "New Fucking York" T-shirt to the office sometimes, or one that says "fuck you, you fucking fuck." He says it a hundred times a day, mostly to make us laugh, and especially likes to pile them on top of each other.

I start the AMOEBA playlist that's mostly for Hunter, with "Southside of Heaven" by Ryan Bingham, a few Sturgill Simpson songs, R. L. Burnside, and Kris Kristofferson's "Sunday Morning Coming Down." Kelsey mixes drinks with the simple combination of ice and vodka. And Savanah starts to order room service.

"Hunt, are you staying long enough to actually eat? I'm ordering you something anyway. It's room service, so it's free."

"It's not free!" he shouts at her. "It's free for you, but not for me. I mean, seriously, what the entire fuck would you three do without me to take care of you?" He has a point. It's a part of our AMOEBA pact.

Before too long he gets bored with our little party and leaves. He claims he is going back to Annapolis and has some business to take care of before it gets too late.

In comfy clothes, we enjoy our lazy girls' night and order milk and cookies that cost $200. Champagne, vodka, and milk probably aren't the best combination, but for women who party as hard as we do, this is a remarkably tame evening.

Sitting on the couches binging reruns of *Friends*, we hear a knock at the door. Puzzled, we exchange glances. We aren't expecting company, unless room service wants to surprise us with complimentary treats. I hop up and peer through the peephole, catching a glimpse of Hunter holding a drink.

I swing the door open, and Hunter appears startled. He throws his drink in the air, spilling it all over the both of us, and the glass shatters as it hits the hardwood floor. Now I'm startled. He looks up at me with a dazed expression. "Jeez! You scared me!"

"Hunt, you knocked on the door. Did you not expect us to answer? Are you okay?"

"I'm fine."

But clearly, he isn't. He looks very different from the Hunter who left us just hours earlier. He staggers in and thunks down on the end of one couch. He's speaking gibberish, not the wild things his brilliant and sober mind comes up with, or the playful shorthand we use with each other, but just incoherent mumbles. He's phasing in and out of complete nonsense, not speaking to us, but seeming to talk to himself. Worry sharpens my senses, and I sit next to him, watching his every move. Across from us on the other couch, Savanah sets her champagne glass down and sits up. Kelsey stands behind the couch, unable to move.

We have never seen Hunter as messed up as he is in this moment. His words are jumbled, and his face seems distorted on one side. I glance at my anxious friends, trying not to show concern on my own face. It's terrifying. Then suddenly, Hunter goes limp, slumping to the floor between the couch and the marble coffee table.

I drop to my hands and knees. "Hunt, are you okay?"

All he can do is mumble, his eyes closed. Part of me wonders if this is some sort of joke. I've seen him consume mindboggling amounts of drugs and never end up in this state. I'm horrified, and more worried than I have ever been in my whole life, but Savanah is frantic, and I don't want to scare her or Kelsey any more than they already are. Somebody has to hold it together.

Five minutes earlier we were drinking milk and eating cookies. Now we might be watching a demonic addiction take our friend down once and for all. I can't help but start praying in my champagne-buzzed mind that our God hears me and doesn't let these be Hunter's last moments on earth.

With Hunter unconscious on the floor, I sit with my legs crossed and cradle his head in my lap, trying to talk with him. His eyes twitch, and he mumbles, but it's all strange and incoherent. Feeling his pulse, I see it bulging from his neck. Savanah brings him a bottle of water. But at the mention of water, he yells out, "Waters of World War II," bolts upright, slams his head against the solid marble coffee table, and passes out again.

"Is he okay? Have you seen him like this before?" Savanah is hysterical, standing over us with her eyes fixed on Hunter. I desperately need someone to tell me it's all going to be okay, but I lie and say he's done this before and just needs to sleep it off. We try to lift him and move him to a bed, but as we do, his delirium intensifies. "Don't call the police," he says, in a panic. So I gently guide his head back onto my lap, reassuring him he's safe, refusing to let his heart race any faster.

We sit there, faced with the horrible decision of calling for help or not. If I make the call and he lives, he'll never forgive me. He'll say he would have survived even if I hadn't called for help, and now, thanks to me, his entire family will be humiliated by incriminating headlines. But if I don't make the call and something happens . . . My gut churns.

Kelsey and Savanah help me get him up, and he seems to come to slightly, but still isn't able to walk or talk properly. He continues to keep his eyes closed. It takes us fifteen minutes to move him from the living room to the bedroom. As we get him under the covers, I see he has passed out again. "God, please help him just breathe."

Curling up next to him on the master bed, I let the girls know he's fine. "He'll be okay after he sleeps it off." Through the night I lie there just watching his chest go up and down, my mind made up that at the first sign of inconsistency, I'll call for help. But once he's tucked in, he appears to sleep, occasionally letting out a snore. Maybe I was right, maybe he does just need sleep. I want to believe that, but sometimes his breathing becomes so faint that I have my phone in my hands ready to dial. Instead, I nudge him until he moves his head or mumbles something, and I at least know he's still there.

At some point during the night, Kelsey goes home. She has to go take care of Gout, but she calls multiple times, checking on Hunter's status and us. Savanah is consumed with worry, but she keeps me company, staying up most of the night talking with me as we wait for Hunter's snoring to become constant. Once it does, she lays down on the other side of the bed, and before long is snoring too.

I stay awake, watching and listening to him. I also cry. It is bitterly painful knowing that someone I care so much about—someone with so much potential and generosity and brilliance—is struggling with this demon of addiction. I cry, wondering if he is even struggling at all anymore, or if he has just given up and let the demon take everything. I cry, knowing that if he doesn't get help, the demon will take him down. I cry, knowing that he has to be scared and somehow his mind managed to get him back to me. A safe place. Someone he can trust to take care of him.

The endless night finally gives way to dawn. Hunter stirs, and it looks like the demon has lost this round. But then he opens his mouth.

"Get me my backpack. I need my coke."

No "Good morning." No "What happened last night?" The first words from his mouth show the demon didn't lose. He actually won. He took Hunter to the brink of death, then let him return to us . . . just to torture him all over again.

I get him his backpack.

He gets up, showers, and comes back like a new man. The old Hunter is back, joking, making wisecracks, and acting like nothing happened. He terrified me the night before, but now, I am just relieved that he is okay, so I go with it.

"Honey, have you all checked out the pool," he asks as if we're on a holiday.

"No, asshole, we didn't have time to. We spent all night making sure you were still breathing."

"Are you mad at me?" he asks, more concerned about me being mad than that he almost died.

Savanah wakes up, happy to see the same Hunter I'm seeing. She tells him he scared the hell out of us, and we describe what happened the night before. "Hunt, you sat up yelling about World War II!" Savanah exclaims.

"Well, at least I wasn't yelling about World War III, right?" he jokes back. "All right, well, it's been fun, but I have to get to the office. Love you, bye!" And he's off.

I wonder if Hunter really knows what he went through that night, what we all went through.

As he walks out, I sit in the presidential suite, looking at the couch where he collapsed, the marble coffee table he smashed his head on, and the bed where I laid next to him, desperate to hear him breathe. And this eerily happy feeling nags at me for a while, until I figure it out.

Last night he could have gone anywhere—to Chain Bridge, to Hallie, or to any friend—but he found his way to me. He knows he can trust me. How damned honored am I?

Chapter 5

He Meant Well

If it bleeds, it leads. That's what they say in the news business, which seems like a pretty disgusting way to talk about news, but in my experience, the people who write the news are vultures, pretty disgusting, so maybe it works.

In Hunter's case, it wasn't so much about blood as it was blow. The media would make him out to be some hopeless "crackhead" consumed by his demons, addicted to drugs, alcohol, women, and living a life he couldn't afford. Hunter has since acknowledged the mistakes and demons that haunt him from that time. But for every story written about that "crackhead" and "fraud," there's a story about Hunter that goes untold, of generosity, kindness, and his giving heart. That's the easiest story for me to tell.

It's a cold day in December 2017 and I've been home all day doing nothing. My phone lights up with a picture of Hunter and Joe from the cover of *Popular Mechanics*. I set it as his contact, thinking it was one of the best pictures of Hunter I'd seen.

"Hey, honey, I'm leaving for New York City today for meetings and could use your assistance. Want to come?"

Hell yes. Even though New York is just a train ride from D.C., I have never been. Plus, when he's in some meetings, I'll be able to see the Christmas lights. I'm ready in an hour. Excited is an understatement.

At Rosemont Seneca, Hunter emerges from the parking garage where he's dropped his Porsche. Patagonia backpack pulled over one shoulder, Nantucket police force hat pulled down, and looking at his phone, he's incognito, just the way he likes it. I hop out of the car and get in the passenger side, conscious of his downgrade from a Porsche coupe to a Dodge Challenger. But not Hunter. You'd never know he owns the most expensive car on the lot. But he doesn't like having to be the one who drives; it means less time to do the extracurricular activities he's packed in his backpack. Playfully pissed, he walks to the driver's side, gets in, gives me the finger, and pulls out.

Before heading to Union Station, Hunter makes a pit stop at the Archibald's Strip Club. I can see from the doorman's reaction that this is not their first rodeo. He greets Hunter with a hug and Hunter asks him the latest. Inside, Hunter pulls a chair out for me at the bar, then slides next to me. Before he can even order his Tito's, girls start swarming. It's like when you feed fish and you throw a piece of bread into the water, then out of nowhere fish swarm and nibble. Hunter is the bread. I order our Tito's and smile at the girls while I sit back admiring how one guy can come into a public place and have everyone's attention without wanting it. Most men are here to see girls naked, but Hunter's here to socialize and see friends, handing out hundreds while making girls laugh and talking through their problems. He's every stripper's dream. But he never stays in one place too long, so before I know it, we're out the door to catch our train.

In the parking garage at Union Station, Hunter starts throwing his stuff in his backpack, dropping one of his many phones between the seats. Even though I tell him, he doesn't seem to care. He just keeps rambling on, telling me not to draw attention and to sober up while in a public place. I laugh, knowing why he's concerned about me making a fool of myself. How does he manage to hold it all together?

As we walk into the station, Hunter has his hat pulled down and his backpack over his shoulder, looking back to make sure I'm rolling my luggage in a straight line. I don't want to let him down and blow his need for blending in. I enjoy getting under his skin, but not enough to purposely humiliate him.

Hunter has this distinctive walk, especially when he's on a mission or under the influence. I first noticed it when he was going down a staircase and his left foot turned a little bit inward. It's not pigeon-toed or knock-kneed, but something in between. His left leg swings out stiff in front of him every so often, and his arms are straight at his side. It doesn't happen all the time, but when it does, it's distinctive.

He's doing this walk real fast, and doing his playful pissed thing again, when I drop my scarf and stop to pick it up. He is halfway down the escalator with the collar of his navy blue pea coat pulled up and shadowing his face when time comes to a standstill. Union Station is crowded, even nearing 10:00 p.m. The alcohol and scarf are making me sort of tangled as I try to place myself on the escalator. And just then my roller bag flies right out of my hands. My eyes double in size. *Boom. Boom. Boom.* My bag is flying past a now very un-incognito Hunter. He throws his hands up. "Are you fucking kidding me?" his face reads. He shakes his head, grabs the bag at the bottom in one swift motion like no one might notice, and stalks off, head down. Never missing a beat. I die laughing as I ride down the escalator in the high-powered spotlight suddenly shining on Hunter Biden and the girl who can't handle a rolling bag, scarf, and a couple of Tito's. If I can teach him anything, it's how to let loose.

I follow as Hunter walks to the Amtrak counter to charm an older woman into getting an extra ticket. Her face says she feels like the only woman in Union Station. She doesn't stand a chance. He's told me his ticket is always free since he's on the board of Amtrak, or something like that. And he certainly doesn't need my ticket to be free, he likes flexing his superpower. I keep my distance till the rolling bag thing blows over, but I smile.

Tickets in hand, he throws his green backpack over his shoulder again, grabbing a now banged-up roller bag that I'm staying away from, and beelines to Uniqlo for armfuls of clothing. For him, packing for a trip doesn't mean grabbing clothes. He gets new things wherever he goes.

Coming out of the restroom nearby, I cross the white marble floor to Hunter now in front of Victoria's Secret, chatting with a couple of girls in black.

"Hey! There she is." He smiles, first at them, then at me. "These girls said they would fix you up. Go ahead. Go find whatever you like." He is generous, and grabs a pair of sweatpants to make it less awkward while saying, "Did you bring enough warm clothes?"

"Oh no! I'm fine!" I hate attention drawn to myself, probably more than Hunter. Plus, here comes my awkwardness. I also don't handle receiving gifts well, especially from someone I am interested in or dating. I don't really know why, it embarrasses me. Plus, I don't want the sales-girls fawning over me and lingerie. Hunter picks up on it real quick, so he doesn't push, and we make our way to the bench to wait for the train.

"I'm going to grab something quick to eat. Are you hungry?" Hunter asks.

"No." I always say no. I'm weird when people offer to buy me things, whether it be lingerie or food.

He pays my awkwardness no mind, and before I know it here he comes with two McDonald's bags and two Cokes.

"Here. I don't care what you say. I'm not eating in front of you without at least bringing you something, too."

Now that I think about it, I am kind of hungry. Hunter knows people. Sometimes better than they want him to.

I follow him onto the train and toward the back. I'm starting to get to know him too. I don't question why he chooses the back of the train; I know. He wants to be close enough to the bathroom that when his demons start calling, he can casually duck in the small enclosure for privacy, and any other passenger will just think he has a small bladder, not a serious addiction. As we ride, I act as if I don't notice the demons dragging him to the urinal every fifteen minutes.

Just about at the Wilmington, Delaware, stop Hunter tells me he has to hop off the train and grab a pair of pants. Yep, pants. He bought armfuls of pants in Union Station, but I guess he needed some special Delaware pants too. "Is pants a code word for something else?" I wonder. He exits to meet his pants contact, and my dad FaceTimes to check in. "Did you see that?" I look up as a blur of Hunter shoots across the platform beside us. Next thing I know he's running through the cars, making his way to the back. Disheveled and a little winded, he plunks down, khaki Delaware pants in hand. Turns out it isn't a code word after all. He catches his breath as I look at him in disbelief. What? Why? Pants? With Hunter, life is a cliff-hanger, and I laugh and hold on.

Like two best friends sitting in our blue leather seats, we ride in the hazy intoxication of more than just being together. We laugh and look at whatever he pulls up on his laptop, as the chilly darkness slides by outside and our breath fogs the window. Even with Hunter in his casual clothes and as modest as he is, I sit next to him thinking my cream sweater and North Face parka aren't fancy enough. Tom Ford Tuscan Leather permeates the air. He has a bottle on him wherever he goes.

On his laptop, we scroll through pictures of gorgeous colonial style homes in Annapolis he is considering renting. I love them, the white columns, the shutters, the peaked dormers and chimneys with just a little soot at the top. I never knew how much I liked colonial homes until Hunter introduced them to me. I never even realized there were so many different housing styles.

Then there is a picture of his mom. We've all heard the story of the tragedy that happened to the Biden family when Neilia and Naomi died in a car accident. I never asked for details because I didn't want him to have to relive a painful story like that. I had heard Hunter and his brother, Beau, were in the hospital with multiple broken bones and a fractured skull while Joe was running to be one of the youngest U.S. senators in history. He was sworn in by their bedside. Hunter is nostalgic. He misses his mom every day, even though he can hardly remember her. He said it felt like he was missing a limb. There is this one picture of her in a bathing suit that reminds me of Marilyn Monroe when she was candid with her soft rolls sort of showing. She is beautiful. It isn't posed. It's real, raw, like a woman and a mom should be. He loves that picture.

Neither of us like to dwell on sad things, so we laugh and pick at each other as the dark night speeds by. We even pull up an old highlight reel from my junior basketball season of high school. I'm boasting, and Hunter can't help but laugh. He tells me about his daughter Maisy and how she plays basketball too. I can see the corner of his mouth turn up with pride as he talks about his children.

Throughout the night a little old black woman turns around every few minutes to smile at our conversation.

"Excuse me," she asks in a voice softened by age, "do you know what time it is?"

He looks at one of his phones. It's 11:00 p.m.

She apologizes for the interruption. "I don't have a watch or a phone with me."

Hunter and I look at each other. The woman is so old, every bit of eighty-something. It is way too late for a woman of her age to be on the train in these big cities, let alone without a phone and by herself.

"You wouldn't happen to know that man there, would you?" she asks Hunter, pointing to a poster above our heads. It is an ad for Joe Biden's memoir, *Promise Me, Dad*. A much younger Biden family appears on the cover. Hunter, in his humble way says with a little smile in his eyes, "I might know him."

"What are you doing on a train so late?" he asks, leaning in a little.

"Well, my nephew, who I raised like a son, was diagnosed with a brain tumor; it's called glioblastoma." Her voice breaks a little as she talks about the same brain cancer Beau died from.

It's over. I can see it in Hunter's eyes. He is about to go above and beyond. He stands, without breaking eye contact, and walks to the woman, wrapping his arms around her little shoulders. She embraces and opens up, because everyone does with him. He attempts to call Joe and allow this woman a phone call she would never forget. It is the Hunter magic. Call the former vice president of the United States to get some comfort for this woman he meets on the train, while still being a kind guy, down to earth, and relatable. That's how he is with everyone.

In a few short minutes he has brightened a dark time for this lady. But he isn't done yet. He finds out she is getting off at the second New Jersey stop, Newark, then walking by her lonesome to the stoplight outside the station, where her family will pick her up. An elderly lady on the streets is bad, but an elderly lady on the streets of Newark at night with no phone, even worse.

"Okay, I'm going to get you there," Hunter guarantees her.

Pulling up to the station, he takes her arm, walks her toward the door, and says, "I'll be right back." There was no way. But how could you not find it real attractive when a guy does that?

So I sit here, again. Doors close, again. Hunter not in his seat, again. And suddenly I see myself in New York, with no one I know, getting mugged on a street corner. And the train pulls out.

Then Hunter comes barreling through the cars and crashing into his seat. Again, he had gotten on at an earlier car, just as the doors closed. He gives me a satisfied little head nod and not five seconds later an announcement comes over the loudspeaker, "Newark, New Jersey, next station."

He freezes, muscles tense, holding his breath. "Did they just say that?" he whispers in disbelief.

"They did." I close my mouth tight to try to keep it in, but I burst out laughing.

For just once in his life Hunter hadn't run late. Nope, this time he was early. A whole train station early.

"Oh my God, Hunt! You just put that old woman at the wrong stoplight in Jersey!"

Hunter isn't laughing, he's devastated. He freaks out, sprints to the front of the train and tries to make them stop.

"We don't stop the train, sir. That's not how this works."

"I'm on the Amtrak board!" he shouts.

"We don't stop the train for anyone."

For once, someone is immune to Hunter's charm. Amtrak engineers. I didn't see it coming.

He is going to lose his mind if he doesn't make it right, and I have (almost) zero doubts this woman won't be stranded for long. He will fix this. He will fix this. Oh God . . . will he fix this?

"So what am I supposed to do?" I ask as he hops off at the next station.

"I'll take care of it. Trust me. Just trust me. I'm going to rent a car. I'll probably be thirty minutes behind you, tops." And he is out, leaving behind my roller bag, bottomless anxiety, and a backpack full of more hmm than I could bail myself out of jail from.

But like Hunter magic, five minutes later a guy working for Amtrak comes up and asks who I am. "Hunter Biden sent me to babysit you." Except he doesn't say the babysitting part out loud. I guess they aren't immune to his charm after all. "I'll get you to Grand Central, get you in a taxi, and tell the driver where to go. You'll be fine."

Grand Central Station is wild, even at midnight. Hunter calls with directions to Luxury Penthouse NYC - SIXTY Loft. "When you get there, they'll have everything ready." So my babysitter gets me and the backpack into the cab and we're off. It isn't actually that far. If Hunter hadn't accidentally left that little old lady to die on a street corner in December, we would be walking there together.

The SIXTY Loft front desk attendant slides me paperwork, and I sign "Hunter Biden." Then one of Hunter's jackets materializes in his hands. How can one man lose that many jackets? I'm not joking when I say he leaves them everywhere. Hunter's backpack, check. His new clothes, check. Delaware pants, check. Drugs, check. Laptop, check. And an extra Hunter jacket, because why not? I need a drink.

The penthouse is so pretty. It has a balcony all the way around, and there are skyscrapers everywhere. The lights are incredible, bouncing off shiny black stairs going up to a beautiful loft with a magnificent bathroom. Downstairs is a fireplace in the middle of a modern studio with an open bar. Not something you'd see in Arkansas.

I put our stuff up, make a drink, and call Hunter. No answer. I try working the TV, punching the buttons on the remote. Nada. Apparently, I need a course just to learn how to get this fancy TV going. Finally I get hungry. I never know when Hunter might show up, so I go to a restaurant next door to get a dirty martini and some spaghetti by myself. I keep calling. Still no answer. Finally, at two in the morning, when I'm back in the loft, still trying to turn on the TV, there is a knock at the door. Through the peephole I see the gold Nantucket police force star on the hat. It's Hunter, but not the same Hunter who left me on the train hours ago. All he had on was a T-shirt and jeans. It's snowing outside! Where was his pea coat? I swing the door open to see the look on his face.

"I saw this homeless guy, and I gave him my stuff." Of course he did. I try not to laugh.

After he sprinted off the train, saved the elderly lady, and took time to talk with her family (of course), he was on his way back when he saw a homeless man out in the cold by himself. Hunter being Hunter (which is to say very kind but out of it), gave the man his jacket. Another jacket bites the dust.

Then at some point, when he was getting close to SIXTY Loft, it dawned on him that his wallet with cash, cell phone, some recreational rocks, his ID, and worst of all, his single most prized possession, Beau's dog tags, are all in the jacket he's just given away.

"We've got to call the homeless guy." He marches around, flinging his hands down.

"Okay, Hunt, but the homeless guy's been ignoring me for hours."

Bless his heart. I know it seems awful, but to me things like this are comical. Not because Hunter is panicking over the dog tags; my heart hurts for him. But because what else can you do but laugh when you hear something like this? I swear, Hunter's tombstone is going to read, "Hunter Biden, He meant well."

We call for hours, and around 4:00 a.m. the homeless guy gives in and answers.

"Hi! I just gave you my jacket and left some things in the pocket. You can keep the money, the wallet, anything. Keep the phone. Hell, I'll buy you a new phone. I'll even put you on my phone plan! Just please let me get the dog tags back," Hunter pleads, my phone pressed to his ear.

Hunter makes a date with the homeless guy for later that morning. I try to get his mind off of it in the meantime and start by rubbing his shoulders. I've got a few drinks in me, which makes me bold enough to make the first move.

A few hours later, a much more relaxed Hunter heads to the homeless man rendezvous and stops by the ATM to get more cash to give him something extra for making the trip to bring back the dog tags. After that, he has a business meeting. But the one he brought me to New York for was canceled, which leaves me at the penthouse.

"Honey," he calls everyone honey. "It looks like a bomb has gone off down here!" He's calling up to me from the bottom of the stairs to the loft. "It's a mess, but I'm running late!" A bomb made of socks, shoes, receipts, paraphernalia, cell phones, and pants.

"Yeah, well that mess'll be here when you get back to clean up, Hunt. It ain't going nowhere." He gives me a stiff-lipped kiss before leaving. I start picking up the place.

As I am straightening up, I see wadded up Benjamins sticking out of my wallet. Hunter wants to take care of everybody, no matter his state of mind, no matter how high he is. It's part of the Hunter package, and you don't feel like a burden, because you aren't asking.

Time for New York. I throw some warm clothes on, grab his blue YETI hat and a scarf and instead of grabbing my North Face parka, one of his blue pea coats with a V.P. pin on it—and I am off to see Manhattan. It is a culture shock, even after years in D.C., but I love it. I love the East Coast, and I love big cities. I wander the streets looking at the giant Christmas decorations and lights, taking it all in. But it isn't nearly as much fun by myself. I feel like a tourist. With him, we would have blended into the scene.

By evening I figure maybe he is back at the loft, and I am kind of tired of being on my own. But as I walk into the lobby, a text pings, complaining that he has to run to another late meeting.

I hear a phone ringing while I'm out on the balcony upstairs, and it's not mine. One of Hunter's phones had slipped between the black leather couch cushions. Who could resist? I fish it out and punch in his password, looking for reasons I should just pack my bags and head back. And honestly, I find my concerns confirmed with lots of women in his phone, but then I open his message app and my heart breaks for another reason. It breaks for him.

"Hunt, I need $2,000 in this account."

"Done."

"Can you pay my rent this month?"

"Okay."

"Can you wire me money, I need help!"

"You got it."

It goes on and on. People just asking for something, asking for anything from Hunter. Demanding. As if he were made to meet their needs. How draining. Not a single person asking how he is or if he needs anything. Takers surround him, and he is expected to comply. No wonder the demons pull him down into numbness and forgetfulness.

Who is there for Hunter? No one. And I do not want him to be alone. I turn off the phone and try the TV again. No go. I am getting ready to chuck the remote into the fireplace when my phone vibrates. It is Hunter on FaceTime. Most times he would FaceTime rather than call. Maybe he needs eye-to-eye contact, or maybe he thinks a FaceTime is more secure and less likely to be tapped.

"Hey, so I'm stuck in this meeting."

"Hunt, where are you?"

"I'm in a meeting. I'll be out in about five . . . fifteen minutes. I'm not far."

He is talking but all I am seeing is the EXIT sign over his head.

"Hunt, where are you? I can see the EXIT sign over your head."

"I'm in a meeting," He emphasizes "in" and "meeting."

"Hunt, there's a mirror behind you and I can see the strippers on the pole!"

Realization dawns.

"What?" he shouts, turns around, pauses for a second to get his game plan together, then click. Hangs up. Solid plan there, Hunt.

I call back, but no answer. He's caught with his hand in the stripper jar. That is a hit to his ego. I'm not going to hear from him again until he's over it. I shower and FaceTime Kelsey.

"Please come up! Pleeeeeease." I mean if Hunter is going to be in "meetings," we could at least see the city or burn up some room service. But Kelsey has plans with Gout, so I am on my own.

Around midnight there's a knock at the door. I'm lying in bed wearing one of Hunter's button-up shirts and some of his boxer briefs; I wasn't expecting company. I check the peephole. It's Hunter. He couldn't keep up with his key. But this time, he isn't alone. He has a man and woman with him, so I run up the shiny black stairs to the loft, put on pants, and come back down.

"What took you so long?" He still has a little glitter on him from one of those long meetings.

"I didn't know you had company. I, uh, had to change."

He introduces them as "friends from the city." The woman gushes that I look like an athlete. Immediately I know Hunter has prepped her for our meeting and told her I played college basketball. I just look at Hunter.

"I swear I didn't tell her! I didn't say anything." Hunter insists, but he lies through his teeth, so who knows.

"Hi, I'm Lunden." I shake her hand. "Nice to meet ya."

I catch a side-eye from Hunter. I can't miss it. I've done something wrong.

There is something in the closet that they are picking up. It isn't drugs or anything shady. It is something they need to give to someone for him, or something like that. Hunter is always randomly helping people get what they need, or he is wheeling and dealing. I can't figure out which one it is tonight.

He leaves them to look for their item, then pulls me aside. Yep, seriously mad. I make the first move.

"Why did you give me that look?" Something is different this time.

"In a situation where you don't know somebody," he says in his clipped voice, "do not ever give them your real name!"

I am taken aback.

"Now would have been a hell of a time to give them a fake name," he says in a shouted whisper, eyeing the closet to make sure they're still in there.

"You introduced them as your friends," I shoot back.

"You gave your real name. You never, ever give your real name," he replies, sort of crazy.

"I thought they were friends! You said they were your friends!"

"Well, they're not," he says, hands flying.

I can't tell if he is panicked or paranoid. But now I'm both.

Turns out the girl's dad lives overseas, and Hunter doesn't trust him. He knows him somehow; he knows everyone. But this guy isn't trustworthy. How was I supposed to know? It isn't a hmm, not hmm hmm situation. We don't have a code word for "nice woman who might or might not be a terrorist."

This is the only time since I've known Hunter that I think he is actually mad at me. And I almost get mad at him. My feelings are hurt because of his reaction, and he knows it. But it's Hunter, so I need to help him.

This is New York, so I don't have a gun for protection, and I can't stop them from killing us, but at least I can make sure they don't take our shit. I slide over to the table in my socks, grab Hunter's Rolex, wallet, phones, and Beau's dog tags, then slip back upstairs.

Finally, downstairs I hear the door shut and things get quiet. Then a minute later, Hunter bolts up the steps and blurts out, "They robbed us!"

I lift my wrist with his $80,000 presidential Rolex watch dangling in front of his face. I was thinking they'd have to kill me to get our things if I had it all on me. But Hunter hasn't caught on yet. "You stole my Rolex?"

"I'm not hoarding your shit, Hunt! I took your things to hide from your friendly guests that weren't friends."

"Oh." He gives his quirky flatline smile and stares at me. Clearly he needs sleep. But we don't get to that just yet.

Hunter rarely sleeps. Anytime I drift off, I wake to him stirring somewhere. The tighter the demons' grip, the less peace and rest exist in his life.

Exhausted from the previous day's chaos, I stay in bed most of the next day, as Hunter tries to shower the demons away every few hours. Once again, I wake to the sound of water coming from the bathroom and a slow little cloud of steam escaping through the cracked door. I toss my oversized T-shirt in the corner and join him in the tan-tiled steam shower, appreciating its comfort and the long bench built along the back.

As we shower, we laugh together about the chaos of the past forty-eight hours, from the Delaware pants, to rescuing the old lady on the train, and the homeless man who saved Beau's dog tags. Even the friendly robbery from the previous night becomes funny. Hunter can't always laugh at himself in the moment; usually he wants to argue his point until you give in, but he can't help but laugh about this series of unfortunate events.

I'm trying to keep shampoo suds from my eyes when there is a little pause and I hear him say, "Ya know, honey, you've got a real problem."

The lightheartedness vanishes like steam on a mirror. "What?" I manage to ask, with that vague feeling he's about to say something he'd rather not, but knows he has to anyway.

"You're in love with me."

I blink, more from shock than suds, as the magnitude of his words sinks in. Love? I hadn't even considered it. But now, here in the shower, he's claiming I'm in love with him.

There's barely a pause before he finishes, "It's going to hurt you. I hurt everyone who loves me."

Everything comfortable between us tenses up, and I question if he's right. And if he is, how the hell does he know?

Before I can gather my thoughts, he slides the shower door open and walks out, head down. Wiping my eyes, I drop to the bench, needing a moment to clear some of the shampoo and the debris from the bomb he's just dropped.

Confusion clouds my mind as I try to figure out what to do next. Most women would follow him out of the shower, wanting to discuss whatever the hell just happened and where he got that idea. But I'm not most women. I struggle with talking about feelings, and maybe he doesn't want to talk about it either.

The sting in my chest makes me wonder if he's on to something. Normally I'd have a comeback like, "Ah, Hunt, you wish!" But I'm left speechless.

What the hell. Am I in love with him? Is he right? Well, he's always right. So I guess I have some things I need to think about.

He calls during the day from his meetings. "It's about time we get out of the city." He sounds paranoid.

An hour or so later he squirrels back into the loft, sniffing around for bugs in the plants.

"Something's going on and I don't want you to be any part of it. The CIA took in Devon Archer." Hunter's voice is low in case someone is listening.

CIA? What the hell!

Then he is out again to another meeting.

Is this real life?

I'm not sure about any of this; it could be his paranoia, or lack of sleep. I'm not sure about anything, what I'm thinking or feeling. I just know I need to get back to D.C. I start packing.

A short time later I sink into the blue leather of the train to sort through the words from the shower that would haunt me for years to come—am I in love with Hunter Biden?

Chapter 6

Sneak a Peek

B ack in D.C., running errands the next day, I'm about to call my sister
to talk things over when I look down and see Hunter's phone wedged
between the seats. I feel the paranoia creep over me. Am I being listened
to? Fishing it out, I double-check to make sure it's turned off, then I wrap
it in a sweater and stash it in the trunk. I don't care if that makes me seem
paranoid, I'm not taking any chances.

I lay low for a couple of days, trying to process things. Fortunately,
before I go insane with my thoughts, Aubrey invites me to a fancy dinner
and dance on Saturday night. I need a night out with friends.

I buy a stunning red formal two-piece dress with a little train, pair
it with six-inch silver heels, clasp some rhinestones around my neck, and
throw on my fur wrap as the signature touch. The event is catered by
a high-end restaurant with open bars scattered around the ballroom.
Dancing and laughing, we party all night, and it's probably about time
for me to get home when Aubrey has to pull the bottom of my dress out
of an escalator. It is so hot it could have caught on fire. But I'm not giving
in, so we tie it in a knot to hide the black streaks and keep on going.

A few shots into the night, I start thinking about going to Annapolis to figure this whole thing out with Hunter. He messaged me earlier, and I told him I have his phone. "Well, are you going to keep it, or are you going to give it back?" he responded. I told him I hadn't seen him, and by shot number five, I'm thinking I should. And after a drink or two more, it's decidedly the most brilliant idea I've ever had.

In my drunken stupor, I manage to call my designated driver, Savanah, who just happens to be in the city. I tell her to meet me at the parking garage where my car is, and Savanah, being Savanah, complies. She's sitting on the hood of my car when I get there, and the downhill slope on the concrete, and the numerous shots I've had, are making it hard to walk in heels. Popping out her phone, she makes a video to send to Kelsey. You can't hear much of what I say over Savanah's laughter, but apparently I ask if she thinks I can take my heels off and walk barefoot without getting HIV on the streets of D.C.

A quick trip to 7-Eleven for taquitos and three country songs later, we are on the John Hanson Highway heading for the Chesapeake Bay area. I sing the entire way, pouring my heart into every song, because when you're drunk and your not-boyfriend/boss tells you that you love him before you know you love him and maybe you're thinking you do love him, well, what else can you do?

Savanah calls Hunter to let him know we'll be there in the next hour.

"She's had a lot to drink, Hunt," she says into the Bluetooth as if I'm not in the car.

"What do you mean? What's a lot? Is she sick?" he asks.

"No, but she is definitely entertaining. She's put on an entire country concert."

"Great. Get Dolly Parton here safely," he says.

We reach Hunter's house, and without really thinking, I head straight to his room. Hunter is in the shower, as always. I find a pair of black Lululemon joggers and a T-shirt to wear, and he comes out of the bathroom and laughs as I'm stuffing my red dress and fur wrap in the trash. I'm thinking it's the hamper. I never do find out what happened to them. I fear the worst.

Two things make their way to the surface of my foggy brain that night. The first is Hunter giving me a hard time about taking so long to bring him his phone. The second is that he has to be in Delaware the next day for something special at church. It's the anniversary of the car accident that took his mom and sister's life, and they're having a Mass.

I vaguely remember getting into the back of a car, maybe, and being woken up again sometime later to walk into a house, but the next thing I'm sure of is slowly rolling onto my back, which makes the painful light that much brighter. Sleeping off last night's drinking on an unfamiliar couch isn't for the weak. My body is sore and aching, but nothing matches the headache.

I finally manage to crack open my eyes when I hear Savanah laughing and Hunter's voice. Then it hits me. The headache is the least of my problems—what did I do? Did I make an utter fool of myself? Trying to compose myself, I follow their voices to the doorway of a bedroom. A small desk is against the wall across from me where Hunter stands. Savanah is perched on the edge of a bed covered in white sheets, with white walls surrounding them. It seems simple, but where the hell am I?

"Do you know you snore like a grown man when you're drunk?" comes a question that is more of a statement from Savanah.

"Where the hell are we?"

"She's right," Hunter says, "that's why you stayed out there last night. Savanah couldn't even sleep in the same room!" He laughs, turning to look at me. It is no surprise that Hunter is already cleaning a stem, standing in his boxer briefs.

Savanah fills in my missing pieces. After trashing my dress in Annapolis, we drove to Beau's home in Delaware, where I slept on the living room sofa. Hallie had even been there but left earlier with her sister. My mind faintly shoots back to hearing a couple of women talking in the doorway, but I shut them out when I crept my eyes open and felt the sting of my headache. I'm now mortified at the thought of everyone hearing my drunken snores.

Walking across the room, I grab Hunter's charger and plug in my phone. It's almost 10:00 a.m. Savanah skims through the pages of a book, and I collapse on the bed next to her, rubbing my forehead. I have never been this hungover. Hunter walks out, but is back in a jiffy, throwing a green-colored beer bottle my way. Stella Artois. Right now it seems hair of the dog is my only survival tactic. It's worth a shot.

As I sit up to take a drink, I hear knocking, "Hunt, did someone just knock on the door?"

"What?" Another knock.

Throwing on some jeans and a T-shirt, Hunter scurries out of the bedroom in a panic. Savanah and I sneak around the corner, following him through the kitchen, far enough behind that he won't notice. Being in Delaware, it could either be family or a family friend, so he is paranoid about not wanting them to see an "under the influence" Hunter, even though I feel like he's pretty good at keeping his composure. Someone's at the door.

Savanah stays put in the kitchen doorway while I creep to a window that I can see through without being seen.

"Who is it? Is Hunt okay?" Savanah whispers.

Hunter's outside, back to the house, facing a man. A man I know. A man the entire country knows.

"It's his dad," I whisper back. Joe stands there, casual in a navy polo and jeans. But I'm focused on his face as he watches Hunter. Heartbreak and devastation overcome him. It's a look I could never forget, a father's intense love for his son who is suffering addiction. One of the most powerful men in the world, and there's nothing he can do to bring his son out of this battle. I retreat from the window, back to the bedroom. No one could pay me enough to listen to that conversation.

Hunter returns, not saying much. Savanah and I act like we never left the room. "Who was that? Everything okay?" I ask.

"Everything's fine. It was just Dad," he says casually, not making eye contact. He doesn't bother going into detail. But the Hunter who's returned is softer. That guard that he always keeps up has seemingly come down. I can tell something is bothering him. It's subtle, but if you know his face like I do, you can see it.

"What's wrong?" I ask.

"I've just got to get to this thing for my family," he says quietly.

"What can I do to help?" Immediately the hangover is in the back seat of my mind and I'm ready for whatever he needs.

"Nothing. I just have to get to this Mass, and Hallie needs me to take her car back to Annapolis, plus mine."

"Why don't I take the BMW back to the Annapolis house, then I'll be able to get my car from there and go back to D.C. . . . and then you drive the other one down when you come so they're both there for you."

"You wouldn't mind doing that?" he asks. It still surprises him that while I love the fun life I have around him, I am always there to help when things aren't so fun.

"Of course I will."

He gives me the keys and gathers his things from the BMW.

"There might be a woman at the Annapolis house, cleaning," he says, pulling his things from the trunk.

"Okay," I respond, standing there watching him.

Then he turns and looks straight into me with those beautiful blue-gray eyes. "Okay, love you," he says, like usual, but instead of giving his normal firm-lipped kiss, his lips feel soft against mine. The walls he surrounds himself with have suddenly dropped.

Savanah and I load up in the BMW, and head south. As we pull into the Annapolis house, the blonde cleaning lady meets us. She doesn't look like a cleaning lady at all, but definitely someone Hunter would know. She greets us and I let her know I'm just dropping the vehicle off for Hunter. As we pull out in my Challenger, I look to Savanah and say, "I hope to God he trusts that cleaning woman, because there is no telling what he's left out."

The shower conversation nags at me for a few days, but the knot in my stomach slowly dissolves after seeing him. Although I'm curious about his feelings (and still trying to understand my own), I decide to let it rest and push it to the back of my mind. I'm planning on staying in D.C. over the Christmas holidays. I don't mind being alone, plus I'm fixing to take on more workload for Hunter full-time. Hallie calls to tell me Hunter looks forward to having me work for him full-time, saying he trusts me wholeheartedly. At times we refer to each other as "best friends since forever," but hearing from others how much he trusts me gives me a different sense of pride.

"I'm fixing to be on payroll, and I just have so much I need to start doing. Plane tickets are skyrocketing and is it really worth driving seventeen hours in two days? We have FaceTime," I tell Mom.

"We will buy you a plane ticket," Mom says, not taking no for an answer.

"No, Mom, I just can't get away right now."

I can hear the break in her voice as she fights back crying. We aren't ones to really cry in our family. It was instilled in me as a child that it is a weakness. It's going to be the first Christmas the entire family hasn't been together, but I'm honestly okay with spending the holiday alone. I'm focused on the future and excited about this new opportunity working for Hunter at Rosemont Seneca.

"You have to go," Hunter demands when we talk about it. He can be very business-minded, but family is first and foremost to his sober mind and heart. "We'll get you ready to work once you're back in D.C. But you have to go. You never know if it's your last, or theirs."

It makes me think about the many Christmases he probably wished he had with his mother. He is no stranger to how fragile life can be, and although his scars aren't visible, they'll always remain.

So, two days before Christmas Eve, I toss a few outfits into a bag, throw on some Adidas sweats, and head out the door. A seventeen-hour trip turns into twenty-three hours as I drive through the night and day, dodging tornadoes.

My sister knows I'm coming. I stop by her house on the way so she can see my parents' surprise. We pull into the driveway, sneak through the garage, and make it inside without Mom or Dad noticing. It's dark, but I hear them watching television. We creep down the long hallway until it opens up to the living room. Dad stands in shock, but once Mom notices, she jumps from the recliner, knocking it over, and runs to me. She grabs me in a hug. I've made their Christmas. Mom even sends Hunter a message thanking him. I enjoy the holiday with my family and am thankful Hunter talked me into going home.

About a week later, I deliver to Hunter a late Christmas present from my dad, a big box of Arkansas "moonshine," deer jerky, a Rob Roberts Custom Gun Works shirt, and hat with a note. About nine months after that, I deliver a present neither Hunter nor I know is coming, though I've already been carrying her for nearly two weeks. And it still hasn't dawned on me yet that he was right. I do love him.

New Year's Day finds Kelsey and me recovering from a night out we could never forget, sitting around my place in Chevy Chase with Savanah, whose nondrinking policy has kept her from a hangover. We're laughing at all the fun we had, when Kelsey holds up her phone with a picture that captures the night—me, in a black dress, with very red lipsticked lips encircling the entire top of an upturned champagne flute. 2018 is off to a bang, and I can't wait for the excitement and my new position that's in store.

On the way to brunch, one of the girls casually mentions starting her period. *Hmm, am I late?* I think for a split second. But I've always been irregular, so I let it go.

Then, driving into the city, a small green metal sign catches my eye. Prego. An Italian gourmet deli. Was that a coincidence? Did I just manifest that from the wild thought I had prior? Definitely a coincidence.

Finally, parking at Chipotle, I notice something when I move my seat belt. "Man, my chest feels sore."

No sooner have the words left my mouth than it hits me. Three coincidences in one day? A sudden unease washes over me. "We, um, might want to stop off at CVS on the way back," I say a little haltingly, to puzzled looks in response.

"Y'all, I think my period is late, and my breasts are sore. Then we passed that Prego place, and now I'm paranoid it's all a sign."

My paranoia makes them laugh. The idea of one of us being pregnant at this point in life is crazy. Still, I stop at the drugstore just to be sure.

Back at my place, I head straight to the bathroom with my test from CVS. After peeing on the stick, I start wiping away the leftover eye makeup from last night, and sort of forget the reason I'm even in there until I look down to see a plus sign, bright as day. "No . . . no . . . no . . . no . . . no," I grab the test. Falling back onto the toilet, I try to catch my breath, unable to process what I'm seeing. This can't be real, can it?

Savanah instantly drops her smile to mirror the shocked look on my face as I walk out of the bathroom. "Oh my God, no."

Kelsey turns around, not putting two and two together. "What happened? Who died?"

"I took the pregnancy test."

"Oh my God, no!" she shouts with Savanah, because they know who's at the other end of that test.

As they freak out, my mind races. God wouldn't do this to me, right? What are the chances of this happening? What do I do? What have I gotten myself into? Why? This seems bigger than me.

Savanah stares at me with concern and pity. Kelsey lightens the mood. "Man, are we sure? Should we take another test? I hate it for you, but I'm so happy I'm not in your shoes." And we all laugh.

We run to the nearest CVS and buy every brand they offer. Five more tests and one extremely empty bladder later, I join the girls again. There was no bad test. If one could be nothing, and two is a fluke, and three is reliable, what is six in a row? All positive.

"I need to call my sister," I mumble, walking back to the bedroom and slowly pushing the door shut. Randi Jo is almost six years older than me and already has two children.

It only rings a couple times, but it seems more like twenty, and with each ring my fear grows. This still doesn't seem real.

"Hey! What's up," says Randi's cheery voice.

"Something big. I have to tell you something, but you can't tell anyone."

"Okay, you know I won't. Everything okay?" Her voice drops an octave.

"I don't know. I think I'm pregnant."

"You think? Have you taken a test?"

"Yes, six . . . all positive."

"Well hell, you *are* pregnant. Is it who I think it is?"

"Well, yeah!"

There's a pause. "Oh, shit." She's processing all of this. I'm trying to as well.

"How far along are you?"

"I don't know! I don't even know when I had my last period."

"It's okay. It's going to be okay. You can call and schedule an ultrasound and they can tell you more."

"What am I going to do? Mom and Dad are going to freak the hell out."

"Listen, it's all going to be okay. You need to schedule a doctor's appointment."

And just like that, a new whirlwind of emotions explodes in my mind. Is the baby healthy? What if it's not? Who's a good obstetrician in D.C.?

Thanking Randi Jo and promising her I'll call back when I know more, I plod back out to the front room with the massive weight of six little blue strips of paper on my shoulders and a tiny new life on my mind.

Kelsey and Savanah's eyes get big when I break down and I bawl.

They listen as I process the news over and over. "I don't want to tell Hunter. Will he be mad? Will he want me to abort it? I never saw myself in this situation in a million years. I'm now a PR nightmare for him and his entire family. I can't just be another scandal for him, another problem. Oh my God, my mom and dad are going to kill me."

After trying to cheer me up, Kelsey and Savanah decide it's best to get me out of the house. They have the perfect place—a small get-together at our friend's apartment near Logan Circle. We arrive around 8:00 p.m. and things are pretty calm, with Lydia and Vanessa at the kitchen bar mixing drinks. Dropping my things on a barstool, I head straight to a large black sectional couch. I can't even indulge in the drinking and fun. I'm the new Savanah.

Reclining on the couch, listening to my friends swap stories, I can't keep my eyes open. I'm exhausted, running on fumes while my body desperately needs energy to create this little human. I have to take better care of myself.

"Lunden! What is going on?" Savanah's voice snaps me out of my thoughts. "Your phones?"

There on the barstool sit my two phones, on two different carriers, from two different states, and both are covered with black and white lines simultaneously. The lines aren't moving, they're just hanging there, almost looking like a barcode. Then one goes black, and a few seconds later, the other does too.

My eyes are locked on the screens, trying to make sense of what I'm seeing. Savanah's default is freaking out, but now I join her. "What the hell? I don't know. Have y'all ever had this happen?" I'm panicking out loud to nobody in particular.

Everyone starts gathering around. "What's wrong?"

"I don't know." I'm pushing the power button on both phones, trying to get something, anything, to show up on the screen. But they're just sitting there in my hand like little bricks, blank, and my heart sinks.

"Oh my God. What is happening? This is so weird," Savanah wails, as she's probably picturing black helicopters hovering over us outside to whisk me away to wherever politicians stash women who shouldn't have gotten pregnant but did. Hunter's paranoia is haunting us.

"I don't know, but your anxiety isn't helping," I hiss, still trying to play the role of the one who keeps everyone calm. But I'm a mess inside too.

I can feel the weight of isolation descending. Just after receiving the scariest news of my life, both of my phones crash. I can't get to Hunter, Dad, Mom, Randi, or anyone else. Conspiracy theories have never really been my thing, but how could this be a coincidence? Were my phones tapped? Did someone know I was pregnant? What was going to happen to me?

"Well, this is a great way to start off the pregnancy, huh," I say to Kelsey. Instantly, Vanessa and Lydia both eye me. The cat's out of the bag. They don't ask who the father is, they don't have to. They know.

In the following days, Kelsey never leaves my side. She even drives to Apple the next day and buys me a brand-new iPhone with her own money. My stress level starts dropping as my iCloud downloads. I check my messages, but something's not right. I swap over to my camera roll. Something's off there too. What about call logs? Nothing.

Half of my digital memories are gone—pictures of Hunter, from Hunter, messages between us (depending on the phone he messaged from), and call logs. Deleted. The only place Hunter consistently exists is my Snapchat photos. Maybe there's some fire to the conspiracy smoke. Maybe Hunter's right to be so paranoid. Maybe I should have been putting my phone down and walking out of earshot to talk about things all along.

Questions swirl in my mind. Had Hunter or one of his protectors somehow found out and tried to erase him from my life? The chaos is disorienting, and I can't tell whether his demon of paranoia has finally gotten into me, or if maybe there really is something to be afraid of.

Googling "ultrasound," I find a place called Sneak a Peek, where you can walk in and have an ultrasound done to check on the baby. They have availability that day. Vanessa and Savanah stop by to check on me and come with us for moral support.

My mind is racing as I walk into the Rockville Sneak a Peek. Kelsey and Vanessa look for a parking spot, while Savanah hops out with me so I don't have to go in alone.

Upstairs in the empty waiting room, I hear the technician with some-one doing an ultrasound. Joy bubbles up from the other side of the door. A couple is listening to their child's heartbeat, and a small burn sinks into my chest. It's not pregnancy heartburn, it's the burning question—will I have the same support this young woman has by her side? Or will I be listening to a heartbeat alone?

The door swings open and a small brunette with long curly hair emerges with a happy expectant father in a green sweater vest and khakis. He has his arm around her, as she dabs at tears with a tissue. A smiling couple emerge, the joyful dad wiping tears from his swooning woman's eyes.

A small Indian woman follows behind. "Ms. Roberts, you may come back." Will I leave the same room with tears of joy? What if she tells me something is wrong with the baby? What if she tells me I'm not even pregnant? I don't know what to expect, and every part of the future frightens me, even as near as the next few minutes.

As I start walking, I notice Savanah still sitting. "What are you doing?" I ask.

"Do you want me to come in with you?"

"Well, hell yeah, I don't want to do this alone." I laugh nervously.

Walking into the ultrasound room, I'm greeted by a large screen, and the technician instructs me to lay on the bed. Savanah stands nervously. Of all the friends in my group, why did they let the one who freaks out the most come in with me?

The technician preps her transducer and pulls up my shirt, applying a cold gel onto my exposed skin. As she presses the device against my stomach, a brief calm takes my mind from the chaos.

"Do you see this sac here? That is your baby."

The words ring in my head. Savanah is now sitting on the bed watching the large screen on the wall in admiration. But I can only manage to get out, "Um, are you sure?" A puzzled look wrinkles the technician's dark tan forehead, as if she's wondering why I would pay to come have an ultrasound if I wasn't sure myself.

"Umm, yes. Let me measure the size and we can see exactly how far along you are. The earlier the ultrasound, the more accurate a due date and conception date I can give you," she explains.

"Are we really sure there's a baby there?" I ask again. Despite her confirmation and the visual evidence, it feels surreal.

"Yes, ma'am. Do you see the screen? That sac is your baby," she says.

"Do you mind doing it again? Could that sac be anything else like a cyst? Are we sure it's a baby?" I desperately cling to the possibility of this all being some hoax.

"Umm, no ma'am. Here, do you see this sac? It's visibly a baby. I've done this for years." She's looking at me as if I'm crazy or insulting her experience. I don't blame her; she doesn't know my situation or understand my paranoia. "I'll give you a second to process," she says, leaving the room.

Breaking the silence, Savanah laughs, "Lunden, I think this is real." For once, she's the calm one. I struggle to tear my eyes away from the screen with a picture of a small white sac crowded by black darkness—this might be the first time I can relate to my child.

A few minutes later, the technician returns, confirming what I already knew, what Savanah knew, and what she knew too. I am pregnant.

She dots points on the sac, getting the baby's measurements. It feels like an out-of-body experience. My mind is consumed with what Hunter will say. I have to talk to him. This is actually real. I'm having a baby . . . with Hunter Biden. I know the state he's in, and how can I add a baby to this equation?

"It looks like you are about five weeks and three days. That puts your conception sometime between December 12 and 15. Your estimated due date based on measurements is September 8." She confirms.

Again, the only words that I can seem to get out follow. "Are you sure?"

"Yes!" Savanah laughs. "She's sure. You've asked a million times. You're pregnant. It's a sure thing."

The technician joins Savanah's laughter, and I can't help but give them the smile they want. She wipes the gel from my stomach and hands me the sonogram pictures to keep.

Out in the waiting room we run into Kelsey and Vanessa. I hand Kelsey the sonogram saying, "I think I need to get her to run it one more time though, just to be sure."

Kelsey laughs. "Umm, well actually it looks pretty sure to me." Savanah and Vanessa laugh too, but all I can think about is when I will be scheduling my next one, just to be sure.

As I sign the credit card receipt, the lady behind the counter hands me a folder with pamphlets about vitamins, vaccines, and crib death (definitely a cheerful pamphlet), a dozen sonogram readings, gestational progress, and detailed notes. Something jumps off the page, "Likely date of conception: December 12–15, 2017"—the New York trip.

Driving back from Sneak a Peek I think about Hunter's addiction and the state that he's in. Early on I'd ask him if he would ever stop. I saw it was hurting him. But he would just give me the same speech. "Honey, I'll only stop when I want to stop. It's my addiction. The only person that can stop it is me and I'm not ready." When I asked with any regularity, he would just begin to shut down. So I did my best to be there for him without forcing the issue. But now the issue is being forced by biology. Fun and games are over. I can't just go party and do whatever without thinking of any consequences. There is a child in the picture now, and I can't raise a child in that world. I start worrying about Hunter, and I start hating his addiction in a new way.

Chapter 7

Not a Clinton

Uncertainty and fear swirl around me as I sit on my bed in my basement apartment. I find myself thinking a lot about women who learn they're pregnant and can tell the father and go through the process together. What's holding me back from telling Hunter? I'm not scared of the Hunter I've gotten to know and love. I'm scared of what everyone says about politics, the conspiracies, and what happens to people who get in the way. I'm not scared of Hunt. I'm scared of Hunter Biden.

Needing advice, I call Don Miller, my loyal Democrat, attorney friend who went to Harvard Law with the Obamas. He suggests meeting at his office over lunch, but I make it known that this is something I'm very paranoid about and I don't want to take the chance of any recordings. I want it on my turf. So I invite him to my house for lunch. He's intrigued, and by noon, he's at my door.

"What is going on? You're scaring me." I don't even have time to officially greet him before I realize my own paranoia has rubbed off on him the way Hunter's has on me.

"I need to talk to you about something. Something I hope can stay between me and you, but I want your honest advice as a friend and as an attorney. What would you tell your daughter in this situation?" I hit him with the opener I've been practicing since I made the call.

"Okay, let's hear it," he says, sitting at my kitchen table.

"Okay, so . . . I don't really know how to give the news so I'm just going to say it. I'm pregnant."

He chokes on the water I just handed him. "And I'm assuming the father is Hunter," he manages to cough out. I nod my head in agreement. His cough turns to a chuckle, and he sits back, crossing his arms and giving me a small, almost sympathetic smile.

"Well, at least it's not a Clinton," he says, and we both laugh.

"Do I have anything to worry about? If I tell him, will he have me killed?" I can't hold it in anymore.

"Killed? This baby is a Biden. The Bidens are known for loving their family and being so family oriented. They can turn a scandal into something to be proud of. It's what makes them who they are."

"I'm just so scared to tell him."

"Maybe you're scared because of the state he's in at this point. Don't be scared. You want my advice? Be honest with him."

While his words are comforting, I still can't get the stress under control. I thought what he said would prompt me to immediately call Hunter and arrange a time to meet face-to-face, and all my troubles would be over. But even after hearing what I needed to hear, I'm still feeling fearful. Maybe it isn't the fear of conspiracies and what he will do to me, maybe it's the fear of letting him down.

Every day I wake up thinking, "I'll tell Hunt tomorrow." But each day is the same, full of tears and fear. I have withdrawn so much. I take days off work and Hunter finally calls Kelsey, asking why I am avoiding him. "Why is she not answering? She always answers!" Kelsey, being Kelsey, makes an excuse. "She just has a lot on her plate right now. I'll tell her to call you."

I don't want to face him yet. For another week I put it off till the next day. And soon the stress finally takes its toll.

The emergency room at Adventist Medical center isn't packed yet. It's almost 7:00 p.m., and I guess the Friday-night rush will start after everybody drinks away the past week's stress. A Stella would be nice right about now, but clearly that's not happening.

A nurse leads me and Kelsey to a small room in the back where I go over everything I told the first nurse already with a second nurse: I had a positive pregnancy test a couple weeks ago and now I'm bleeding. Kelsey is absolutely perfect in this moment, trying to help manage the stress and worry that probably put me here in the first place. She downloads the Heads Up game app on her phone so we can pass the time not thinking about what's happening inside me, as I sit there in my hospital gown, BCBG sweatpants, and black Adidas shoes.

Before long the doctor comes in for conversation number three, except he says the word I've been dreading from the second the bleeding started. "Miscarriage."

"It's not certain," he says, "Let's get an ultrasound."

More Heads Up as we wait. I think to myself, miscarriage is the only answer. What else could it be? Google says it. The doctor just confirmed I had all the symptoms. I feel defeated, almost. How could I have already grown somewhat attached to this little thing? The ultrasound tech rubs the cold gel on my stomach, and I hear the sonar, wondering if it's picking up what used to be my baby.

The doctor returns, saying I'm six weeks along and it's possible I'm miscarrying or experiencing complications, but there isn't much anyone can do. "Go home, rest, and hopefully it will resolve. If not, your body will pass the baby on its own." Those are the least comforting instructions I've ever received from a doctor.

Riding back to Chevy Chase I start thinking about the miscarriage and the possibilities of what's to come. Thirteen days ago, if you described a woman in my situation to me, I would have thought that a miscarriage might fix it all. But tonight I am remembering the ultrasound and how I desperately wanted the doctor to say nothing was wrong with my baby.

The picture of me with the emptied champagne flute somehow comes across my mind. What if I caused this? Suddenly a wave of regret hits me for the way I've been living. If I hadn't taken that test, my lifestyle could have killed my baby, and I wouldn't have even known.

Pregnancy might've been the last thing I wanted, but the instinct to care for my unborn baby has officially awakened. I still don't know exactly what to do, but I know I want to protect it.

After a few days, I stop bleeding and text Hunter. "We need to talk." No reply.

My friend Peyton asks me to come visit, and after spending days in bed, watching movies with a friend sounds great. I'm still packing when she comes by to pick me up. She's as pretty as ever, with the looks and personality of a Kardashian, except Peyton is someone I trust. I don't think I'd trust Kim K with the biggest secret of my life, but I do Peyton, so I let her in on it.

"*You're pregnant! How?*" I laugh, because, well, we all know how it happened. But I know what she means. How could this happen to you? Running her small hands through her long black hair, it hits her. She grabs the *Popular Mechanics* magazine from my dresser with Hunter and Joe on the cover. "Oh my God. Do you know how big this is? Bitch, are you okay?" she somehow manages to ask with her jaw on the floor.

"I know . . . I know! I don't need to hear that right now. My stress has already landed me in the emergency room," I say, and she gets things back under control.

On the drive to her family's place in Maryland, we stop at a mall. Victoria's Secret is having their semiannual sale. Peyton has grabbed some PINK sweatpants and is wafting freshly scented perfume strips under her nose while I lean back on a table piled high with underwear. My new phone vibrates, and then everything PINK starts fading when I see the text from my dad. "The scans came back, it's prostate cancer."

Suddenly everything is blurry, and I have to concentrate to get through the rest of the message. " . . . prostate . . . 1–10 . . . aggressiveness . . . hopeful but . . . 8 . . ."

"Are you okay?" I mumble something to Peyton in response and call Randi Jo, grasping for a lifeline. She's optimistic and everyone around Dad is too. He's going to have the surgery, but they don't have dates. She's comforting, knowing everything I'm going through. As we walk to the car, I fill Peyton in. She's a good comforter too. It feels weak needing comfort from so many people right now. That used to be my job.

Peyton's family is a godsend and getting out of the D.C. partying lifestyle re-centers me. Her mom and dad make me feel at home, and so does her German shepherd, Stella. I grew up with German shepherds, and was missing my dog, Ada.

My second night there, as Peyton and I finish our nightly routine, Kelsey calls.

"Hunt's in Dupont Circle. I just met him on the street. He even went to Mpire looking for you. He walked up and the doorman asked how he and you were doing. Hunt said everything was good and he was actually trying to get ahold of you, but then the doorman said he heard you were sick and that started Hunt's wheels turning. He wants to know what's going on."

"What the hell!" My tone startles Stella and she's immediately by my side. So is Peyton.

"Yeah, he was obviously worried about it when we saw him. I told him I'd call you. It's probably time you tell him before he finds out from someone else." She's right. I scrape together as much willpower as I can find, pull up Hunter's number on my phone, and use every ounce of courage I have to move my thumb half an inch to the call button.

"Hey," I hear through the phone's tiny speaker. "I heard you've been sick. You okay?"

"Yeah, Hunt, I'm fine. I sent you a text the other day saying we needed to talk. Can we link up tonight, maybe an hour?"

"Sure. I'll wait around here. Let me know when you get to Dupont. . . . Honey, you should've called me."

"I know . . . ," I say, trying not to let my voice break. "I'll see you in a bit. Love you, bye"

"K, love you, bye."

Peyton and I scurry around throwing on some clothes that look presentable. Sweats and messy buns might not cut it in the city. We hop in her red Mercedes coupe and are at Dupont in under an hour. As Peyton parallel parks on M Street, I see Hunter walking. He's still there. No telling what bars have occupied his time in this last hour, but I'm thankful he waited around.

"Fuck. Time to face the music," I say to myself as my anxiety explodes. He's walking the other way, but I know it's him because I'd know that walk anywhere. "Hunt," I shout a couple of times before he turns around. He comes up and throws his arms around me, then leans back holding my arms and looking in my eyes. "Honey, how are you? Feeling okay?" This time, though, he's not asking in general. He knows something. I don't know what Savanah and Kelsey have said.

"There's a lot going on, Hunt, but we need to talk."

"Honey, your dad is going to be okay. You know that, right?" He claims he worked with some prostate cancer foundation or something. I immediately know Hunter hounded Savanah and Kelsey until they had to give him something, so they told him about my dad's cancer. "The prostate can always be removed," he goes on, sincerely trying, and completely failing, to make me feel better.

"We've got to talk about more than that, but not here in the middle of Dupont."

"I'm going to the Annapolis house. Coming?"

"I'm with Peyton right now, and I told Kelsey I'd meet her before I left Dupont. Give me an hour and I'll meet you there."

"Okay," he says, grabbing my hand before I walk off. "Honey, it's going to be okay."

"I hope so."

I link up with Kelsey at Surfside. She and some of the other girls are heading to the MGM casino. They invite me, not realizing I'm about to drop the bombshell to end all bombshells on Hunter. Peyton is all for going. I don't want to take away from the fun she could have, so I push her to go. She's dealt with me the past two days; she deserves it. I pull Kelsey aside and ask if she will go with me to Annapolis. I need someone I trust, possibly someone he trusts, and someone who knows everything to go with me—I need Kelsey. Through her eyes I can see she's weighing her options—should she go with some girls to the casino or come watch me drop this bombshell on Hunter? "Okay, I'll go. We can take my car."

As we speed back toward Maryland, Kelsey asks, "Okay, so how are you going to do this?"

"I'm just going to tell him."

"Well, I'm here to support you, but I'll leave you two alone when the time comes. I'll let you guys have that moment. What do you think he'll say?"

We both give our best impressions of Hunter and his responses. "Honey, I knew it!" "Honey, it all makes sense now." "Honey, we will get through this." "Honey, have you heard of Planned Parenthood?" We can't help but laugh at our impressions of him and his Delaware accent.

"I don't know really. I mean you don't think he will have Big Boy come kill me and drop me at the bottom of the Potomac?"

Kelsey laughs hysterically, and I can't help but join in, but I'm starting to sound like a conspiracy theorist. "You know Hunt could never do that to you," she reassures me.

His silver two-door Porsche greets us in the driveway, and when we let ourselves in, Hunter greets us at the top of the stairs wearing boxer briefs and a black leather jacket. He looks like a biker that lost his pants. Kelsey and I start laughing. "What are you doing?" I ask. He goes into a spill about how the jacket emphasizes who he is, "the black sheep, the bad guy" of his family.

We spend the next fifteen minutes in small talk, sitting in the gray-blue accent chairs in his room, facing the windows that let in the most beautiful sunset views over the Chesapeake. But right now, it's pitch black.

My anxiety dropped a little after I called him, and again after I saw him at Dupont, because both times I was able to put off the inevitable. But now, the anxiety starts spiking again. And when Kelsey says she has to go make a call and gives me a wink, my anxiety goes through the stratosphere. It's now or never.

"Hunt, I have to tell you something."

"Okay, okay, I know, so what is going on?" he asks, and the kindness and compassion in his voice remind me why I've cared about him so much—why I really do love him. He scoots his chair closer, taking off the leather jacket, and leans forward in his boxer briefs to comfort me.

"I'm pregnant."

And just like Ross did on *Friends* when Rachel tells him she's pregnant, Hunter's brow furrows. His eyes freeze after locking onto mine. I don't know if he can even move. Did he hear me? Five seconds go by and still nothing.

"Did you hear me?" I ask.

He simply nods, not taking his eyes off me.

"And I'm sure it goes without saying, it's yours," I say, also just like Rachel. He pauses a couple more seconds, then snaps out of it. There he is.

"Honey, I know that! I'm not questioning that! I know it's mine! What do you want to do?"

"I honestly don't know what you want me to do, but I also know I don't think I can do anything else other than keep it," I say, trying to be a peacekeeper just in case I'm about to see a side of Hunter I've never seen before.

He pauses for a moment, but it's not a moment of doubt. It's more like he's arranging pieces in his mind. "Okay. Well, honey, whatever you decide, I'm here. You let me know what I need to do. I want to be there for you emotionally, physically, spiritually, whatever I can do."

I feel like a weight has been lifted. I've finally let the cat out of the bag, and he's supportive. We're going to be a team for the baby. I'm not alone. This should be a happy time.

"I've been getting sonograms done to check on the baby's progress. We've got one set for this week, and they say we will be able to hear the baby's heartbeat. I'm excited after all the complications. Do you want to come?"

"Absolutely, I'll be there—whatever you need." He's kind, affectionate, and passionate that night.

Finally, Kelsey walks out of the bathroom. "So, Ross and Rachel, we're really doing this, huh?" She laughs. I can't help but laugh too.

"Yep, I guess so. I didn't know if Ross was gonna snap out of it though!" We both laugh.

But once Hunter does snap out of it and assures me he knows it is his, and he will be there for me, I know everything will be fine.

What I don't know is that a year later he will totally deny this, but for now things are looking up.

Chapter 8

You Can Always Come Home

Over the next few days, my anxiety levels return to halfway normal. I'm still single, pregnant, and have a dad with aggressive prostate cancer, but at least it doesn't look like the former vice president's son is going to try to kill me for getting pregnant. In fact, we see each other a few times, and it's sweet and intimate, with him knowing I'm pregnant, and knowing the baby is his.

The day for the heartbeat ultrasound arrives, but Hunter is a no-show. He assured me again that he would be there and do whatever I needed, but I asked him to come hear our child's heartbeat for the first time, and he stands us up. When I call to see what happened, he claims he planned on being there, but things came up. And then he tips his hand.

"I'm in a horrible place, honey, just like you are, and I don't want to hurt you. I'm so fucked up and have so much going on . . ." He describes the problems going on in his family. My heart sinks.

A few days ago he was going to be responsible and do what was needed for me and our unborn child. Now suddenly he's a victim who's worried about hurting me. Now I'm the one telling him we will get through this and being there for him—when I need him the most.

A couple more days pass and no sign of Hunter. He reaches out to Kelsey for help. I ask her to go check that he's okay. He can't call me because I've become a burden. My heart starts to break, piece by piece.

Kelsey meets him at the Annapolis house early one afternoon. When she gets inside, he's already a wreck.

"I know, honey, I should have been there for Lunden. Don't even start with me! I know. I should have been there. I'm just a fucking loser and my life is shit right now. Is she mad at me?"

"Yeah, you should have been there. She drove herself, went alone so that you two could be together for it. Hell, she even made the appointment in Annapolis so it would be easy for you, and you still didn't get your ass over there to support her!"

"I know . . . I know. But look at me, I'm not in a good place, Kelsey. How do I bring a baby into this? I'm a walking disappointment. If I could go back and go with her I would do it but I can't."

"She has a recording of the heartbeat, ya know? She sent it to me and told me I could play it for you if you wanted to listen." Kelsey doesn't reveal that I think maybe the heartbeat will jolt him into realizing he needs to step up for this child.

"She did?" he asks, shocked that it's possible I would do that for him to process on his own time.

"Yes. She said it's totally up to you. You don't have to listen if you don't want to. Just an option."

"Yes, I want to hear," he replies, exhaustion and defeat in his voice.

She turns up her phone speaker and the gentle but rapid sound of a tiny baby's heartbeat fills the room.

Hunter listens, staring blankly into the distance, then silently leaves the room. Worried about what might have happened to him after hearing the heartbeat, Kelsey searches the house. He's in his room, curled on the floor in the fetal position.

"How am I supposed to have a child out there and be in this state? How can I have a child and not be a constant in its life? How do I clean up my mess," he says, eyes teary.

The heartbeat got to him. Suddenly it's all real, and Hunter knows it.

"You can do this," Kelsey comforts. "You don't have a choice. If you need help, get help. You don't always have to be a mess. You can clean it up and be a good dad. You have been to your other three children, right? You can be present for this child's sake, and you need to."

He stares off into nothingness, then walks out of the room, the house, the conversation, mumbling that he has to go get something. Kelsey calls him, but you only get to Hunter when Hunter wants to be gotten to, and right now he doesn't want to be reached. He leaves her at his own house.

A couple of days later, Hunter resurfaces and asks to meet me at a sushi restaurant on the waterfront near Rosemont Seneca. I arrive and wait, but an hour passes with no sign of him. Finally, my phone vibrates with a text.

"I'm on my way down now. So sorry."

Five minutes later he walks through the door, full of apologies for everything—being late, missing the ultrasound, everything. He asks to go to the bar instead of sitting at our table, and I follow. He orders his usual Tito's, double, and I sit, listening to his excuses. Despite my own need for help, I still want to help him. I let his excuses slide and assure him everything will be okay. I want to believe he's telling the truth. I know he's in a bad place, but deep down I wonder if I'm enabling this behavior for the future.

We switch topics to talk about business. Katie Dodge, his other assistant, and I have been preparing for me to take over the official role of his executive assistant. He's moving Rosemont Seneca out of the House of Sweden, much to the relief of every Swede. They don't like him there, or any of us who visit. They see Hunter's office as some human-trafficking drug destination, because he has his friends over there to have a good time. The only party thrown in that building after Hunter moves out is probably the one the Swedes throw to celebrate his being gone.

He wants Katie and me to take the move off his hands. But as we talk, I notice Hunter's subtle hints about how bad his personal finances are. He goes so far as to claim he's "broke," and sprinkles references like that throughout the conversation.

I can't help but feel offended. He thinks I'm after his money? Does he honestly think of me like that? Because I got pregnant? Does he think I did this on purpose?

He pays for his Tito's and insists we walk to Rosemont Seneca. On the way he asks, "So how did this happen? Do we know?"

"The pregnancy?" I ask, confused. He's a smart man, surely he knows how.

"Yeah, I mean, I thought you were on the pill," he replies, almost questioning me.

"I am . . . or I was, rather. But I did some research and found that an antibiotic I was taking for my skin could have messed with it."

"Oh, I see. Well then it sounds like it was meant to happen," he says, kind of laughing. Then turning to me he asks, "How are you? Do you feel okay?" What would have been his normal caring questions leave me feeling uncertain. This time it's different. It's all about him.

In the penthouse, he takes off to his bathroom and I wait. When he comes back to his office, I know what he's been doing. His kryptonite. Normally he'd do it in front of me, but because I'm pregnant had the courtesy to go to the bathroom.

"Honey, this is how bad I'm doing." He sits down at his desk. "Finnegan needs a new MacBook, and I can't even get that for her. My dad is having to buy her a new laptop because I don't have the funds. How pathetic am I?"

It's bullshit. He thinks my intentions aren't pure, and I'm pissed and quite frankly ready to get out of here.

"Hunter, I'm not asking you to put a down payment on this baby. I'm just asking you to be a dad. I don't have to be this burden you're making it seem. I can always go to Arkansas and raise this baby. I just hope that you would choose to be in its life."

He stares at me intensely. I stare back, not wanting him to see my hurt, not wanting him to see the strength it took to utter those words without a break in my voice.

"Honey, I know that . . . Go back to Arkansas though? How can I have a child out there that's half of me and not be in its life? You really think that low of me?"

Think that low of him? I've gathered why he's throwing out he's broke, because he thinks that low of me. There is no winning.

"No, Hunt. I don't. I just don't want to feel like a burden, and this baby shouldn't either. I know the state you're in. And I'm sorry, but this is where we are now," I say, standing.

I tell him I will get with Katie Dodge this week to coordinate the move, then I go home and crash, completely emotionally and physically exhausted.

On the phone with Kelsey later I say, "He's acting like he's broke and making financial excuses as if I am after his money because I'm pregnant."

"What? He seemed so heartbroken at the house when I saw him."

"No, he's looking for a way out. And there's something else going on. I'm not sure what, but something. He seemed sketchy. A different sketchy than the usual Hunt Sketchy."

Vanessa calls out of nowhere the next day and asks if we can meet. It sounds like she has a problem that might distract me from the dump truck of chaos parked in my life's driveway. We meet at our usual parking deck in Dupont, and before Vanessa opens the door to get in my car, I can see she's dreading this talk for some reason. Rather than her usual smile, her head is weighed down with what looks like shame and regret.

"I've got something to tell you," she says and sighs heavily. "But please don't be mad at me."

Nothing she can say is as crazy as what I'm already going through, I think, but before I make it to the end of that thought I hear, "Hunter called me last night."

My palms instantly start sweating, and my body prepares for fight or flight.

"He wanted to hang out. He said he'd been having a rough time and just wanted someone to talk to. So I went over to his place."

I sit dead still, eyes never leaving her. The pressure in the car builds.

"We hung out for a while and drank. . . . We drank a lot."

There's enough pressure to crush a nuclear submarine.

"And . . . things just kind of happened. . . . We had sex."

Now I'm the submarine. I could explode.

My nonresponse makes her go on. "We would have never done it if we had been sober! It was a mistake!"

She looks at me scared, like I might hit her with a right hook, or completely lose it. But I don't. I just look at her. She knows I'm pregnant. She knows the baby is his. She is my friend. I don't yell or cry. I just quietly say, "It's okay, we've all done stuff we might regret."

I'm mad at her, but I am furious at him. In that moment, I feel sorry for her, sorry for myself. We've both fallen victim to Hunter's charm. She knows what she did was wrong, and quite frankly, I respect that she fessed up and apologized.

The pressure is slowly seeping out of the car when the phone on her lap starts buzzing, shattering the silence. We both look down. It's Hunter.

"What do I do?" she asks timidly.

"Answer it."

"You sure?"

"Why not?"

Vanessa's hand almost trembles as she slides her thumb across the screen and puts it on speaker.

"Hey . . . what are you doing," comes Hunter's voice.

"I'm sitting here with Lunden."

"You didn't tell her, did you?" he says.

"Yes. She knows. You're on speaker."

Silence. Click.

We both look at each other and laugh. Typical Hunter.

Then the unexpected. Hunter starts blowing up my phone. Normally he would avoid something like this, especially with me being such a burden lately. I let the first six or seven calls forward to voicemail.

After Vanessa gets out of the car, I drive, trying to process the anger, hurt, and betrayal, then finally answer.

"Hey, where are you?" comes the voice of the guy who just slept with my friend while I'm carrying his child.

"Just left Vanessa. What's up?"

"Will you pick me up at the CVS on the corner?"

Is he seriously going to act like nothing happened, like I don't know he knows I know? But somehow through the anger and pain, I find the word "sure" coming out of my mouth.

I pull up to the Dupont CVS. "Hey honey, do you have cash? I'm trying to get a Gatorade and my card is messing up. I can go down to the ATM, but do you have cash by chance?" I should let him die of thirst, but I hand him my card.

Before I know it, he jumps in my Challenger with his Gatorade and my credit card. Heading for the waterfront, I park on K Street when Hunter breaks the silence.

"Honey, I'm sorry. I'm such a fuckup. I'm a loser. I hurt everyone around me. I'm just a fuckup. It's all I am and all I'll ever be."

Now my turn. "Hunt, that's such bullshit! I know you've got your demons and you're in a horrible place right now. You've been in a horrible place since before we met, and all this time I've stood beside you. I've never judged, and quite frankly I've loved you through it. Now I'm in a horrible place. I'm clearly going through it alone and where the fuck are you?"

My cheeks are wet with tears. My head crashes into my palms and I sit sobbing, finally letting it all come out. It takes me a minute to realize that Hunter is hugging me, and he is crying too.

"It's going to be okay, Lunden. . . . It is."

I don't feel like it's going to be okay. I have no clue what it's going to be like, and that's what makes it so scary. The unknown. I only know I am going to have a baby, a whole human relying on me for everything, and I can't rely on anyone, especially the other party accountable for this little human.

"I'm tired, Hunt. I've got to go."

He steps out of the car and comes around to the driver's side, opening my door. Then dropping to his knees with head against my chest and arms around my waist, he says, "I'm sorry. . . . I love you."

"I'm sorry too. Love you." I mutter back, exhausted from the chaos and the toll it's taking on my body while I'm growing another human inside.

The next morning, I go to the office to start moving everything out of Rosemont Seneca. I don't hear from Hunter, but the chaos of the movers distracts me. Katie Dodge packs the back room where I first met Hunter, while I handle his office personally. Who knows what he has stashed, or where, and we wouldn't want random movers to come across it.

As I'm boxing up Hunter's desk, I hear a knock on the glass wall beside the open door. A mover looks a little uncomfortable, like he has bad news.

"I'm coming to you," he tells me, "because when you introduced yourself earlier you said you were his friend before saying you were his assistant . . . and I think this is something for his friend."

"Okay," I say, wondering where this is going.

He pulls out a small box I recognize. "Did you open that?" I ask.

"Yes ma'am. I found it with some, um, paraphernalia . . ." He opens the box to show me the glass stems and the rock that I knew would be in there next to a torch lighter and some copper wire. "Now listen, I'm from the streets and I ain't no snitch."

"It's mine," I lie, without missing a beat, standing to grab the box.

Eyeing me for a second, he responds with a slight smile, "Well, I guess that's why you introduced yourself as his friend first. You're a good friend."

Yeah, some kind of friendship, I thought to myself. I'm pregnant and taking the blame for the white ghost he randomly leaves around the office, and meanwhile he's parading around with my friends, having too good of a time to even check on me.

The next day, the movers bring in a huge crane. Hunter has a sofa he claims was a gift from Joe, or possibly had been in the White House at some point. Who knows if he's telling the truth, or if he just wants to get under the skin of one of the head Swedish ladies who is pacing back and forth on the roof, cursing Hunter under her breath. She's terrified the crane will damage the glass architecture and wants us to cut the sofa in half and carry it down the stairway to the nearest dumpster. She's lovely.

As I'm dodging nasty Swedish looks on the rooftop, I get a call from Randi Jo. I step over to the edge of the roof so Katie won't hear.

"So I just came across this name and I love it. If it's a girl, how about Navy?"

"Oh, I love that!" She knows I'm hoping for a girl, but every indication is that I'm having a boy. I've had dozens of ultrasounds, and one of the technicians was confident she could determine the gender as early as eleven weeks. Both times I've seen her, she said she saw boy parts. Hunter and I had gotten a cup test from CVS before he started avoiding me. Green for girl, blue for boy.

"What color is it?" he wanted to know, and laughed when I said it was a blue, plain as day.

"I want a girl I can dress up," I say. He already knows this, which is probably why he thinks it's funny. But the thought also nags at me that if this is Hunter's only son, he might try to take custody.

So, while I love the name Navy, my dream of a girl is fading. "Wait . . . I can't do that. Hunter was discharged from the Navy. People will think I did it for that reason."

"What people? Who cares what people think? You know otherwise, and so will Hunter."

She has a point. People will think what they want. I'll learn that the hard way.

And as it turns out, I pick out my daughter's name on the rooftop of the Swedish Embassy. The place it all began.

I see Hunter again over the next several weeks, him dropping in to see me, or me driving out to his Annapolis house. We still connect deeply when we're together overnight, but the times in between become longer. I don't hear much from him after a while. Nobody does, not even the AMOEBA clan. One evening, I pass the Chain Bridge house on the way to a friend's place. Hunter's Porsche is parked out front, but backed in and out of the way, like maybe it isn't in use. A weird feeling comes over me. A few days later on the way to see Kelsey, I pass the house again. The Porsche is in the exact same spot but covered in snow. I start wondering if maybe Joe and Jill sent him to rehab. I'm hoping.

Many times I think about stopping, punching in the gate code, and letting Joe know what is going on. I don't want to be a scandal. I don't want to bring the family down. But I know they don't know. Hunter isn't going to tell them in the state he's in. I can only pray that someday he will.

In mid-March, I'm three months along, and Vanessa, Lydia, and I take a small trip to Virginia Beach to relax on the beach and listen to the waves.

Mom texts while we're there, asking how everything is going. "I'm fine," I respond, but she isn't one to check in much, so something must be off. I need to decompress after a trip home to Arkansas for my birthday, where I wore baggy sweatshirts the whole time so my parents wouldn't notice.

While I was there at a family dinner, my mom's oldest sister and best friend sits down next to me and whispers, "Your parents know."

"What?" I ask as my eyes get big. "What do they know?"

"They know you're in love with Hunter, it's obvious, and that you're together."

"Ohh," I sigh, as every muscle in my body simultaneously unclenches.

"Why, what did you think I was talking about?"

"Oh nothing," I casually reply, turning away a little.

"Oh my, Lunden. You're pregnant. You need to get out and come to my house tonight."

I go and we talk. "Is it his?" she asks, and I tell her it is. "Lunden, what have you gotten yourself into?"

I don't know, and I'm scared. She urges me to tell my parents. "I know I need to," I say, but I can't. My sister got pregnant before she got married, and my mom acted horrible to her, like she was damned and the entire family was going to hell. I've always been the golden child, the one they were proud of, and now I'm not only pregnant, I'm in a situation that's going to be a public scandal.

As I board the plane back to D.C., my aunt calls. "Did you do it?"

"No, I couldn't. Mom was so happy I was home for my birthday, and I just couldn't disappoint her." I cry on that flight.

My aunt, uncle, and sister have been calling every day since, checking in, making sure I'm not at a Planned Parenthood. They know I'm not, that I would never do that, but that's just our personality. Morbid.

While we're roasting marshmallows by our fire, trying to forget it all, my phone vibrates. It's Dad calling. Now I can sense it. They know.

I'm relieved. My sister and aunt must have told them.

Having no idea what to say, I walk out onto the beach and sit on a long piece of driftwood. The sun's setting and I pull my ball cap down over my eyes, wishing I had a blanket to cover me against the ocean breeze. I take a deep breath and call Dad back. He picks up on the first ring.

"Hey what's going on?" he asks.

"Oh, nothing . . ."

"Sounds like a lot is going on, actually. I heard the news."

"Yeah . . ." I reply, with my knees tucked to my chin, looking out at the ocean.

"Well, how's everything going with that?" He's my rock. I can hear it in his voice.

"Umm . . . okay, I guess."

"What do you mean?" he wants to know. "Is he okay with everything?"

"I don't know . . . He's not in the best place right now, Dad." My voice breaks the tiniest bit.

"Well, you know you can always come home."

"I know." I feel the steady lifeline. I'd been thinking about coming home before our call. Hunter's car is still parked in the same spot at Chain Bridge, and I have barely heard from him.

My dad and I say our goodbyes, and I get up off that long piece of driftwood and slowly walk back down the beach to our campfire. Vanessa and Lydia greet me with a hug and ask if I'm okay. For the first time in a long time, I feel like I am. The warmth of the fire creeps back into my cold arms and legs as I sit there knowing I've made my decision.

I'm going home.

Before leaving D.C. I meet with Diane, a woman who has become like a mother away from home. She's a world-renowned animal communicator and reminds me of my Grandma Tomi. But animals aren't the only thing she talks with; she connects with spirits and can see things that are coming. Because I trust Diane so much, I ask if I can come sit with her for professional advice rather than the mother-daughter advice she gives me daily.

I'm aware what the Bible says about consulting with mediums, but when you're as desperate as I am for some sort of answer, there's almost nothing you won't resort to, especially when it's within your reach.

Diane meets with me at her home. She's on the phone when she answers the door, and stops long enough in her conversation to say, "It's a good thing you're so pretty, since you're going to be on TV." This isn't the normal Diane I'm used to. This is Diane the medium. She's already in her zone.

"What?" I think to myself. She doesn't even know anything about my situation.

As we sit and talk, she tells me a spirit has arrived. It's a blond woman with big hair who smells like cigarettes.

"That's my Grandma Tomi," I say, laughing.

"Yes, I can tell she's related to you," Diane says. "She's very concerned with your father's health."

"That would make sense," I reply, "he has cancer."

Next Diane says, "There's a lot of chaos surrounding a baby." Pointing at me she asks, "Are you pregnant?"

"Yes," I tell her, getting hopeful for some answers.

"Is the mother of your baby's father deceased?"

"She is."

"I can sense her here with us. Does he have any siblings who are deceased?"

"He does,"

"His brother is here. They want you to know that they're here to support you and they're here for the baby. That's why they showed up." She continues to stare at me while I try to hold my composure, then says, "Is the father of your child someone of authority or influence?" Her question hits me.

"Well, yes he is."

"I can tell. I keep getting pictures of the White House."

So that's when I decide to tell her.

"Oh, hell," she says.

"Yeah," I think to myself. "No kidding."

Chapter 9

Burisma Baby Briefcase

A small, black briefcase is slanted against the wall, with a large "Biden" sticker printed in big blue Garamond letters on the cover, and "President" in thin red letters underneath. A small enamel badge outlined in silver sports the pacific blue and white logo of Burisma.

I flip open the briefcase to vinyl lining and a silver Burisma name tag.
BOARD MEETING
June 3, 2016—Monte Carlo, Monaco
HUNTER BIDEN
Business papers, ADP earnings statements, and one of Hunter's old journals fill one side. Oh, what the media would give for those. But far more valuable to me is what's on the other side—our baby's sonograms.

Coming back to Arkansas doesn't stop the darkness from closing in. I held it off as long as I could, but by the time I get home to the South, the light is fading fast. Pinpricks of hope feel out of reach, like lightning bugs that should be easy to catch, but recede into blackness.

My once heroic, robust father, who slayed deer, ventured on safaris, and built a custom gun empire is now wearing a fall-risk bracelet. He's been my rock, but every day cancer erodes his strength, bit by bit. While Dad fights for his life, Mom's brutal disappointment has her barely uttering a word to me. She was hard on my sister and me growing up, but now she makes sure I know every single day that she disapproves of me and "the situation you got yourself into."

A cold war of icy glares and tense silences rages, punctuated by hot zones and catty comments shooting across the room like barb-tipped arrows from a compound bow. Sometimes I let one fly back at Mom, but most of the time, when an insult zips through the air, the bow is in her hands and the target is me. I'm a lot like my mom in ways. She loves hard but doesn't know how to express it in the right ways. I know I've disappointed her, and she only expects more from me.

I'm working at my dad's shop, Rob Roberts Custom Gun Works, and living in the loft at Mom and Dad's house too, so there's no escape. It's like I'm living alone, but with my family. It's so dark.

Things come to a head on a Sunday afternoon in May as Mom and I drive a winding country road home from church. The car is silent as I stare out the passenger window watching the fence posts pass. I'd like to trade places with one of those cows. Then Mom's sharp voice snaps me back into reality.

"Do you even know what you're namin' it," she asks, even though she already knows I'm having a girl.

"Navy," I say quietly, still looking out the window.

"Navy? Spell it."

"N-A-V-Y, Navy." There's a long pause. I glance up to see a disgusted look on her face. She doesn't like it.

"Navy what?"

"Navy Joan, J-O-A-N." I stare into her face to see her reaction. The look of disgust turns to hurt mixed with guilt and sympathy after I spell out my mom's middle name. She does a remarkably good job getting us home for someone who appears to look out the driver's-side window the entire rest of the trip, so I don't see the water in her eyes.

I trail behind as Mom leads the way into the house and clicks the master bedroom lock, shutting herself away from the world. Randi Jo later confides that mom cried behind that door the rest of the day, touched by the fact that I would be naming my daughter after her.

Something shifts after that. It doesn't magically fix everything, or maybe anything at all, but from that day forward, the darkness doesn't get any deeper on that front.

Sparks of hope light up other places too. Dad starts improving. Diane has become Navy's fairy godmother, and she tells me, "He will be fine. Ya know why he will be fine? Because he will not leave this earth knowing what you have ahead of you. He's your protector, and he will be your daughter's too." The doctors manage to operate and successfully remove his prostate. Hunter is right again, and the darkness is held at bay there too.

But growing in me is the certainty that Joe is 100 percent going to run for president in 2020. One day in the gun shop, one of the men working in the office casually talks about politics.

"Who you got winning the primary for the Dems?" he asks as if it's March Madness and I have a bracket filled out for betting.

"Joe. That's a no-brainer," I shoot back without having to think about it.

"Really? How do you . . ."

"And he will pick Cory Booker or Kamala Harris."

"Huh? You serious?"

"Yeah. I actually know it for a fact. I have some inside insight on it," I say grinning. In time, he will know. Might as well have some fun with it.

Seva and Brandi, my two best friends since sixth grade, have gone through all seasons of life with me and are such a comfort. One night, I break the news to them over dinner. "I'm pregnant, and Hunter Biden is my baby's father." They spit out their red wine. They've seen posts of us on social media, but as far as they knew, Hunter was my friend and I worked for him.

"I mean we knew y'all spent time together, but damn sure wasn't expecting that! What are you gonna do?" Brandi asks.

"Well, I'm gonna have a baby. I don't really want it to get out who the father is with Joe planning on running. Right now, I just want to focus on growing this baby. I'll handle the hard stuff after."

When the word does get out that I'm pregnant, like good friends they act clueless when asked who the father is. Even though it's no one's business, small-town Arkansas folks tend to think otherwise.

During the summer of 2018, Joe is doing his American Promise Tour to gin up support for the coming campaign. When they hold the Memphis rally, I don't know exactly why, but I decide to attend.

Joe works the crowd masterfully and talks about hope. For some reason his sermon on how we need more love and fewer lies doesn't motivate me quite the way it does the rest of the non-Biden-impregnated crowd. Go figure.

I'm not even sure why I'm here. Probably desperation. Halfway through the rally I decide that if he does a handshake line or a meet and greet afterward, I'm going to get to him, tell him everything, and beg him to have Hunter contact me. But there is no line, so I go back home completely devoid of the hope he preached about. He was one hundred feet from his granddaughter, and completely oblivious.

The threat of scandal grows along with my baby, as the possibility that Hunter's father could become president means I might be having one of the nation's first grandchildren.

After my last lunch with Hunter, he jokingly said, "I have no doubts you can go to Arkansas and handle any redneck that comes your way, but what if you come home to ISIS on your living room couch?"

I don't know. I'm scared.

The mere thought of the Oval Office connection catapults a manageable pregnancy into a realm of craziness. I find myself planning where to keep guns in case some crazy person decides to hold the granddaughter of the POTUS hostage. Pregnancy and anxiety are a nasty mix on top of feeling like I have to keep it a secret to protect Hunter. The less people who know the details, the better.

Kelsey calls one night with a flashback from my past. "Hey Lunden, listen to this." She's at Mpire in the dressing room with the dancers and I can hear through the speaker phone. They're talking about Hunter and how many of them have slept with him. I'm almost numb, but now it's more than hearing about an ex-lover. He's the father of the baby inside me, so it's like hearing them talk about a family member.

Then I wake up one morning rattled by the notifications on my phone. I have nine missed called from Savanah, a couple missed calls from Kelsey, and texts saying, "Call ASAP."

"Savanah, what is it?" I ask with my heart in my stomach.

"I was out at this lounge last night," she says, "and a man in a suit started asking me questions about you. I didn't think anything of it and didn't tell him anything, but he came into the bathroom behind me, and he put his arm up against the wall and wouldn't let me pass and kept asking about you. He said something about working with the CIA and had an official presidential pin on his jacket. It said Trump! It was the gold one like Hunter has of Joe! It freaked me out!"

"What do you mean he kept asking about me? What was he asking?"

"He kept asking what I knew and where you were. He wanted to know who all knew, and I just kept asking what he was talking about. But he knew I knew he knew and said something about hearing you went back to Arkansas."

Now to be fair, Savanah freaks out a lot. Once I jokingly told her that her flu symptoms were symptoms of AIDS, and she spent the night in the ER getting tested. But this call sounds different. I don't think the guy can be both CIA and wearing a Trump pin, but if anything she's describing holds any truth, then it's terrifying. And I completely trust Savanah.

Of course, I also have to worry about everyone finding out in my small town too. Independence County, Arkansas, is Trump country, and while the town is good and I've known these people my entire life, I don't want anyone knowing I'm carrying the grandchild of their archenemy.

"Hey Lunden," a text pops up on my phone one day. "Can you run and pick up some paperwork for me and run it to Hunter in Annapolis?" It's Katie Dodge.

"Hey Katie, my dad has cancer, and Hunter let me come home for a little bit." That was always my excuse to her, but part of me wishes I was in D.C. I would have done it. I hadn't talked to Katie since we packed up Rosemont Seneca together. I'm not sure what she knows and doesn't know, but I figure I need to say something about being in Arkansas before she asks me to run another errand. Working for Hunter wasn't being at an office every day. As his assistant, I could handle most things by running errands or over the phone or online.

A couple days later I get my teeth cleaned, just to take care of myself in the midst of the darkness, and my Aunt DD who works in the dentist's office calls afterward. "Lunden, I need to come talk to you."

When she arrives to my parents' house she says, "The receptionist who does the insurance at the office pulled me aside when you left today and told me the craziest thing."

Oh, hell, what now? DD's a funeral buzzard, always circling the latest crisis, and I have no idea what she might come up with.

"She said 'DD, I thought Lunden worked for the government or something.'"

DD knows I've been working for Hunter. She knows I've been seeing him, and just like the rest of my family, she is well aware I'm carrying his child, but she plays it cool.

"Well, the weirdest thing just happened," the receptionist relays. "I had to call her insurer and the girl on the other end mentioned the insurance was for Lunden's employment at a boating company based in Moscow, Russia, and she was listed in their records as a head of the company!"

Top-tier anxiety level opened.

"What the hell? What does that even mean? I've never even been to Russia! She had to be mistaken!"

As if the rest of the stress isn't enough, now I am head of a Moscow boating company. What the hell have I gotten myself into? What other companies do I work for? A coffee company in Brazil? An oil refinery in the Gulf? Who knows! But I also know, my aunt has an inclination to exaggerate some stories, it's part of the small town tendencies and I'll hope that's the case here.

Trapped in the insane world of Biden benefits, I need to get my insurance updated since I'll be having a baby soon. So I call the carrier and the lady who pulls my information takes one look and says, "Um, I'm not allowed to talk to you about this policy."

"So y'all can't talk to me, but you can talk to the lady at my dentist office about my plan? I just need to know what to do since I have a baby coming."

"Ma'am, I really can't talk with you. I don't have the clearance to view this account. I will have to transfer you. Please hold."

I get passed around more times than a basketball in a motion offense, and finally get connected to someone with "clearance."

"Yes, I'm trying to find out . . ."

"I'm sorry ma'am. What was your name? Are you a James?"

"Do I sound like a James? No, I'm Lunden Roberts."

"Oh okay, ma'am. I'm sorry, I can only speak with a James or Jimmy about these policies."

"James? As in James Biden? Why would you have to discuss my insurance policy with him?"

"No ma'am, we're not allowed to discuss further details. I'm sorry. Please have Jimmy or James contact us for any changes."

"Yeah, sure I'll do that. By chance if you talk to them before I do, tell them the baby and I are doing fine." Click. I hang up in defeat.

My CSI nosiness kicks in. I might be miserable right now, but at least I've got a mystery to solve. Just who is Lunden Roberts of Moscow, Russia, and why can't she talk to anybody about her own insurance policy?

For the next couple of weeks, I research what I've really gotten myself into. I go off what I know about him and what he shared with me through his divorce. I try to get in the mind of Hunter Biden. I know him well enough and paid enough attention to details to know how he names things that mean the most to him, including his love for the Finger Lakes. I always thought he felt some connection to New York, because that's where his mom was from. The Finger Lakes were special to him. I look into his family's past and any companies I suspect he might have.

The Moscow boat company is a revelation. James Biden, or a guy named Jimmy, managing my insurance is a revelation. But the be-all and end-all is when I turn up the GPS coordinates that belong to one of Hunter's companies. I punch them into Google Maps, and the company is headquartered under the Potomac River, probably with all those Clinton enemies.

Then I get a call from a friend in D.C.

"Are you okay?" he asks.

"Uh, yeah why?"

"Because tonight I was out and overheard a conversation from a couple of people on Trump's campaign. Something about Trump has a bombshell he plans on dropping on Joe Biden *live* during the debate, and it had everything to do with a woman who worked with Hunter then fled back to Arkansas, pregnant with his baby. And he wants to tell Joe and the world that he has a grandchild in Arkansas he doesn't know about."

"Oh . . . shit."

"Now I may not be smart, but I can put two and two together. You were with him a lot, and now you're back in Arkansas . . . pregnant!"

"Hmm, coincidence," I laugh.

"Hell no it ain't no coincidence! It's you, isn't it? You're the girl I overheard them talking about! Are you okay?"

No, I'm not okay.

So now my baby and I are allegedly a secret Trump can use as a bombshell to destroy his political rival. I have to protect Hunter, because if I don't, this small-town girl from Arkansas could possibly cost his dad the presidency, and quite frankly I'd never do anything to promote a Trump campaign.

I just keep beating myself up. Hunter let his guard down, I took that trust, and now my pregnancy is not only going to hurt him, but also his family. It's all my fault. He is going to hate me. I've let him down bigger than I knew.

But at the same time I wonder, how did I ever put myself in this predicament? To get fooled into falling for someone who didn't care anything about me. And here I am, still caring for him, determined to protect him even though there's no way he'll protect me.

Don Miller was right. After he assured me I should talk to Hunter, he also told me before I left, "Don't forget he was raised by one of the greatest politicians in this lifetime. He knows what he's doing, and he can charm himself out of anything. That's the politician in him."

For the last couple of years I've had such hopes for Hunter, his huge potential, intelligence, kindness, charm, magnetic personality, and million connections. He loves to help people and desperately just wants love and appreciation. All things being equal, he should have been an enormous success, praised for helping others. But all things aren't equal.

As a child, Hunter lost his mother and sister in an accident that he and his brother survived. He came away with a fractured skull, traumatic brain injury, and survivor's guilt. His dad, who kept campaigning instead of helping his sons process that nightmare, had himself sworn into office from the hospital room where Hunter and Beau were being treated, in what could have been perceived as a photo op.

Then Joe married someone else's wife in what seemed like a bit of a rush job to support his bid for reelection, and insisted the boys call her "Mom," when it's been said she didn't act like much of one to them. Hunter wasn't interested in politics, or even business. He wanted to be an artist and to help people, but he had to put that aside to help cement the family legacy. Beau was tasked with handling his father's political legacy, while Hunter would handle the business deals. And then, finally, cancer claimed Beau.

Take every tragedy and put it under the media spotlight for more than forty years, and what do you get? A man in extreme pain, tormented by his guilt, self-medicating his demons, needing approval, but thought of as the family's black sheep.

Now, with this little bit of distance between us, I realize I thought I could be the one to draw him out of all that. He trusted me more than anyone else, like Hallie claimed. I loved him, desired his love back, and believed I could stabilize him. He resisted getting help, but I never gave up asking because I knew it had to happen for him to have any shot at recapturing that gargantuan potential. I fought to protect him. I kept his secrets buried, and I enabled him.

But he hasn't changed. I haven't rescued him, and now I'm about to become a mind-blowingly big scandal for him . . . *another* scandal. I feel like I'm the exact opposite of what I wanted to be. Instead of loving him through and out of his problems, I've just become the biggest one yet. My heart breaks as my hope of helping him recedes back into the dark.

That darkness has eclipsed every hope I brought with me from D.C., and every hope I thought I was returning to in Arkansas.

Chapter 10

Mustard Seed

It's a bright afternoon, so bright that I need to shield my eyes to make out the faces of the people sitting at the little tables all around me. But before I raise my hand, someone walks up and pulls out one of my table's empty seats. I know his face, but we've never met. It's Beau.

"I'm so sorry," I tell him. "Sorry for everything," the apologies flowing like melting winter snow.

"Why are you sorry?" he asks, with genuine interest in his eyes. "You were chosen for this."

I stare in awe, trying to comprehend.

"I've held her before you have," Beau says, with a moment of reassuring serenity on his face, and I gasp and bolt upright in bed.

Pregnancy brain is a real thing, and with it come the wild dreams that help with processing the many emotions. But I wasn't ready for that. Dreams are fleeting, gone within minutes of waking, but the clarity of that connection with Beau is something I'll never forget.

A few weeks later, I visit Dr. Chang, a small Asian man with a thick accent and a constant smile. He's referred to as the best obstetrician in

Little Rock, where I decided to have my baby to avoid the small-town talk.

"Do you see here, Ms. Roberts?" he asks in his soft-spoken voice pointing to the ultrasound. "You can see here that you're having a girl."

Beau was right.

"I don't think so," I say to Randi Jo over pizza by the river on a muggy summer evening. She's in big sister mode and wants me to have a baby shower.

"Your friends want to do something for you," she urges, and I know the church wants to do one too, but mom would be against "flaunting" the baby, since we weren't married.

"Bullshit." Randi shoots back. "Either way, this baby is a blessing!"

I don't bother to tell Randi that I'm not planning on being a mom for very long after the birth. I've made up my mind. I could never hurt my child while she's inside me. After all, I'm not going down to Planned Parenthood to abort her. But after I've seen this through, no one needs me hanging around much longer.

"Just leave it alone," I say. "None of these people know what's going on, and I don't want their sympathy. Besides, I don't have the energy."

If I did have the energy, I would tell Mom she's right about not celebrating sin, but also my baby isn't a sin. Hunter and I weren't married, and if we're going by the Bible, which Mom likes to do, then our "union" wasn't holy. But that sin created the most beautiful, precious little life imaginable. So yes, Mom, condemn the sin, but how about we love and celebrate the wonderful thing that came out of it? After all, the Apostle Paul wrote "God causes everything to work together for the good of those who love Him, and those who are called according to his purpose."

"Have you been on social media?" Randi asks, knowing what people are saying about me and my baby.

"Not a lot. Some asshat said instead of a gender reveal, people should start doing a father of the child reveal. I assume that was targeted toward me."

"If they only knew . . ." Randi trails off.

"If only . . . It wouldn't change anything except instead of calling me a gold-digging NBA whore they'd call me a gold-digging politician whore," I chuckle.

The rumors started when people found out I was pregnant and my family and close friends weren't talking about the father. People said I didn't know who my child's father was. That conspiracy made me laugh, but honestly, I expected it. Lately, the rumor has become that I'm carrying a black NBA player's baby, and my family is ashamed. That conspiracy sends me into a rage. Their racism infuriates me. How could anyone think that low of me and my family? For the first time, I'm ashamed of where I come from.

Even though Hunter once told me he was the blackest person I know, even claiming that if we were dropped in a black community he would fit in better than anyone, I am reasonably sure we aren't going to produce anything other than a blue-eyed, non-NBA baby.

But then one day the theory changes. My sister calls to fill me in.

"I just talked to Tara, and I have to tell you what she just told me." I take a deep breath. "The nurses at the dentist office were having breakfast in their conference room and talking about your whole situation . . ."

I butt in: "The local dentist office has nothing better to discuss than my pregnancy this morning? What miserable lives they must live."

"Just wait! So apparently Lisa tells them you're having an NBA baby, but Martha tells everyone that she had actually heard it was Donald Trump Jr.'s baby!" She's laughing so hard I can barely gather the name.

"Trump Jr.? What the hell?" I don't know whether to laugh or be offended, but that's hitting a little close to home.

I let people talk, and they make up the most awful things about me. They say I'm a ho who's been knocked up and left with no father for my unborn child. But I don't defend myself. I take the heat to protect Hunter.

Things get dark, and rumors are the least of my issues. I'm growing a baby whose future is so unknown, and in the back of my head is a constant worry. I'm worried about Hunter. I wonder where he is and if he's gotten help. Worry steals any light I could find in pregnancy.

"My biggest regret with my pregnancies," my sister tells me, "is not taking enough pictures. I only have one picture of me pregnant with Brooks. I get that it's hard right now, but one day Navy's going to find joy in a picture of you pregnant with her. It might end up being one of her most prized possessions."

Maybe Randi is right. It's my last trimester and I've hardly taken a picture. Maybe I should do a maternity shoot, not for myself, but for my baby. It might be one of the few pictures she ever has of us together.

I order a dress, and being from the beautiful natural state of Arkansas, we don't have to look far for a backdrop. The White River is less than five miles from my house, with a sandbar that gives our town its own little beach. The last time I waded into that river, I was a different person. No D.C., no Hunter, no pregnancy, no idea just how much life would change over the next couple of years. Now I'm not just a different person. I'm a different person carrying another person. I literally couldn't be more different than I am now, and I want to own this change. This is the perfect spot.

I traded my Challenger for an off-road Jeep when I thought I was going to need a mom vehicle, and we drive that out onto the river. Climbing over sand and rocks with ease, we find the perfect spot just off the sandbar and into the water.

Randi snaps hundreds of pictures of me in a light blue floral dress, off the shoulders and fitted to show my growing baby. I pick my favorite and post it on social media with the quote, "No man ever steps in the same river twice, for it's not the same river and he's not the same man." Everyone who talked so horribly about me before, suddenly wants to congratulate me. They have no idea I know what they've been saying. They also have no idea that the baby's birth is about to be overshadowed by tragedy.

I grew up in church but am still not really sure what will happen when I die and face my maker; so, it's probably time to make good with Him. Throughout my pregnancy journey, my faith has become stronger than ever, despite my plans for after the baby comes. I figure, as long as I can keep a good relationship with God throughout my last days, He might just forgive me for what I'm about to do. That's how the praying starts . . . that and desperation.

Long drives in my new Jeep make me fall more and more into prayer. It's an escape, alone with the trees, pastures, country roads, and God.

I find myself praying for my dad, for his health, that God will bring him through the cancer. I pray for my Navy baby. I pray that she's healthy, that her future will be bright, and that she'll be a good person, someone she will be proud of when she looks in the mirror. I pray for Hunter. I pray that our situation will work out the way it's supposed to, that he will beat the addiction and self-destruction, find himself, and be a father for our child.

One scorching July afternoon, a wall of emotional bricks collapses onto me when a Kesha song, "Praying" comes on the radio. The lyrics are so relatable, yet so devastating that I have to pull over and catch my breath when the song talks about going through hell and fighting for myself, hoping that he's out there somewhere praying and changing, and wishing him farewell.

And while it's up to God to forgive Hunter, I'm convinced that I am unforgivable. There's no typical journal on my bedside table, but when emotions start to overcome me, I grab a white Burisma notepad from the briefcase and drain them onto the page. In just a few days, Navy Joan will be born, and the weight of my life feels like it's going to crush me to death.

8/11/18
I'm scared, filled with doubt, lost hope, depressed under this forced smile, ashamed, unpure. I feel like I've lost all credibility to my name and who I am. I've begun to question who I am, who I thought I was. A waste of potential. Beyond all of this, I have to find the blessing within. It's hard. Praying to God has become my only "sure thing" of everyday. I know he will listen—and I just need to be heard. Among all this, I've lost my voice. My happiness. I pray for this child, sweet Navy Joan. I wonder who she will be. Will she blame me for bringing her into this situation—this cruel world? I pray for my parents—their strength through this, their health. I need them . . . . I pray for him. Wherever he is, he's lost. Will he ever show up? I miss my friend. If he does show up what turmoil will come to light? Will I be the bad guy?

I've lost the person I was. I miss her.

Still no hugs. Still very much alone. Still scared. Still a disappointment.

. . . . and she will be here soon.

Just hitting nine months and I'm miserable, not only from the chaos in my mind, but I'm too oversized for this Arkansas summer heat. An acetabular fracture in my pelvis has me crawling on elbows and knees, up and down the stairs to my parents' loft for the incessant bathroom visits.

Then, on August 28 at 2:04 a.m. my eyes pop open, but this time something is different. The only sound is the gentle blowing of the air conditioner working hard to keep me cool, and everyone else in the house safe. Wobbling, I stand from my bed when a splash hits the floor and splatters onto my legs and bare feet. Panic strikes, since I don't think I've ever peed my pants before. But it isn't urine, and it keeps coming.

Grabbing a towel, I wobble downstairs with it between my legs.

"Mom!" I call as I slide her door open, "I think my water just broke."

The covers burst off the bed like rocks erupting from a volcano, and I hear, "Are you sure?" being yelled from somewhere under the explosion.

"I don't know! But if it hadn't broken before, it sure has now. You've scared the hell out of me!"

Punching the emergency line saved in my contacts, I call my doctor. "My water just broke. I'm like thirty-nine weeks, should I just come in? Is that what people do?"

"That's fine. Go ahead and c'mon in! Dr. Chang will call you soon!"

Wrapped in four or five towels, I manage to hoist myself into my Jeep with the car seat, the hospital stay bags, and the diaper bag. Before I head out, the doctor calls.

"Hello, this is Dr. Chang. Is everything okay?" a man on the other end asks in a very American voice.

I hesitate. The accent is gone. Is this a setup? "Umm . . . I'm sorry, I think I have the wrong Dr. . . ."

"I'm sorry," he laughs, "I should have been more specific. I'm your Dr. Chang's son, Dr. Chang. I am a doctor who works in his clinic. I heard your water broke. Just come in. Dad will be at the hospital by 5:00 a.m."

After waiting for my mother to do her makeup, I drive an hour and a half on the uneven interstate with more water breaking onto the seat at each bump. My mom faces me from the passenger seat, like a hoot owl staring at any movement or reaction I might give. She knew that I hated looking vulnerable and that I'm completely stubborn, so she didn't even bother offering to drive. We both knew what I'd say.

The long miserable haul comes to an end around 4:30 a.m., and we arrive just in time for the nurses' shift change. They put me in a gown and a hospital bed, taking bets on which women will still be in labor by the time they come back for their night shift. I'm on the list for still being very much pregnant. The labor is slow, but by the time I'm hooked up to everything, Dr. Chang is coming through the door.

"Would you like Pitocin to speed up the labor?" he asks. But I'm not expecting the kick that comes with it. Within thirty minutes, everyone on the floor must think our room is an active crime scene, as one screaming person murders another person who is weeping. Both people are me.

"I can't do this, Mom," I moan and cry, sitting cross-legged at the foot of the bed.

"Too late now. You got yourself into it, and now you've gotta get yourself out." She doesn't say it out loud, but I'm 100 percent sure I can hear her thinking it.

Surprised to see me still sitting cross-legged, Dr. Chang schedules an epidural. He also gives me a shot to protect the baby from the developing antibodies in the mother's bloodstream due to an Rh factor in differing blood types. When they asked me about the father, I had a vague recollection that Hunter said his blood type was rare, or maybe I just thought it was, because that would be like him. It's a good thing we take that precaution, because Navy has the same rare blood type as her father.

At 11:00 a.m., Dr. Chang comes in to check me. "Okay," he greets us with his thick Asian accent, "it's time to get the room ready. She's ready to push."

Instantly, the relaxation fades. Randi's been telling me I'm going to have a ten-pound baby. All Roberts babies are ten pounds or more, and one of our relatives was almost eighteen pounds. It's game time. It's the fourth quarter. I've been down by two the entire game, but now the ball is in my hands, and I'm taking the last shot. I thrive under the pressure.

I don't want anyone in the delivery room. I've gone through the entire pregnancy alone, and it's only right that I finish it alone. But Mom doesn't leave. I tell the nurse to get her out of there, but the nurse laughs.

Within an hour, I deliver Navy Joan into the world. She's tiny for a Roberts, just seven pounds. Mom cuts the umbilical cord, and the nurse hands me my baby to do skin-to-skin contact and build the initial bond, but I cut that short. I know we won't have much time together. It's already unfair for me to deny Navy a mother, but why make it worse by letting her bond?

"Does she look like me?" I ask as Mom stands over me, observing Navy's face.

"Well, she doesn't look like anyone I've seen in person," she shoots back with a grin. I know what she means. Navy may have had a head full of dark hair like I did when I was born, but my mom thinks she looks like Hunter. And she does.

Mom leaves to meet my dad and sister, who had rushed to the Little Rock hospital, and when the nurse returns from taking Navy to the nursery, she finds me flopping my legs alongside the bed to stand. Both are still very numb, but I'm determined to get them working.

"Ma'am, what are you doing?" the nurse asks, frantically rushing over to me.

"One of my legs is really stiff, but can you help me get to the bathroom and get everything cleaned up? I'd like to change clothes."

"Are you sure? You just had labor. Why don't you lay down and rest a little?"

"Yes. I'm sure. My family will be here any minute and I don't want to look like I just went through labor. I want to look normal."

She looks confused, but she removes my catheter all the same and helps me clean up. I've seen women postdelivery before, and they look miserable. I've got a fresh change of clothes, and I'm not about to let myself look that weak and helpless in front of anyone, even my family.

"What the hell? You don't even look like you've just had a kid," my sister exclaims as she and my parents enter the room. I'm sitting in bed cross-legged, wearing a light pink floral gown and robe, hair in a messy bun. I contemplated putting on makeup, but I was too exhausted.

"We spotted her right off," Randi says. "She was a little shrimp screaming."

"Yeah," Dad chimes in, "all the other babies were just being babies, sleeping in their cribs, and Navy was screaming bloody murder. Giving the nurses hell. We knew it was her."

I haven't told anyone I went into labor, but over the next few hours, my aunts, uncles, and cousins arrive. My mom has been spreading the news. My youngest cousin is holding Navy when the nurse walks in saying, "Okay, it's time to feed the baby." I've decided not to breastfeed. I don't want there to be that attachment. So the nurse hands me a bottle, and I hand it to my cousin.

"No," the entire room erupts. "The first feeding should be by the mother."

"It's okay. She can feed her," I say quietly. I can tell everyone might think something's off, but I don't think any of them realize just how far off it really is. Through the rest of the afternoon and into the evening, the family takes turns holding her as I sit in bed.

Finally, that night after things calm down and most of the family has gone, the nurse gives Navy Joan her first bath, then carries Navy to me while she screams to the top of her lungs. "Hold her where she can hear your heartbeat. The two things that will make her most comfortable are your heartbeat and your voice," the nurse tells me.

As I think about my heart being the key to her comfort, it starts to sting. I'm not sure why. Maybe it's just sad because in a few days my heart will be still and hers will be broken.

Chapter 11

Seven-Pound Hunter

Overwhelmed and exhausted, I spend the first night of Navy's little life lying in bed, thankful that my mom stayed to help. I don't know the first thing about what I'm doing, and I need her.

Navy sleeps peacefully in the clear bassinet next to my bed, only waking for mealtimes and diaper changes, which I'm unaware of because Mom is tending to her. I'm in my own head, and the exhaustion sends me into a coma for most of the night. I'm worn out.

Managing to shower first thing in the morning, I put on yoga pants and an oversized shirt. What they don't tell you before having a baby is your baby bump doesn't immediately go away.

A lady walks in with papers. It's the birth certificate. I've been dreading this part, going back and forth. I want her name to be Navy Joan, and we can call her Navy Jo. That's what I'm sure about. But what about her last name? I consider Navy Joan Hunter Roberts, to give her something from her father, and even think about giving her her father's last name. It keeps going back and forth in my mind.

"If you want to give her her father's last name and add him to the birth certificate, you can," the nurse explains. "We can even send him an 'Acknowledgment of Paternity' to finalize everything; you'll just have to give us his address."

I don't know Hunter's address. I don't know where he is, and I'm ashamed to admit it. The safe thing is to name her Navy Joan Roberts. We can always change it if we need to.

"Good morning, Mama," another nurse chirps as she walks in the door. I let out a sigh of relief as the paper lady packs her things.

"Morning," I respond, but it doesn't feel good, and there's not much spirit in my voice. The darkness has grown deeper than anyone knows, stealing my will to live. I've let everyone down, and I don't want this little baby to be next, but I feel like I've already let her down by bringing her into this situation. Keeping myself alive to bring Navy into the world was my goal. I could never hurt her, so I could never hurt myself as long as she was in me. But I've planned on ending my life once I gave birth. My misery and disgrace will somehow go away if I do. I don't want to live. At seven months pregnant, I wrote letters to the people closest to me for them to find once I'm gone, and they are about to find them.

Mom and Dad will take care of Navy and give her the best life. And who knows, Hunter might eventually get involved and give her a parent. But I won't be around to be anyone's problem anymore. Everyone will benefit from me being gone, including Navy.

The nurse picks her up from the bassinet. "So we're just gonna check on the baby real quick. It looks like all she has left is the bilirubin test. Once that is over and all is good, we can get y'all out of here!"

The needles are laid out on the bed across from me, and the nurse sets Navy next to them and unwraps the blanket swaddled around her. She's lying there in a soft white gown with "Navy Joan" written on it beautifully in cursive. I bought it for her ride home from the hospital, and a matching beanie covers her ears. Her big blue eyes stare up at the ceiling, and she lies there, never making a sound.

Then comes the first prick. Navy screams. At her cries, a feeling creeps up from my chest and into my throat. A lump takes shape as I sit there just watching.

"Sorry, I'm not getting the best sample and we have to get a good one in order to discharge y'all." She pricks again, and again . . . and again, the cries getting louder each time.

The lump in my throat escapes into tears pouring from my eyes, and I'm hit for the first time with an overwhelming sense of being a mother. I want to kill this woman who is hurting my baby. Leaving the room before the anger completely takes over and I tear the nurse apart, I pace in the hall, praying it will be over soon. With every scream, I find myself walking further away, my heart hurting because I can't save her. This isn't a hunger cry, or a scream from a dirty diaper; this is pain, and I need it to stop.

Finally, I hear the nurse say she got one, and I'm in the room in an instant, scooping up an inconsolable Navy, whispering to her it's going to be okay and rubbing her little cheeks. We lay back on the bed together, me holding her tight, and her pressing her perfectly formed ear to my chest. Once she's in my arms and against my chest she begins to quiet down. Staring up at me, her brows furrow and she gives her pacifier hell. She's pissed. I let out a laugh looking down into a small face that looks so familiar.

As her breathing returns to normal, my mind drifts back to those dark clouds that overshadowed my thinking for months. I gaze at her little fingers and toes. A radiant shaft of light pierces the clouds. It's not big, but it lands on a tiny seed I hadn't known was there. Nine months ago, it began to put down roots inside me. It was so small I wasn't aware of it. Now this little mustard seed finally breaks through the surface, gleaming in the light, changing everything. I have to take care of her. I'm her protector. I'm her everything. It's just me and her.

Friends and family flood my parents' house in the first few days of Navy's life. Rana, one of my dearest friends, comes over with her daughter Harper. I watch as Rana's daughter holds mine and think about how a mother and daughter should never have to endure what they've been through. Chase, Rana's husband and Harper's father, committed suicide. Left to pick up the pieces, Rana grieved his decision, while finding the strength to be the best mom to Harper and trying to meet her every need. I admire her for that, and I feel convicted.

Until the last nine months, I never understood how a person could get to the point of thinking that the world would be a better place without them. But darkness creeps in without warning. Mental health is fragile and has to be protected. Even when it gets dark, each person has to find a reason to come out of that darkness. My reason is Navy.

When Rana and Harper leave, I go to the loft where I've spent so much time in a horrible headspace. I take three crisp letters from the nightstand. There's one to my dad, one to my mom, and one to my sister, telling them what they've meant to me, forgiving them for where they've hurt me, and asking them to forgive me. I sit and cry reading these letters, knowing how much they care. But there isn't a letter for Hunter. I only wrote them to people who I thought would miss me.

How could I let myself get to this point? I've witnessed Harper grow up with a hole in her life because of her dad's decisions. And I resented him for what he did to my friend and this little girl I loved so much. How on earth could I do that to Navy? I am her Rana. It is my job to muster up the strength to pick up the pieces and be the best parent I can be.

I'm ashamed of even letting the mere thought overcome me. Navy is my purpose. I know this now more than ever.

At Navy's first doctor's visit, her weight has dropped from seven pounds to five. Given her Roberts heritage, the smallest clothing we've bought for her goes to three months. I hadn't counted on her Biden blood. Hunter used to tell me that he was five feet tall until he went to Georgetown, where he shot up to 6'1". And when it came to playing football as a kid, he said it was a good thing he was fast. If he hadn't been, they would have killed him. So I go out and buy preemie outfits for this little doll baby who is half me and half him.

Early in my pregnancy, Hunter claimed he was upset with me for not giving him proper updates on his unborn child. After he missed the ultrasound, I guess I didn't feel he cared enough to know. But Hunter deserves to know at least that his daughter has made her arrival. And who knows, maybe I'll get a response and Navy will get a dad after all.

As I'm driving around one sunny October afternoon less than two months after having her, Navy sleeps in her car seat. I think about reaching out to Hunter as I wind around the same country roads I drove so many times to think and pray. It seems like forever ago, but maybe that's just because my mindset has completely changed. I don't feel alone now. I'm not anymore.

I send a text message to all the phone numbers I have for him—Hunter Biden, Hunter Biden New, Hunter New Cell, Hunt Other, Hunter New New, even sending it to his iCloud accounts. Whether on an iPhone or a MacBook, somehow he would get this iMessage.

It says, "Last we spoke you were upset because I hadn't kept you updated. That was in February. I've called numerous times and sent a few messages as well. I understand you despise me and want nothing to do with the decision I've made. However, I still felt you deserved to hear about it from me. Since it's nearly impossible to reach you, a text will have to suffice . . . in hopes that you even read this—

"Baby was born Aug 28. Beautiful and Healthy. If you ever become curious and want to know more, I can send pics, details, or whatever you may request. I know that's a long shot and you'd much rather avoid the whole situation, but I just wanted you to know the door is always open for you in the baby's life.

"I have left my 'D.C. lifestyle' in the past as I have decided to come home . . . ."

I've never sent catty comments to Hunter before about not being able to reach him, or him despising me and my decision. I'm angry. No, that's an understatement. I'm furious with him. Not only do I blame him for the dark place I was in months prior, but how could someone not want to be there for this perfect baby? She deserves the world. She deserves a dad who knows how fortunate he is and chooses to be present.

Over time, the rumors around town lighten up and so does Navy's hair. Her once black hair turns golden, and when people see a bright blue-eyed baby with skin lighter than mine, their NBA conspiracies die away. But people paying attention notice that something's still a little off.

In every post on social media I make of my daughter's arrival, I do not show her face. I get comments and messages, "Let me see that baby's face!" "I'm ready to see that sweet face of hers." And so on. Then talk starts stirring around town. "Why won't she show that baby's face?" "What is she hiding?" "Is something wrong with it?" As the rumors trickle back to me, I ignore them. I know why I'm not showing her face.

Even though he's not a part of her life, Hunter's presence is there from the beginning. The truth can't stay hidden forever, and even though I can withhold the name of Navy's father for now, I can't hide all the ways she's like him. All it would take are a few small slips for the word to spread like wildfire, especially since the truth is so much better than every rumor going around.

While Navy is still an infant, she has digestion and sleeping issues. I spend every night for months in a recliner, holding her to me. She won't sleep any other way. After extensive research, I find that chiropractic help could solve our problem. I haven't slept in days, so I'm open to trying anything. It reminds me of her father who constantly had a crick in his neck, needed massages, and was always rubbing the spot where his shoulder and neck met. It's at the chiropractor's office that I let the first slip happen.

"Here you go," I say to the receptionist, sliding a plastic clipboard across the counter. I've filled out at least six different sheets of paper just to get Navy looked at. The receptionist flips through the papers, double-checking insurance and all information I've filled out. I watch intensely, waiting. I can see her stop and try to digest what I've written. I know which part. She looks up at me, back down at the page, then back up again. Her eyes narrow for a moment, then she asks in a professional voice, "Is all this information correct? Insurance?"

"Yes, ma'am."

"Father's name . . . and phone number?"

"Yes, ma'am, to the best of my knowledge."

More narrowed eyes, then clacking on the keyboard, storing one of Hunter's many cell phone numbers in that Arkansas chiropractic clinic's computer system. I wonder what she'll get if she tries calling it.

"Right this way, Ms. Roberts," she says, following Navy and me to the treatment room. We've been here for a while, and so far we are the only patients she's done this with. "She's so pretty," she coos, looking Navy over.

"Oh, thank you."

Her eyes scan Navy, looking for any sign of . . . I don't know . . . a presidential birthmark? "She has such beautiful eyes . . . I don't know if I've ever seen such distinctive eyes."

"Oh yeah? Ever watch CNN?" I'm obviously testing my luck with this secret thing.

"That's it," she laughs. "Is her dad in her life?" She avoids eye contact just a little, because she knows how transparent her fishing expedition has become.

"He does his part, and I do mine."

And this exact pattern repeats every time we show up there. And I always say the same thing to anyone asking about Navy's father. "He does his part, and I do mine." It's meant to deflect, but more so to defend. Even after everything Hunter has put me through, I defend him to people who don't even know he's the father, or those who've possibly heard and suspect.

Randi might have given me a hard time for being the golden child growing up, but when it comes to politics, I'm the black sheep of the family. My entire family is very conservative, and if we start discussing politics, I get called a liberal. I like to think of myself as mainstream, an old-fashioned Arkansas Democrat, and when the 2020 election rolls around, Navy and I both support her grandfather from afar. How many children can say the first ever election since they were born had their grandfather on the ballot as a candidate for president of the United States? And how many can say their grandfather won?

When the time comes to vote, I dress Navy in a mustard-colored velour jumper, with a "BIDEN for PRESIDENT" pin on the sleeve. We walk into City Hall, and I let her choose her grandfather's name on my ballot.

Navy and I support her grandfather, even if her grandfather, and father, don't support her. If they could only see two-year-old Navy toddling around telling her conservative side of the family "No Trump! Let's Joe baby!" in her tiny baby voice. And every time she hears the name Trump, her brows furrow, just like her father's, and she shouts, "let's Joe baby."

For all they know, I have her dressed head to toe in MAGA gear, but I don't. Never would. I still care for Hunter and his family, and Navy takes her cue from me. Her paternal side will always be treated with respect, especially around her.

She knows my dad is her Pappy, and she knows the man on the TV we are cheering for to win is her other grandpa. She doesn't understand how that works, or why one grandfather wants to see her nonstop, while the other has never once seen her. But just like her dad, Navy is quick to love, and even though she's never met her grandfather on the TV, she adores him from a distance.

When I was pregnant, and things were dark, Kelsey called one day to encourage me.

"You know your baby is going to have some of Hunter's qualities," she said. "What qualities of his do you want her to have?"

I didn't hesitate. "His heart. His generous and caring heart. I want my baby to have that."

"What qualities of his don't you want her to have?"

"His feet! He has these two toes that are in a straight line with each other and then two more toes in another straight line. It's gross. That's probably why he can't dance."

Well, Navy got his heart . . . and she also got his feet.

Another distinct trait of Hunter's was the way he connected. "Honey," he'd say to everyone in his slightly nasal Delaware voice, "Honey, are you mad at me?" He constantly wanted everyone's approval and would ask just to be sure everything was good. "I love you," he'd always offer without being prompted or whenever he left a situation. He wanted you to know he loved you, and he needed to hear it back. Having grown up in a family that didn't say it much, I admire that Hunter instilled it in the people he loved.

Navy does the exact same things. She's her father through and through. They have never even been in the same room, but somehow he's present in her.

The first time I hear her Barbies calling each other "Honey," it catches me off guard. I'm standing in the dark hallway, admiring her in her room as she plays. Her soft blonde curls hang to her shoulders, and her animated facial expressions make me laugh. "Honey," she chirps as she holds a Barbie in each hand, "wanna go shopping?" It's her father. She sounds just like him in a tiny voice. "Honey," I ask walking in her room. "Where'd you learn that?"

"I just like that name. I call them all that," she says. Nature over nurture.

Kelsey comes to see us at least twice a year.

"This kid," she laughs, "is so much like someone I once knew. Being around you two and hearing y'all go back and forth, it's just like two people I knew back when!"

"Can't deny that," I laugh.

"Kelsey, are you mad at me?" Navy's little voice asks.

"Mad at you? No, Navy, I'm not mad at you," Kelsey says.

"Mom, are you mad at me?"

"No, Navy, I'm not mad at you. You haven't done anything to make anyone mad," I assure her.

Later she finds her way from her room where she's been playing by herself, to where we are in kitchen just to check in.

"Kelsey, I love you," the little voice says. "Mom, I love you."

"I love you too," we both say.

"Oh my God, Navy you're giving me PTSD," Kelsey says with a laugh.

The similarities aren't just verbal. They're physical, sensorial, and temperamental too.

From the very first steps Navy takes, she has that exact same Hunter/Taylor Swift walk, foot turned inward, stiff leg swinging out every few steps, arms straight at her sides.

One day in the office, my sister is flipping through channels to check on the latest murder trial on court TV when something catches her eye.

"Oh my God, is that Hunter?" she asks.

I look up at the TV to see Hunter leaving a building and getting in a black SUV. "Yep, that's him."

"Do you know how I knew? My God, he walks just like Navy Joan!"

"I know," I laugh.

Sensory issues must be genetic too. Hunter despised clothes when he was battling addiction. When he was high, the first thing he would do once he had some privacy was take his clothes off. He spent more time in his boxer briefs when we were together than any other clothing.

Navy and I have nuclear-level meltdowns over her pants being "too hard." She's convinced she can't function if she's wearing something uncomfortable. Sometimes it's cute, hearing her negotiate like a little politician. "I'll just take these pants off, Mom," she says in a convincing voice before preschool one day. "I need to take them off so I can learn better, okay?" It would be funny, if sometimes it weren't debilitating, like the time I think we have to go to the hospital because she is crying so hard from the sensory overload that she can't catch her breath.

She also manipulates her teacher into helping her better deal with nap time.

"Mom, we can bring our own blankets to school for nap time," she says one day as I put her hair in pigtails.

"You can? Ms. Shauna didn't tell me that."

"Yes, the ones they give us are scratchy and I can't sleep."

They are allowed to bring a stuffy to keep in their cubby for naptime, but I haven't heard anything about a blanket.

"Okay, well you can take your blanket and I'll ask Ms. Shauna when I drop you off."

As we pull into the school, Navy gathers her YETI jug and her blanket. We walk up to the door and as soon as Ms. Shauna appears, I ask, "Hey, Navy said they could bring blankets for nap time?"

"Umm . . ." Ms. Shauna is caught off guard.

"I was thinking if I brought a smaller stuffed animal, the blanket could just fit in my cubby and I could keep it there until nap time," Navy says.

"Well, that works, I guess," Ms. Shauna says.

I stand and watch. She's a master manipulator at four. I imagine her father being that way at that age.

Like Hunter and I, Navy is as headstrong as a hurricane. I know early on that I will have to lay down some fundamental ground rules for things she will be taught that are nonnegotiable. I settle on three—respectful, kind, and honest.

When Navy gets in trouble I ask her, "Three things, Navy, what are they?"

"Respectful, kind, and honest," she answers.

She then goes on to tell me why she's in trouble and which one of those traits she failed to live up to.

I believe those are the three most important traits in any person. Respectful. Kind. And honest. I won't raise her any other way.

Chapter 12

Strap In and Hold Tight

Time passes. I've been holding out hope that Hunter is getting clean, and I'm certain if that happens he'll do the right thing.

Sometimes he visits me in my dreams. Hunter and Navy know who each other are and interact together while I sleep. In one recurring dream, Hunter sits slumped in a chair. He's trying to stay awake, but he keeps dozing off, head falling to the side. Navy approaches him, pleading, "Daddy, wake up . . . Daddy, watch me." He does his best to hold his eyes open, but for whatever reason he can't.

In another dream, Navy and I go to D.C. so she can spend time with her dad. We visit the Annapolis house, where Hunter and I spent so much time, and he's there with Hallie and his daughters. He avoids making eye contact with me, and his daughters observe from their perch on the couch as Navy walks in and plays with Beau, Hunter's youngest child. Over and over, she leaves her play to run to Hunter, giving him hugs and kisses, telling him she loves him. She is so happy to finally spend time with her paternal family. But again, Hunter is exhausted. Something keeps pulling him down, and even though he tries for his children, he can barely stay awake.

One afternoon while I'm dressing two-month-old Navy in a little rose-covered outfit for an outing, Savanah calls.

"Hey, Ummm . . . . so Hunter just called me. He wants me to drop my pin. Says he is sending a private vehicle to come get me and leave my phone."

"That's odd."

"What do I do?" she pleads, as if she wants me to tell her don't go. I don't.

"Put your phone on the fuckin' counter and get in the fuckin' private vehicle," I say as we both laugh, knowing who I am mocking.

"Okay, is there anything you want me to tell him?"

"Yeah. Step up. Take responsibility."

"According to Kesley, he's sober. At least that's the last thing she heard."

"Well, you'll know in no time," I say.

"Okay, I'll call you once I'm back with my phone."

That day moves slower than cold molasses. In the evening, I call Savanah. Nothing. I pace all night, unable to sleep. As I watch Navy's peaceful little face on her pillow, my heart breaks, knowing she has an absent father who may or may not be sober and may or may not ever want to be in her life.

After a long night, the sun comes up, as it always does. Savanah calls me in the morning, because she fell asleep. Some things never change.

"Is he sober?" I ask first thing, as I tuck Navy in her swing for her morning nap.

"Oh, no. He's not." She sounds sad.

Deep down I knew it. My heart sinks. I've wanted what was best for Hunter all along, but now, a part of me just wants him to be better for Navy. She deserves a dad.

"But, umm, I do need to let you know you why he wanted to meet." I can hear the hesitation and dread in her voice.

"Okay?"

"He wanted to talk about you and Navy. I told him y'all were fine and how beautiful Navy is, but . . ."

"But, what?"

"I told him he needed to step up and take responsibility. But he tried to avoid it. He said, 'Savanah, how do I know I'm even the father?'"

"What?" Rage takes over.

"Yeah, he was trying to avoid everything, but I shut it down. I said, 'Hunt, get real, you know you are the father! Take responsibility.'"

"Good. What did he say to that?"

"He said he knew it. He said, 'Honey, you're right. I know I am. I'm just stressed right now. I'll do the right thing.' He solely did that to try and make the fact that he's not taken responsibility make sense."

I'm livid. Knowing Hunter as well as I do, I know exactly what he's doing. He's throwing doubt out there to make it seem like he didn't know if the baby was his. He knew. He knows. He's known it from day one. This is just his way of deflecting and avoiding.

Although I'm furious, Kelsey laughs when she hears about Hunter's new tactic. "He knew he wasn't going to get one over on me," she says, "so he thought he would try Savanah." Hunter had called Kelsey too, but she didn't answer. He texted her and said, "We need to talk," only to get a response saying, "Who you need to be talking to is in Arkansas taking care of your child." Then she sent him the quote from his recent article where he said, "I am not a victim. By any standard, I grew up with privilege and opportunity, and fully accept that the choices and mistakes I made are mine, and I am accountable for them and will continue to be." When he replied to that with the message, "Don't text. Call me," she called and he didn't answer.

Another dream plagues me as well. In that one, Hunter isn't visiting me, I'm visiting him. He ignores Navy and me with a vengeance. As his daughter pleads for his attention, he walks past her, so harshly that it makes me question if he can even hear her. He completely avoids eye contact, almost as if we are the ghosts of Christmas past. It turns out dreams do come true, and not just the good ones.

Days after Savanah's call, I'm plopped in a recliner at Mom and Dad's with a gently sighing Navy asleep on my chest when my phone buzzes. This sound no longer actively triggers my brain to think, "Maybe it's Hunter," but that hope still quietly lurks in the background. The screen lights up and my heart jumps into my throat. One message from Katie Dodge. Is Hunter out of rehab? Can he be a dad now?

"Hi Lunden. Hunter wanted me to relay that as of today you are terminated from payroll and health insurance. You will need to get new coverage."

My heart drops from my throat into my gut. It's a short trip, but it lands like a ton of bricks. Navy stirs a little, maybe feeling my blood pressure spike.

If hell hath no fury like a woman scorned, how great is the fury of a woman who watches her baby daughter be scorned, too?

Within seconds of reading the message, the "A" word pops into my head. Attorney. I'm going to need one. This message could only have come if Hunter was out of rehab and ordered Katie to handle me. So now he thinks he can just make me go away like every other inconvenience in his life. Well, he can't just make a baby go away.

My wrath is hot and fast, but I take my time in responding. After days of contemplating, I decide a subtle text is best, but one I know she will relay to Hunter.

"Thank you for the update you sent on Nov 18. I have reached out to Hunter over the past few months and have yet to get a response. I will be meeting with a team of lawyers within the next week or so to discuss my options. As his assistant, will you please relay the message to him that my lawyer will be in contact very soon so our situation can be handled appropriately, he will know as to what this is regarding to. Thanks, Katie."

In other words, strap in and hold tight, you parrot-wearing asshole, because I'm not going away and neither is your daughter. I protected you and cared about you for so long, while I went through hell, and this is how you respond? I'm not protecting you anymore.

Agatha Christie wrote, "A mother's love for her child is like nothing else in the world. It knows no law, no pity. It dares all things and crushes down remorselessly all that stands in its path." I can relate. Get ready, Hunter, I'm coming for you, and I don't care if I have to bring hell with me. You will take accountability.

Something finally breaks, and with it comes the freedom to let go and move on. While I start my search for an attorney, I also find my heart moving toward a new man, Brock. It's tentative at first, as there's so much going on in my life, but over time he begins to fill a central role that's been missing. His presence is a comfort at first, as I take the next steps of holding Hunter to account.

Hanging with Bicycles and Big Boy is preferable to meeting with attorneys, but I proceed to see what steps lie ahead. After sharing the entire sordid story with Lawyer #1, and before I can take a breath at the end, he says, "Okay, now give me the story again."

"Excuse me?"

"Tell the story again. If you give me the same story twice, I'll know whether you're telling the truth or not."

No client wants an attorney who questions whether they're telling the truth. But I do it, solely for my own sake. The confirmation is worth it.

"Holy shit!" he exclaims. "You're telling the truth."

No shit, but if my attorney is already against me, there is no coming out on top. I leave that meeting quickly and dodge all his phone calls trying to get me to be his client.

Lawyer #2, however, makes Lawyer #1 look good . . . or at least safe.

"Sweetheart, let me let you in on a little secret. Bill Clinton and I are golfing buddies. I've got the connections to find Hunter Biden, and we'll get to the bottom of it. All I need is your standard $25,000 retainer to begin."

"Bill Clinton," I think. "How do I politely leave this office without it hitting the Clintons' radar that I have something that could hurt the Biden family?"

Attorney hunting isn't going as well as planned. The others are dead ends too. I didn't realize that politics would come into it so much. Some are Democrats, and I question their loyalty to my daughter and our case because of the election on the horizon. Others are arrogant jerks who talk down to me. Some are both. And they all want $25,000 or $35,000, even $50,000 retainers.

I'm holding out hope, but wanting to give up, when two family friends recommend the same attorney. "He's a pit bull," one says. He destroyed her deadbeat ex-husband. The other guarantees we can trust him completely. He's the reason her husband has sole custody of his children, which is rare, especially around here. A trustworthy pit bull sounds just like what I've been looking for.

Clint and his wife Jennifer are the attorneys at Lancaster & Lancaster. His curly dark hair, thick black beard, and happy disposition don't quite hide the killer instinct underneath. He's a big guy, and a former Marine. Jennifer is gorgeous, dark haired, and down to business. It feels like he might do the killing in court, and she buries the bodies afterward. There is definitely potential here.

I meet with Clint first, and he greets me warmly. There's no bluster like with the other jack wagons I've met so far; he just says, "All right, so tell me what's going on."

"So, I have a child with Hunter Biden."

"Hunter who?" he asks as he types the name into Google. So far, I'm liking this guy.

As I unravel the saga, he listens intently, never interrupting, only nodding.

"I've hoped he would stand up and do what's right, but he's conveniently avoiding," I tell him. "My daughter deserves the world. He can't just make her go away like he does everything else. . . . And I've also been warned through friends that Trump's campaign may know and might use it against the Biden campaign. I don't want that to happen."

"Okay. Well, first, I'm so sorry this is happening to you." He's sincere and I'm relieved. "You and your daughter both deserve better. You have options here. I can walk you through those."

"I just want him to take accountability," I say. It's all I really want.

He lays out my options, and I feel more comfortable and confident than I have in a long time. I'm almost won over, and then he seals the deal.

"I'm going to suggest you go home and pray about this before you choose an attorney and before you decide to take action," he says as things are drawing to a close. "God will give you comfort and lead you in the right direction, whether that's our firm or someone else."

Done. What kind of killer attorney cares enough about you being comfortable that he urges you to pray about it before hiring him? The kind of attorney I want.

Clint immediately begins tracking Hunter down, which is a daunting task, because, well, you don't find Hunter, Hunter finds you. It's no surprise when he comes back with a list of possible phone numbers longer than the Big Boy Steam Train that came through Arkansas.

I don't want this to be a scandal. I don't want Hunter to have to go through a public paternity suit. I just want him to be with his child, and for it to be something that's accepted. So, in one of the most pitiful moments of this whole sordid mess, I donate to the campaign online just so I can include a message. And then I do it again days later. I describe the situation and ask someone to please reach out so a scandal can be avoided. I'm hoping they will, but I know the chances are slim.

Days pass and not one word comes back to me.

Everything changes one evening at Mom and Dad's. My phone buzzes, and Clint's on the other end.

"I got to them," Clint says.

"To who?"

"Joe and Jill."

"Really? How?"

There's no door to the loft, so I scoot downstairs and close myself in the bedroom Mom and Dad keep for my nephews so I can concentrate. I'm sitting in the dark, a lone orb of light from the streetlamp illuminating a window-sized space on the floor.

"We finally found their personal email accounts, and I sent them both a message where I can see if they've received it or not. Joe hasn't opened his yet, but Jill has been opening hers . . . eleven times so far. They're probably trying to figure out if it's a hoax."

"Oh, why didn't you call sooner?"

"Well, because I also reached out to Katie Dodge to get in touch with Hunter, and just minutes after I did, Hunter's attorney reached out. I just got off the phone with Mr. George Mesires."

This is actually real, I think to myself. This is going to work. "And . . . ?"

"I told him everything, that this is the real deal, a woman in Arkansas had Hunter's baby, and he's going to be served. He called Hunter and called me back."

"And? What did he say?"

"Hunter wants to know if you two can talk and work things out privately. He doesn't want the media or attorneys involved."

He wants to hush me, I think.

"What do I do, Clint?"

"Honestly? He's known you were pregnant from the beginning. Now the baby is here, and he's not done anything to step up. I think he will avoid all of this unless you use the law to bring him to heel. You want accountability. Make him take a paternity test, so there can be no more opportunities for avoidance and denial."

"Okay, make it happen." I'll never know what would have happened if I had just given Hunter the chance. Maybe if he was sober, he would have done the right thing and stepped up on his own. Maybe I could have avoided so much regret if I had just listened to him before pulling the trigger. But I don't.

"I'll take care of it," Clint promises. "Be cautious. Once there is a filing in the court system with his name attached, the media will get ahold of it."

A new anxiety triggers. I don't want media attention. I just want my child's father to do his job.

Chapter 13

Lick the Stick

Clint files the paternity suit in May 2019, but since the media doesn't follow the state of Arkansas closely, they don't pick up on it immediately. It's impossible to know exactly when they first see the court documents, but on June 20 they release the story, four weeks after news of Hunter's new marriage comes out.

The headlines read "Arkansas Woman Files Paternity Suit Against Joe Biden's Son Hunter Biden" and "Joe Biden's Son Hunter Is Ignoring a Baby He Fathered in Arkansas," exploding all over the world.

The timing makes it look like I'm a scorned former lover trying to ruin Hunter's newly sober life. No one truly knows what has been happening behind the scenes over the last couple of years. All they know is I'm officially the woman suing Hunter Biden. And the news starts a spiral of tension in my relationship with Brock. Hunter casts a big shadow, and Brock doesn't respond well to the strain of living under that.

I had warned my family of what was to come from early on. Ignore the media and don't argue online. Turn the other cheek and act like you don't see it. In all honesty, I learned that from Hunter. Let people think and say whatever they want.

When Clint calls that day and tells me to be ready to get out of Dodge, I don't appreciate just how wise he is. I'm at the hospital with the rest of the family eagerly awaiting the arrival of my new nephew Boone.

"We're not going to make a big deal about any of the media," I tell my parents. The attention today should be solely focused on my sister and the birth of my nephew. I don't want her to even know about everything going public and have it take away from her special day.

But in the midst of her labor pains, Randi calls my phone while I sit in the waiting room.

"Dude, you're on the news!" she screams in between heavy breaths.

"I know. Don't worry about any of that."

"Are you okay?"

"Seriously? Today isn't about any of that," I say.

She isn't the only one calling me. My phone rings with a New York number.

"Is this Lunden Roberts?"

"Who is this?"

"I'm with the *Daily Mail* and am calling regarding the paternity suit you recently filed. Would you be willing to answer some questions?"

"No."

"Do you know where Hunter Biden is presently? Could you comment on him?"

"I'm sorry, I won't comment. Please respect our privacy."

"Yes, I understand this is very sensitive for you. How is Hunter doing?"

Click.

My phone keeps exploding with calls from different area codes.

"Who is that?" Dad asks.

"Some media source. It's officially out, I guess."

"No shit?"

Ring.

"Hello?"

"Is this Ms. Roberts?"

"Who's calling?"

"I'm with the *New York Post* and . . ."

Click.

"Dad, this is no—"

Ding.

Ding.

Ding. Ding. Ding.

Normally I have a handful of missed calls each day and a few unread messages. But by the end of this day, I have 73 missed calls, 903 unopened texts, and thousands of emails. Journalists find my phone number, and everyone else calls and messages through my social media accounts. People are just curious at first, but then the brutal stuff starts coming, with death threats and forty-five-minute voicemails about how I'm a whore for sleeping with Hunter Biden.

My anxiety levels climb more than normal. There are people who believe everything they read and some of those people can be crazy, or cruel. They feel like they know you, they stalk you, they harass you, then the possibility of harming you or your child tends to increase.

"You may want to get out of town," Dad recommends.

"I will," I say, but I'm not going anywhere until I hold my nephew. I grab a hat out of my purse and pull it on my head to hide the fact that I look like the girl whose face is now plastered over every news source. It'll have to do.

My phone buzzes again, but with a familiar number. Ladana is a trusted friend who recommended Clint.

"I just saw the news. Are you okay? If you need a place to get away come stay with us in Alabama."

"Are you sure? I'm at the hospital now, but I'll go home and pack once my nephew is born, then head that way!"

"Yes, c'mon. I'll have Abby's room ready for y'all to stay. Nobody will know you're here and y'all will be safe! We look forward to seeing you!"

I give my sister the time she deserves, cradle baby Boone in my arms, then pull my hat low and head to Gulf Shores, Alabama. It's an eight-hour drive, and if nothing else good comes from the world finding out, at least Navy Joan is fixing to have her first beach trip.

So I escape for a couple weeks to the Heart of Dixie while my family vigilantly fends off the media for me.

Meanwhile, Hunter sits down with *The New Yorker* and gets a twenty-four-page story about his redemption. Clint fields a call from the reporter before the story is released.

"Hunter claims he met Ms. Roberts in D.C. in 2017, but that the two of them did not have sex, would you or your client like to comment?"

After protecting him endlessly, this is how he repays me?

Over the next few months, Clint builds our case, while Hunter skillfully dodges everyone we send to track him down. His paranoia must be driving him crazy as we have servers sitting outside every one of his half dozen properties and looking for all his known vehicles for weeks. It's costing us more than everything else in the case together. Clint thinks he's trying to bleed us dry, and says we need to make a statement to create public pressure. "If you don't want to do it, I can," he offers, and my anxiety makes me just want to avoid it.

Clint applies constant pressure through the media. "If Hunter's not the father, then what is he running from? The DNA test will prove everything. Now that he's married, owning his addiction and standing in his truth, what about the child in Arkansas?"

Congressman Tom Cotton even goes on a podcast and shames Hunter, saying he's running from an Arkansas woman trying to serve him papers. He blasts Hunter for running from paternity, saying that shows everyone a lot about his character.

After months of evasion, we find an address for an apartment in his new wife Melissa's name. A man answers the door, and because of some state law, we're allowed to serve him on Hunter's behalf. Now that he's served, I know he will have to take accountability, but one fear remains. Hunter has power, he comes from a powerful family—will he somehow tamper with the DNA? How far would he go to avoid the truth?

Clint assures me we will go to great lengths to make sure the DNA test is honestly and professionally done. His love for Donald Trump makes it impossible for him to be a fan of Hunter or his father. And that means he won't take a deal under the table to secure Joe's campaign, tossing what is best for my daughter to the side. He and his wife have two little girls themselves, and I know they will take care of mine the way they would want someone to take care of theirs. Plus, Clint doesn't like to lose; that's also in my favor.

Hunter files a general denial to the court, asking that the case be tossed, then later questioning whether he had even been in the country at the time of conception, or if he had been on an extended stay in the Ukraine. He proclaims this publicly to the media, then one day he takes all this rejection to a new level and goes from simply claiming we never had sex, to telling his attorney that he had met me once at a strip club, but we never slept together.

Is this just a political PR scheme for handling a scandal, I wonder. Is this what he is telling his family, or do they know the truth?

Overwhelming anxiety and heartbreak consume me, but not because of what he's doing to me, it's what he's doing to his daughter. How can anyone deny something so beautifully perfect? How could he break her heart?

It's starting to feel like I'm in one of those movies where in the end I'm the crazy person, and this was all a dream. Do I need to check myself into a nuthouse?

I call Kelsey.

"Hunter's denying everything," I blurt out before she can even say hello.

"What do you mean? Denying what?"

"He's denying the baby. He's denying having sex. Hell, Kelsey, he denies even fucking knowing me! Did I dream this? Have I lost my damn mind?"

"Okay, whoa calm down. You're just letting him get in your head. Obviously it's real. Obviously it happened. If you dreamed all this up, where did Navy come from?"

"You're right."

"Hunter can tell you anything and you believe it. So now he's going to tell you this never happened and you're just going to believe him? Now I am concerned about your mental health. You have issues," she says, laughing.

I let out a sigh. "Why is he doing this?"

"He's just covering his grounds. You know he hasn't told his family the truth. I'm sure that's where this is coming from. It only takes one test and the truth will come to light. He won't be able to deny it anymore. Matter of fact, how about you leak a picture of her face? The test won't even be needed," she laughs again. This time I'm actually able to laugh with her. She's right. Patience. He's been served. He has to take the paternity test.

After extensive research on DNA testing, Clint tells me Hunter could send his DNA through the mail.

"Is that a joke?" I ask. "He'll pay off somebody at FedEx, have it intercepted, and there's no telling what Joe Blow's DNA we'll be comparing my daughter's to!" I'm not having it.

"I found a facility in Oklahoma City," Clint says. "They will allow you and Hunter to take a DNA test together. We can keep our eyes on DNA samples so they can't be swapped, and we can sit and watch for the results. It takes about five hours."

"I'm sorry, did you say *me* and Hunter? Why do I have to take a DNA test? Does he think I'm driving someone else's kid up there to get swabbed?"

"It's part of his conditions; he wants you to take a maternity test. Also, it's a pretty expensive DNA test, and under the circumstances he will be paying for everything. However, he claims if the results come back and he isn't the father, he wants to be reimbursed."

I laugh out loud. "Well, I don't plan on bringing my checkbook. I won't have anything to pay for, and he and I both know it."

"Do you think you'll be okay with you and Navy being in the same room with Hunter?" Clint asks.

"I don't think there are enough Secret Service agents in the world to keep me from clawing his eyes out right now," I spit back. Then I sigh. "Yes, I think I can handle it."

Clint laughs. "We'll take the precautions to keep y'all separated," he says. "But there's the possibility of running into each other."

I know I won't see him, though. He can't look at me right now and face the lies he's told everyone.

Then Clint brings up another issue. "You know how this guy operates. He's used to getting out of problems. So I'm curious, how far do you think he would go?"

"As far as it takes to get this to go away," I reply. "That's why he won't face me. There's nothing too far that he wouldn't do."

"Would he consider buying a body double?"

"What? Hell, I wouldn't think so. Do they even make those?" A new fear courses through my bloodstream. I hope it doesn't throw off my DNA; I have a maternity test to take.

The drive to Oklahoma City feels farther than it is. My mind is less occupied with whether or not he will face me, than it is with whether or not he will show up. Will he find a way to get out of this last minute?

Sweet Navy rides in her pink car seat with her favorite pacifier, "Dirty Duck," holding on to her little Elmo. I struggle to keep the tears at bay. She has no clue . . . but someday she will. Most of the ride is consumed in prayer, not for the DNA tests, but for Navy. I pray for her future, for her little heart, for the guidance to handle everything and give her the best life possible.

We arrive at the facility, and I throw a blanket over Navy as I get her out of the car. If this is leaked to the media, I don't want them to photograph her. Plus, I'm not ready to share her beautiful face with the man who denied her, in case he happens to be lurking nearby. Anger consumes me at the thought of Hunter.

Meeting me at the door, Clint ushers me to a conference room set aside for us. Hunter and his team are in another one. Clint helps to uncover Navy, seeing her for the first time. "Well, there's no denying that," he exclaims, as she looks up at him with her big blue Hunter Biden eyes.

"Yeah, she looks a lot like her father," I laugh.

Navy is dressed in a pale pink and cream little business suit outfit, with a pink bow holding back her curls from her face. Her matching pink shoes are secured with gold buckles. She is ready for business.

"I'm gonna step out and do Hunter's test. Jenn will take care of anything you need. I'll let you know when it's your turn."

"Okay, sounds great. Hey, Clint?"

"Yeah?"

"Thank you . . . and please let Hunter and his team know that we will give them some time . . . a week, before we let everyone know the paternity, so he can tell his family and set the record straight."

"You bet!"

I don't want this to be a scandal. I never did. I'm rooting for Joe in this next election, and I'm not part of a conspiracy trying to bring down the Biden dynasty. It would just be nice if Hunter would tell the truth and give my daughter the father she deserves. I've seen his potential from the beginning, even through his addiction, and still have high hopes for who I believe he is capable of being. Navy deserves that potential.

Clint stays with Hunter's DNA as the technician comes to get Navy and me after Hunter has been walked out. His attorneys observe me for the first time as we pass. I've never dealt with an opposing legal team, but I've dealt with opposing teams in my basketball days. I walked past with confidence, knowing this might be a buzzer beater, but I'm on the same side as the truth, so I'm winning.

Hunter's attorneys mumble something under their breath that they clearly don't want me to hear. Are they critiquing my snakeskin blazer? Am I fitting the stereotype they have of me? Honestly, I don't care at this point. I hope my black snakeskin boots fit their picture too.

While signing papers in the lab tech's room, she flashes a picture in front of me. One of those ones that comes out the other end of a camera and you fan it. Clint made sure Hunter wasn't a body double. I know the guy in the white shirt standing against the gray door, but oddly enough, he looks more distressed now than the last time I saw him. He should be glowing, now that he's supposedly clean and standing in truth. But he looks distraught, run down, and downright pitiful.

"Dang, looks like he had a long night," I whisper to Clint.

"Well hell yeah. He's been saying he's got the truth on his side. I'm sure he doesn't want to have to admit to everyone he's been lying."

"Is this the Hunter Biden who allegedly fathered your child?" the lab tech asks as my legal team and Hunter's sit quietly watching.

"Yes, he's my child's father. That's Hunter."

"Okay, I'm gonna need to take your picture too."

Navy and I stand against the same gray door so I can prove to Hunter my maternity. It's our first family portrait.

She swabs Navy first, but not without pissing her off. I give her the "Dirty Duck" pacifier as the same furrowed brow expression I just saw in Hunter's picture flashes across her face. Holding her while I get swabbed, I watch closely as the technician labels the DNA samples and puts them next to Hunter's.

"It's done." Clint stands to walk me out of the room and explain the next steps.

They're going to put the samples in the machine and Hunter's attorney and Clint will sit and watch. The technician says she will know in about fifteen minutes if they're a match but can't officially confirm it until the test is finished. My part is done though, and I don't need to stay.

"Bye, Lunden," Jenn says, joining us in the hallway. "Y'all have a safe trip home."

"Jenn, what are you doing?" Clint blurts out, "If I'm out here who's in there with the DNA samples . . . other than Hunter's attorneys?"

"Oh, crap," she exclaims and frantically bolts back into the room, trying to make it look as casual as possible.

Clint and I both laugh as I cover Navy in her plush pink blanket and head for the door. On the drive back home, I think about the DNA spinning in the machine, and how for the next five hours the lab tech will be the only person in the world who knows if the future POTUS will be adding a new grandchild to his family. But she's not the only person who knows; I know too, and so does Hunter.

Navy is asleep and my mind has barely been on the highway when a message flashes across my CarPlay.

"Test results are in! Nothing is tampered with. We will call as soon as we can."

I breathe. For the first time, I breathe without my chest being so tight. Thank God. Obviously, I've known he is the father, but until this moment it has been the word of the former vice president's son against the word of me and three of my friends back in D.C. As I look at the text, I realize there are tears in my eyes and a smile on my face. They're tears of joy. I look back at Navy and caress her soft hand. Today is a day she will want to know about someday, and I don't want to forget anything about it.

Clint calls as I'm taking deep sighs of relief.

"Hey, Lunden! Not that you didn't already know, but Hunter Biden is Navy's father." He laughs.

I'm so thankful.

"When you walked by, Hunter's attorneys mumbled, 'Yeah, the baby is his.' It wasn't because Navy looked like him. They hadn't seen her yet. They just said you were definitely Hunter's type."

"Oh," I laugh. "I thought they were saying something negative."

"And something else funny. The results show Navy is 99.999999% Hunter's child and only 98.9999% yours," he chuckles.

"How the hell does that work? My body created her for nine months and her DNA is closer to his?" I shake my head, but I'm definitely not surprised.

"Thank God it's over," I breathe. "Now what?"

"Well, there's still a hard fight ahead since he's a Biden. But I told his attorneys you want to give him time to set the record straight with his family. In a week we will file a motion to establish paternity in the court. I think it's very gracious of you to do that. And keep in mind the media went crazy when you were just a woman claiming Hunter fathered your child. Now it's scientifically proven she's his daughter, so once this gets out, be careful."

"Great." My chest tightens a little. Here's the next hurdle.

Chapter 14

Happy Birthday, Joe

Now that paternity has been established, I've been thinking Hunter would try to connect with his daughter, but nothing happens. I'm giving up on the idea that he's ever going to reach out, but instilling in Navy that they love her from a distance, when Clint calls.

"Hunter's attorney just reached out."

"What is it?" I ask, worrying about whatever strings I'm sure Hunter's pulling.

"So Hunter claims to be broke . . ."

"I don't care about that," I cut in. It was just proven that he's the father, and the first thing he comes back with is "I'm broke." How about "I'm sorry?" How about taking accountability for your child? I don't care if you're broke, and your child won't care either. All she wants is a father.

"But that's not the biggie," Clint says, hesitating to drop the bomb. "He wants to know if you would like to single-parent adopt Navy?"

"Adopt her? Are you fucking kidding me? So then he has no obligations and avoids responsibility?"

"Yes. They even asked if you would sign an NDA to not discuss the results."

"Oh, hell no. They can shove that NDA up their ass and their fucking offer." Hunter has hurt me before, but this is a new hurt, a mother's hurt for her daughter, my heart breaks for her.

"They said he's willing to add $250,000 to the deal."

My jaw drops to the floor. I've never felt so much heartbreak and anger at the same time.

"How the hell do you put a dollar figure on your own daughter?" I ask. "What the fucking hell, Clint? He wants out. He wants to keep everything hush, not be a father, and continue to humiliate me in public."

"I know . . . I'm so sorry, Lunden. How do you want me to respond?"

"I wanted to do this the best way to not harm him, but fuck him. You tell him I said eat shit, motherfucker. Do whatever you have to do."

"Not a problem. We'll file the motion with the court to establish paternity. I'll send you the details before we pull the trigger."

"Don't bother. I trust you. Word everything however you think it should go, and I'll sign whatever you need."

"You're sure you won't want to review what we put . . ."

"No, I'm sick of this shit. Chew him up and spit him out. I don't care about the details."

I get off the phone and I lie on the bed next to my sleeping daughter. Caressing Navy's blond curls, I can't hold back the tears. How could anyone not want this perfect angel?

Seven days after the DNA test, I'm pushing Navy in the buggy through TJ Maxx, helping my attorney friend Brie decorate her new home, when my phone starts blowing up again. It doesn't take long to figure out why. Googling my name, I discover the *Arkansas Democrat Gazette* found the motion to establish paternity with the test results and is running the headline "DNA Test Shows Hunter Biden Is Father of Arkansas Woman's Baby."

Picking up my pace, I look for Brie. As I grab a couple hats to throw on my head and Navy's, Brie catches the look on my face. She was randomly assigned as my roommate in college and has been my confidante ever since.

"What's wrong?"

I hand her my phone.

"Oh, they've found the motion . . ." she says. "Let's get out of here."

We're hiding out at her house, hoping this will blow over, when I get a call from Clint.

"Hey Lunden, we have a hiccup."

Acid dumps into my stomach.

"The media's talking about the president getting a grandchild for his birthday this year."

The headline in *The Sun* reads:

"YOU ARE THE FATHER Hunter Biden DID father child . . ."

Turns out we filed the court documents with the DNA test results on November 20, Joe's birthday, and didn't know it. I look so conniving.

"I'm wondering if you have a comment on this report, and court filing, out of Arkansas that your son Hunter just made you a grandfather again," Fox News' Peter Doocy asks him.

"No, that's a private matter and I have no comment . . . only you would ask that," Joe retorts. "You're a good man. You're a good man. Classy."

Yeah, I think there's a difference between respecting privacy and keeping someone private and hidden.

Within twenty-four hours, the local Hampton Inn has become a media hot spot. Friends messaging me, people I haven't talked to in years, say the media has been reaching out to them, even showing up on their doorstep asking if Navy and I are there or asking questions. Do they know me? Are we close? What am I like?

The media doesn't know where I'm living, and I assure you they don't want to pull down my daddy's drive. As the owner of a gun business, he takes his Second Amendment right to the extreme, especially when it comes to protecting his family. People hiding in the woods behind my sister's house get the message real clear when shots are fired. Not at them, but near them. They don't come back. One media source even sends flowers to an old address they find for me, knowing I don't live there, but hoping I will pick them up. They are purple and yellow because I'm a Lakers fan, and they're signed "Jill." All this because everyone wants to get a picture of Navy and see if she looks like her father.

One day driving to my dad's gun shop, I pass two people in a small, white SUV on the side of the road by a cemetery. I don't have to look at their out-of-state tags to know they aren't from around here. They're lost on a country back road. I pull into the gun shop and back in to hide the "Lunden" license plate I got when I turned sixteen. Soon I see the small white SUV pull in. I'm thankful the windows are tinted so they can't see me. As they walk up to the office, Doug meets them at the door.

"We don't comment on any of that," I hear him drawl, "and in Arkansas, I only have to give you one warning to get the hell off the property until I'm legally allowed to take action." He raises his shirt over the holster on his pants, making the Sig Sauer visible for the out-of-towners.

I can't help but laugh as they drive off terrified. "You handled that well," I shout to Doug, hopping out of my rig.

"Well, they ain't the first nor the last to get that greeting. Fuckin' Yankees."

It's becoming more and more obvious, especially with a court date approaching in just a few days, that the media will not be letting up. They're getting worse. Although this is our life now, I'm not ready to share Navy with the world just yet. Especially before her own father has seen her. So I pack Navy and me some clothes and head somewhere no one will find us, Spanky's cabin. If they manage to even find the small janky dirt road leading there, which they won't, their two-wheel-drive cars will never make it across the creeks and over the ruts.

I shudder every time the trees scrape my Jeep on the tiny path. Normally, I would take my dad's hunting rig, but under these circumstances we needed to leave, and we needed to leave quickly. The small cabin sits beside a flowing creek with four wheelers, kayaks, and all things outdoorsy. It's miles from civilization, and at nighttime, when it's dark, it's scary dark. The big windows overlooking the creek make me wonder if anything is out there looking back, or if I walk out onto the back porch, I might hear "Dueling Banjos."

Things calm down a bit while I'm hiding out, but toward the end of my stay, while Navy is singing along to Barney tapes while wearing a coonskin cap she pulled off the wall, Clint calls.

"Don't let this get to you," he says, as I am sitting on the front porch of a cabin in the middle of nowhere. Clearly, it's all gotten to me.

"What's happening now?"

"I just got a call from a reporter who heavily implied you need to get your story out there now, or your narrative will be whatever they write about you."

"Psh, no. I won't talk. She can get back with us when she's got something more than 'Lunden needs to talk.'" My anxiety level drops a little when I realize that I'm in control.

"That's not all," Clint says, and my anxiety skyrockets again. "She said they've been given an anonymous tip."

"Okay."

"She just said that if you're going to talk, you need to do it now before it all comes out."

"What the hell is she even talking about? They know about Navy, they know the paternity, so what is she talking about?"

"I don't know, but I did threaten that if they make any claims that aren't true about my client we will be suing for defamation."

"No, we won't. Let them print whatever. Suing for defamation will just add to the media and the drama. I hate drama. And I just want all this to be over. When Hunter takes accountability publicly, let's leave this in the past."

Two days later it hits on Page Six of the *New York Post:*

"Hunter Biden's 'baby mama' Lunden Roberts was stripper at club he frequented."

Imagine living in a small town, being mysteriously pregnant, and then having a bunch of self-important media writers make up a secret life about you that they reveal to the world. Lunden Roberts seduced Hunter Biden at a strip club and became a one-night-stand fling. It doesn't matter that it's not true, for them, the juicier the story, the more money it makes.

One reporter goes as far as to walk into my garage while I'm working out with Seva, Brandi, and Rana. He doesn't come much closer once he hears the click of the pistol. One warning.

The horrible messages come pouring back in. Slut, scum, dirty, better off never born, better off dead. My social media and inboxes are jam-packed with trash like that from people who've never met me and · just want to hurt someone.

Thank God I don't have the time to fixate on this fresh hell. The first hearing is Monday morning, just twelve hours away.

At Clint's suggestion, I arrive at the courthouse early, going through the back door. A judge offers me his office to hide out. Perks of a small town. I sit by myself watching the media set up camp outside the courthouse, awaiting my arrival. I've been told Hunter will not be in attendance. He opted out. How could someone not show up for their child, I wonder, but at this point I'm not surprised. It actually eases my anxiety knowing he won't be there.

Going into the courtroom I nod to the police officer as he runs me through the security scan. As the doors open, I feel everyone's eyes lock on to me. Jenn sees me coming down the aisle and meets me halfway. The front row is filled with men with little notepads who all pay a little too much attention to me. Media. I wonder if more crack reporting is coming, like how my sweater's black and I'm in white pin-striped pants. Dad sits right across from them, watching their every move.

"Where's Clint?" I ask Jennifer.

"So, he's in the judge's chambers with Hunter's attorneys. Or his used-to-be-attorneys. Hunter apparently fired his legal team last night," she replies with a smirk.

"What? He fired his legal team the night before court? Is that so he can postpone everything?"

Jennifer laughs. "Honestly, I have no clue. They came anyway, because apparently, he doesn't have anyone to represent him. I've never been in this situation, so we'll have to see when they come out of chambers."

This definitely sounds like a very Hunter thing to do. It isn't quite as quintessentially Hunter as putting the old lady off at the train at the wrong stop, but it's close. I know through the media outlets that Hunter's attorney used to be the attorney general here in Arkansas. I initially thought it was some form of an intimidation tactic. But I learned through Clint he took the case because he used to be friends with Beau.

Like everything else in my life, this hearing is off-the-rails insane. Hunter may have fired his formal legal team, but it turns out he has an informal team member no one knew about—the judge.

Judge Don McSpadden is tough on dads who are back on their child support. That makes me optimistic about him even though he's a diehard Democrat.

During the hearing, McSpadden makes a spectacle of me and my counsel, calling out the docket and condescendingly informing us that he will hear other cases first because we aren't important. He's right that we're not more important than anyone else, but is belittling us in front of everyone really necessary?

Then the bomb drops. He takes the paternity test, with 99.9999% certainty of Hunter being the father and just tosses it into evidence.

"Is that normal?" I ask Clint.

"Um, no. When you have scientific certainty, that isn't evidence; paternity has been established and the court should rule that."

But McSpadden isn't done. He demands five years of my tax returns.

In most child support cases, the court requests the last two or three years of tax returns. Child support isn't even the main purpose of our case, it's a paternity suit.

The *Daily Mail* covers this:

> Hunter Biden will now have to hand over FIVE YEARS of financial records—including his time at Ukrainian oil company—and his baby mama has to disclose her stripper tips at DC club where the two met.

Clint says the judge is demanding the returns because he wants to know whether or not I was a stripper. That's one of the cons of a small town—people are just nosy, or maybe he's looking for something he can use against me to help Hunter.

After court, Clint tells me to get to the car, trying to avoid the media as much as possible. He and Jenn will call once they are on the road. Before I can walk out with Dad in front of me, someone stops me. It's the former attorney general, the one Hunter fired. He holds out his hand sympathetically.

"Ms. Roberts. I'm so sorry you're going through this. I just wanted to tell you to be strong; you are a very pleasant young lady."

"Thank you," I respond, shaking his hand.

We exit through the wheelchair access, but the media is onto us. They take photos of me in my black pea coat and black sunglasses, descending the back steps of the courthouse. I try to keep my head down as I ignore the reporters yelling out questions about Navy's whereabouts and how she is. *The Daily Mail* reports that the world is being introduced to Lunden Roberts for the first time as I make this public appearance. Up until now, they have been using a college basketball picture from ten years ago:

Daily Mail

> Hunter Biden's baby mama Lunden Roberts, 28, looked glamorous as she left court in Batesville, Arkansas on Monday morning. She wore a black zip-up coat over a white top and a pair of white pinstripe pants. Her long blonde hair cascaded halfway down her back.

Climbing into Dad's truck to await the phone call from Clint and Jenn, I'm just thankful it's over.

"Hey, so how do you think that went?" Clint asks on the phone.

"Um, I'm not really sure. I think not establishing paternity is pretty weird."

"Well, Don made it very clear in his chamber that he's rooting for Joe in the election, so paternity most likely won't be established until after that. He's going to help them prolong this."

"What the fuck?!"

"Yes, he also had a lot to say about you. He went as far as to tell me that you post your daughter online all the time saying, 'Look at this, I have a special baby because she's a Biden.'"

"What in the hell is he talking about? I've never posted my daughter's face. And anything I post about her is a typical mom post. Hell, I've never said any of those words a day in my damn life! He's ludicrous!"

"You're not wrong about that," Clint says.

The next morning I'm back at work at Dad's shop when Clint calls.

"I'm sending you the latest from McSpadden. He's going to try to settle not just paternity but also custody, visitation, and support at the next hearing."

"What?" I shout loud enough that the guys running the lathes on the shop floor can hear. "Can he do that?"

"He can try, but I'm drawing up a recusal motion. He's not going to be fair to you and clearly he's got a God complex if he's trying to arbitrarily settle custody, visitation, and support without hearing a single word of testimony."

Motionless, I hold the phone to my ear, frantically beginning to wonder if some Podunk judge is going to take my baby away.

"Are you there?" Clint asks after I don't know how many seconds of silence.

"Yeah," I reply in a weak voice, "Hunter hasn't even asked to see her, but the judge is throwing custody and visitation out there for grabs? Yeah, do something, Clint. Sad to say, but Navy won't go spend weekends with someone who hasn't even taken the time to get to know her."

"It's going to be okay. I'm filing a custody motion by the end of the day so we can get this settled ASAP. He's never even seen her. I mean, Hunter couldn't even pick her out of a lineup."

"Will that do what we want done?"

"I'm going to write it so that there's no question that little girl belongs with you."

"Do whatever you have to do. I trust you."

I hang up and breathe a sigh of relief but don't realize that before all's said and done, I'll regret telling Clint to go full-on pit bull.

We turn in all the documents McSpadden ordered within a week, but he rejects them. Hunter hasn't turned in anything yet, but McSpadden says both of us should bring our toothbrushes to the next hearing—meaning he is going to throw us in jail. It doesn't make sense, but I assume he thinks I'm lying because he didn't get what he wanted out of my tax returns.

Clint refuses to stomach any more treatment like this. He delayed filing the motion for recusal because he has a plan. He sends the withering unfiled motion to McSpadden, giving him a choice. "Either you recuse yourself voluntarily, or I will file this. And everyone—and I do mean everyone—will see it in the most public paternity case of the year." My family isn't convinced it will do any good; this judge has never once recused himself from any case. But I guess Clint had enough on him, because six days after Christmas, McSpadden recuses himself and we have a new judge.

Holly Meyer takes over the case, and from what I hear, she's a no-nonsense judge who doesn't care who you are or how many connections you've got. She solely goes by the rules. I like the sound of her already. I need a judge who doesn't give in to bullshit.

The first thing Meyer does when she takes the case over is establish paternity, like a real judge serving justice to the legal system, not making a mockery of it. Used to having McSpadden go along with him, Hunter asks for more time to avoid his deposition.

He and his new wife, Melissa, who is now pregnant, are photographed pulling up to the Waldorf Astoria for lunch and getting out of his Porsche. A source close to Melissa says to the press that she wanted to be respectful of the paternity suit and what we had going on, which is why they hadn't announced they were expecting earlier, but I have a hard time believing it had anything to do with respect. But Donald Trump Jr. posts on his Instagram that Hunter has impregnated another woman and gotten out of his Porsche at one of the most expensive restaurants, but he can't afford to support his child in Arkansas.

Hunter even goes so far as to claim he can't be present for the deposition because of COVID-19 and his wife's pregnancy. But Meyer isn't having it. "Mr. Biden will be in attendance for his deposition. I don't care if his hair is on fire, he will be in Arkansas."

Things begin to happen at a breakneck speed. It becomes clear that Meyer understands Hunter's games and isn't going to let him play with her legal system.

It's late Sunday afternoon, and Hunter's deposition is tomorrow morning in Little Rock.

Now it's on him. Either he settles tonight on something I agree with, or he has to be in Arkansas tomorrow and be deposed by my MAGA-loving attorney about his finances. Clint thinks Hunter will settle, but I don't care. Paternity has been established. I don't care what amount he wants to pay me for child support. I just want him to take accountability.

My phone rings. "Hey, Brent Langdon called, Hunter's new attorney," Clint says on the other line. "Hunter's asking to settle. I told you he would avoid depositions."

"Okay, let's settle."

"Not until we make him sweat." Clint's smile comes through the phone.

"So how do we do that?"

"Well, unless we settle, Hunter has to be here at 8:00 a.m. So I'm going to put him off for a while. I promise you, Langdon thinks this is all about money. They have no clue, and it would never occur to them that all you wanted is for Hunter to be honest and take accountability."

But that really is all I want. When Judge Meyer asked me if I wanted to do the backpay to Navy's birth at the lower temporary amount of $3,000 per month or wait until we settled on something higher based on Hunter's taxes, I was fine with taking the lower amount.

"They don't think like that," Clint says." "They think you want to soak Hunter and he's trying to get out of this without hurting his father's campaign and probably without his family knowing the truth."

"I'll never see how accepting and loving your child and grandchild could damage any campaign."

"Yeah, well . . . I'll keep you updated on how this goes. Keep your phone by you."

Time ticks by and the stress has me on edge. My phone jumps to life next to me, and I almost jump out of my skin.

"You're going to love this," Clint says. I can hear from the swagger in his southern drawl that the last few hours were probably very rough for Mr. Brent Langdon.

"Langdon called about fifteen minutes after we talked and offered $5,000 a month in child support to settle. I told him that wasn't even worth talking to you about, but I'd run it by you when I got a chance. So he called me back saying he's gone to Hunter, and he's authorized to offer $7,000 per month in support."

"So we've settled? Great!" I exclaim, genuinely happy it's over.

"Uh, no! I told him I needed to talk with you, but that at the moment, I was going to have spaghetti with my kids and try to find the time to talk to you after that. Langdon freaked out and told me he needed an answer. I told him there was no rush, if we didn't settle, we'd just see his client in the morning. We don't need to do anything at all. If you guys want this settled, it's on you."

"So did you take it?"

"It's up to you. Personally, I'd put the heat on him. Think about all the lies Hunter's told—how he doesn't remember you, you didn't have sex, you met once but nothing happened, he met you at a strip club, and he isn't Navy's father. If I were you, I wouldn't settle, I'd bring his ass to get deposed tomorrow. Sit that sucker on the stove and let him simmer a while. But I work for you, and I'll do whatever you want."

I'm still mad and hurt. Even though we've won at this point, I haven't forgiven Hunter. Those reminders make me sweat with anger.

"Okay, do what you do best. Put the pressure on."

While Clint sweats Langdon and Hunter, I work my way through a soup of emotions. Anger over the situation, bitterness over past wrongs, relief at being so near to the end, and sadness that even though we've proven who Navy's father is, he hasn't acknowledged her and is acting like she doesn't exist. Once again, he just wants his problems to go away.

It's nearing 11:00 p.m., and I've been lost in my thoughts for hours. I pour a bath and try to relax when my phone rings.

"Hey, it's us again, you're on speaker," Clint says. "Are you sitting down?"

"Uh yeah," I reply, not mentioning that he caught me in the bathtub. I sit up carefully, trying not to slosh too loudly.

"Well, I think it's settled," he says.

"It is?" I ask, waiting to hear the details.

"Before I called Langdon back, I decided to have a little dessert with the kids. I got three missed calls while eating ice cream. On the fourth call, I answered and told Langdon I hadn't gotten around to confirming a final figure with you yet. He was totally silent for a second—it sounded like disbelief to me. Then he said, 'Look, no kid needs $10,000 per month, but we will go that high . . .' I cut him off before he could even finish and said, 'No, here's the deal. You double that and maybe my client will take it.' His next words were 'Fuck, let me check. I'll call you back!'"

"Clint, oh my God," I laugh.

I can hear him cackling on the other end. "So then he calls back a couple of minutes later and asks 'Is it a deal, or not?!' I kind of hated to disappoint him, but I responded with, 'And he covers Navy's insurance, right?' 'Fuck, I'll call you back.'"

Clint pauses and I can tell something big is coming from the swagger building in his voice.

"So did you make the deal or not?"

"Yes. He doubled the $10,000 and kicked in health insurance."

The ringing in my ears makes it hard to tell, but it seems like there is a gentle splash from my jaw landing at the bottom of the tub.

"Damn, he really didn't want you to depose him," I say.

Chapter 15

Studhorse in the Shadows

It's after dark on a weeknight, and the Batesville, Arkansas, Walmart is pretty quiet. I'm trying to stay out of the spotlight and protect Navy from all the prying eyes who want to see her because of who her grandfather is, so I do my shopping pretty late.

"Hey, Jack," I say waving a hand and trying to keep Navy from pulling my buggy into the green beans.

Jack was our high school janitor. I've known him half my life, and he had always been good to me, cheering me on at basketball games, or greeting me with a basketball move in the hallway. But this time is different. No warm silly greeting back. He fixes his eyes on Navy as if he has seen a ghost and avoids me as he walks on past. Awkward.

I let out a sigh. Most people don't act the same around me anymore. I'm not the hometown girl who grew up here and everyone knows; I'm the girl flashing across CNN headlines who has a daughter related to the Democratic candidate for President of the United States. And not many people in this small town voted for him. I'm getting outcast vibes. But carrying on is something I've grown accustomed to, and that's what I do.

In the next aisle, Navy sings me one of her favorite songs from her seat in the buggy, "Day-O" by Harry Belafonte.

"'Gin, Mama? Want me sing 'gin?" she says after getting a positive reaction.

"Again?"

"Oyay, Mama. 'gin," she repeats, jumping right back into it.

We continue whizzing through the aisles, and after loading a bag of dog food on the bottom of the buggy, something catches my eye. Jack is back. This time he's way down at the other end of the aisle with a phone in his hand. He's not holding it like he would if he were texting, but in a way that I know I'm being recorded. Once he sees that I'm on to him, his gear shifts into nervousness. Too late, Jack.

I'm overcome with anger. My mama bear senses come to the surface, and I walk quickly toward him, still pushing an oblivious Navy in the buggy.

"This might be news to you, and this might be entertainment to send to whatever group message you planned on . . . but this is *our* life. I've known you my entire childhood and you have the audacity to record my daughter and me? Why? What do you plan on doing with that video?"

"I . . . just . . . well, I mean, you can't blame people for taking pics and stuff now," he stammers while scratching his head.

I really would've thought an apology would come, but instead it's a "Can you blame me?"

"Yes, I absolutely can blame you. I can't even go to my hometown Walmart without getting this treatment from a guy who watched me grow up! All over a child. Children are off limits! You should be ashamed of yourself." I walk off before causing too much of a scene, but not without walking past his puzzled wife.

"You sure got you a keeper, ma'am. A guy that likes to record little girls." I keep walking, leaving that for her to ponder.

Another day in that same Walmart, I push the buggy to the paper towel aisle where I come across a man in his later years, probably eighty-something, going on to a younger woman who looks like she's coupon shopping that he hopes she doesn't support the Democratic party.

"I'm telling ya, young lady. They're evil. *Pure evil.* Anyone who votes for that damn guy is damned for hell. Y'all young folks just don't understand." The young lady is trying to be polite but looks like she wants to get away. As I approach, we exchange smiles. He shifts to me.

"I mean the guy is evil. His damn son is evil. It's in their bloodline. That damn Biden family came straight from the devil himself."

"I don't believe that," I retort as I grab my Bounty, not even giving him the satisfaction of eye contact.

"Oh, well, you're crazy," he shoots backs defensively while I read the label on the paper towels as if I've never bought them before. "The deals his son has had, hell the deals he's had. His son came to Arkansas and got a stripper pregnant then won't claim the damn baby. They're pathetic and quite frankly, pure evil. That entire bloodline is evil!"

I'm done listening to his bullshit. "Well," I fire back him, "I happen to know that man you claim is evil, and he's the furthest thing from it." I look him in the eyes and his face falls while his eyes grow bigger. "I'm the woman you're talking about, and this baby here is their bloodline, and one of the greatest blessings God sent to earth. And as far as him being pathetic, he actually does his part and I do mine. So yeah, you're wrong." I don't give him the chance to say more and start pushing my buggy away from the aisle. I can't get far enough away from him.

The young lady he had been talking to prior hadn't moved. I think she stayed out of curiosity. She gives me a high five as I pass. "You go girl." We both laugh.

So this is my life now . . . a curiosity in the spotlight, and an outsider in my own town. Once upon a time it had been fulfilling to walk into a gym and be recognized, to be an athlete little kids looked up to and kids my age dreaded playing against. But it's a lot less fulfilling to walk into my hometown Walmart and feel locals I've known my whole life treat me as an outcast. I'm not a small-town celeb for being an athlete anymore; I'm famous in a small town for sleeping with Hunter Biden and having the president's granddaughter. My old life casts a long shadow over the new life I'm trying to create.

In June 2020, Jill Biden publishes *Joey*, a children's book about the life of Joe Biden. I don't think anything of it or plan to read it, but a copy arrives at the house. And the next day, another copy. That's how it's been since the media attention. People I don't know send me things. Stuff about Hunter and his family. Stuff they think I will like. Some write letters wishing me the best, saying they're praying for me. One woman from upstate New York sent a yellow envelope with a twenty-page letter about Hunter's mother, Neilia, and what it was like watching Hunter grow up. She was really encouraging, and so kind to Navy, saying she hopes Navy will move mountains. Over the span of a few weeks, I collect about ten copies of Jill's book.

Hanging on to a copy for Navy, I pull it out one night after bath time. She loves when I read to her, and this is a book about her grandfather. I want her to know how remarkable her family heritage is. When she's old enough, she will appreciate that.

We snuggle into the big cushions in the bohemian egg chair in her room, her blonde curls wet against my chest, and I soak up the softness of her little pink sleeper, and the smell of Johnson & Johnson's baby lotion.

But opening the book, I see the dedication and my heart sinks.

"To my grandchildren: Naomi, Finnegan, Maisy, Natalie, Hunter, and Beau."

Jill has dedicated the book to all of Joe's grandchildren, excluding one, my sweet Navy. Why could it not have been dedicated "To all of my grandchildren?" Why did she have to list them and purposely leave out a name? Had I known that, I wouldn't ever have picked this book to read to Navy. Or I would have told her, "This was written by some woman named Jill who is not your grandmother."

What a classless, tasteless move. I have to gather myself.

"Read, Mama," Navy says in her innocent toddler voice.

I kiss her on the head, trying to console myself enough to get through this book without her knowing I'm holding back tears. I have to breathe. Her little hand comes up to my face, grabbing my cheek softly.

"Mama, read?" This time it's more of a question.

"Yes, baby," I say, as I catch my breath. Someone told me the hardest thing they've ever done is be a mother while their heart was breaking. I agree. My heart breaks for the one thing I love most in the world, my daughter.

I finish the book and am rewarded with claps on Navy's end. She loves it.

"Aw done," she says.

I tuck her in, giving her a kiss on the forehead, the hand, and the forehead again. I can't show her enough love in this moment. Despite who may not love her, she has a mama who will always make sure she knows she is loved. "Love you, sweet girl."

"I wuv you, Mama," she says, snuggling her stuffed animal she named Slothy, and settling into her pillow.

Walking quietly out of the room, I head straight into the bathroom, lean back on the closed door, and fall to the floor. Tears start flowing.

Someday my daughter will be able to read this book. How will she feel knowing all the president's grandchildren were intentionally listed, but Jill left her out, purposely? I always thought that a quality of a First Lady is to handle herself with class. But this is distasteful, and borderline cruel. Navy deserves better. This little girl is innocent in this scenario, and she should not be treated this way, especially by a matriarch who is supposed to pull the family together and love them.

In mid-October Peyton tips me off that someone's posting these horrible, never-before-seen photos of Hunter. When she sends me the screenshots, my stomach drops at the sight. They're being leaked from somewhere, picture after picture, and my heart breaks when I realize who's reposting them—my friend, Aubrey. So with shaky hands I message her.

"Aubrey, that's someone's father—my child's father! Why would you promote this if you're supposed to be one of my friends? I hope my daughter never comes across these pictures. When you have your child, you'll understand where I'm coming from when I try to protect mine with everything in me. These pictures hurt not only him, but his innocent children."

She apologizes but the damage is done. I'm left with the wreckage of a friendship and a sick feeling in the pit of my stomach that more pictures could be coming . . . and maybe the next ones will feature me.

Twenty days before the election, massive news breaks. According to a computer repair shop owner, Hunter dropped off his laptop for repair but didn't bother to return for it.

The *New York Post* headlined the story with "Smoking-gun email reveals how Hunter Biden introduced Ukrainian businessman to VP dad."

No one knew about the drop-off and abandonment until October 14, 2020, when the *New York Post* ran a bombshell article based on "a massive trove of data recovered from a laptop computer."

Can this be true? It would explain the pictures Aubrey and now lots of other people have been posting.

Hunter never went anywhere without his laptop, and with his paranoia, I cannot imagine him leaving it somewhere and allowing anyone access. When we traveled it would be in his backpack. When we were at Chain Bridge it would sit out on the counter. And when we stayed at hotels it would be out on the desk or dresser, open. What . . . what if he had been recording *everything*? Our conversations? Pictures of me? Videos of us being intimate?

Another new level of anxiety jolts my mind. The best therapist in the world won't be able to help me if anything like that leaks. But there is some hope. None of this sounds like Hunter.

Texts and calls start flying between me, Kelsey, and Savanah. We're all wondering the same thing. But in the midst of our panicked discussions, Savanah asks a million-dollar question: Why would Hunter drop off his laptop for repair?

CSI mode kicks in again and I start trying to put the pieces together. This isn't his MO at all. He doesn't get things repaired; he just buys new ones—like the phones. We've never seen him repair anything other than Kelsey's car the morning after we met at Rosemont. Did he actually do something this careless? Even when high, Hunter never let that laptop out of his sight.

If it's not Hunter's MO and he's not that careless, how did this happen? We come up with three theories ourselves.

One: It's not his laptop. It's some kind of October surprise that Trump or his surrogates have set up to demolish Joe's campaign. Two: It's Hunter's laptop, but it got to the shop without him knowing. Three: Maybe it's Hunter's laptop and he dropped it off and abandoned it *on purpose*.

Three is pretty far out there, but if it's true, he had to have done it for a good reason.

Everybody already knows Hunter struggled with addiction, drugs, alcohol, and a crazy party lifestyle. He's been candid about it, owning it publicly. Nothing on the laptop would be surprising but everything on the laptop would be attention-grabbing. Was this a red herring? There was no way to know. But more importantly to me, there was no way to know if pictures or videos of me were about to begin spilling out onto the internet for the entire world—and someday for my daughter—to see.

I had seen the demons of addiction and paranoia oppress Hunter. I had caught the demon of paranoia from him. Now the demon of anxiety is stalking me. The form it takes doesn't even matter. It's there whispering that I'm a disappointment, a failure, and any day now I might literally be exposed to the entire world. The trauma from the last two plus years is starting to show and it's taking me down again. I'd never ever consider harming myself while my daughter is on this earth. The anxiety isn't that severe, but it is brutally painful living with a demon on your back.

Early on election night 2020, someone is beating on my front door. I've moved out of Mom and Dad's place and gotten a home for Navy and me. Cracking the door open, I see my dad standing there looking like Rambo. Four large rifles are strapped around him, and pistols are in the holsters around his waist.

"What the hell is going on?" I ask, scared and confused as I open the door further.

"Sheriff in town just called and said for me to get over here. There's been some threats about if Joe wins the election . . . he said if y'all were his daughter and granddaughter, he'd have you in hiding for bit. So pack a bag."

"Why? Hell, we were fine until you showed up in Rambo mode." I'm annoyed, I didn't think in my small town that we were going to have to take cover.

"Not takin' the chance. I want you in my sight. There's a lotta crazy people out there, especially in this area that will do anything if Joe wins. You and Navy are easy targets."

Navy runs over to greet Rambo Pappy while I go pack an overnight bag. As I'm throwing things together, anxiety creeps in. Is this what things will be like for the next four years?

Hiding away at Mom and Dad's house, the night drags on as I stay up watching the votes come in. When Joe wins, I celebrate, but I want to be back in my own home. I hate having to live in the shadows, I'm really not scared, and I don't think that Hunter would let anything bad happen to us. Even though we don't have a security detail like all the president-elect's family members get, our case is so public that anything that happens to me or Navy would fall back on Hunter and his dad, and I don't think he'd let that happen. So I call my soul sister Brie to come stay with me at my house. I convince my dad that it will be fine, I'll take home more guns and more ammo, and I'll have an extra shooter. He isn't convinced, but gives in, settling for Rambo Pappy drive-bys throughout the night.

The next day, when CNN makes their announcement, I lift Navy Joan in the air above me on the sofa, and Brie captures the perfect candid picture of her and the TV in the background reading, "President-Elect Joe Biden." Not many little girls can say their grandfather is the leader of the free world, and hers just made history. How iconic.

Nobody in our small town ever harasses us about Joe being president. In fact, the locals actually show a lot of respect for Navy and her paternal family, but only after many made fools of themselves during my pregnancy.

A couple months later Brie and I watch the inauguration from my house, and the shadow creeps over again. On stage, Hunter and his new wife are holding their little boy Beau, while Naomi, Finnegan, and Maisy all enjoy the historical moment their grandfather has accomplished. I look down at Navy sitting on the floor playing with her Peppa Pig house. She's not old enough to quite understand what's going on, but nonetheless she watches from over one thousand miles away, the only grandchild not included. I don't see what would have been hard about acknowledging a child, or grandchild, and allowing her to be a part of this moment. Especially a family that won America over with their love for their family. Accepting Navy should be a feather in their cap.

I'm not asking to be a part of it, I am of no relation, but she is their blood, and she deserves to be there with them. I don't know who is to blame for why that didn't happen, but once Joe is in office, Jill decides to exclude Navy again.

It's late November the following year and I'm sitting on the floor wrapping presents with Brie after putting Navy to bed when my ears perk up to the news on TV. Brie eagerly grabs the remote and turns up the volume so we can hear clearly.

A reporter is talking about the White House Christmas decorations and how the First Lady always designs them. It's one of her many duties. Then right before my eyes, they show a picture of a White House fireplace full of garlands and striped stockings hanging from the mantle. I sit there speechless as the reporter finishes reading the names on all the stockings. Every grandchild of the president is mentioned, except the one most important to me. Even the dogs have their own personal stockings hung by Jill, but not Navy. Jill did it again. She snubbed a small innocent child, and a family member. I can't conceive the number of prayers I will need to ever forgive this woman for publicly snubbing a child she should be embracing. My heart absolutely breaks for Navy, knowing someday she will see this.

Jill's not the only one who forgets Navy exists. Joe makes several public statements that he has six grandchildren. The media rakes him over the coals for excluding his seventh grandchild who lives in Arkansas.

About five months later, another shock wave hits when a friend texts me a link to an article. "Tomorrow Night! Exclusive interview with Hunter Biden on his new memoir, *Beautiful Things*. Tune in 8 ET/7 CT."

I can hardly get my mouth open before it comes out. "What? No freakin' way."

Then it's all a stream of consciousness. How will he portray having a child that he earlier denied? Will he tell the truth about everything? He can't say too much since he had told everyone prior to the book that we only met once, and no sex was involved, an obvious lie. There's no telling. Then it dawns on me—he will go with whatever story he's told his family about me, and probably anything else that discredits me.

When it hits the shelves, I don't buy a copy. But I do read the articles that soon follow. "Hunter Biden claims to have no recollection of baby mama," they say. Well played. It's like being on a witness stand and not wanting to admit the full truth. It's easy to say "I don't recall." He can't make it go away, so he just pretends he doesn't know. He describes me as an Arkansas woman who filed a paternity suit and says he has no recollection of our encounter. He sets that up by talking about the downward spiral he was in and how it led him to many girls he spent time with that were "hardly the dating type." Anyone who reads this will think I was just a one-night stand. It's infuriating.

His whole point with *Beautiful Things* was to own his past and live in his truth. But this part of "his truth" isn't the truth. He's still lying to his family. And heaven forbid he tell his wife that when they got married he was fully aware of a child he had and was avoiding. I'm sure those lies came from a place of guilt and shame, but I also won't make excuses for him anymore. Navy is my sole priority, and I won't take the snubs coming her way lightly.

When the audio book comes out, I download it, but my palms start sweating on the steering wheel when I hear the voice. I hadn't realized Hunter read his own book, or how much simply hearing him would send me into fight-or-flight. I just want to pull over and go to sleep. One minute into the audio and I want my money back.

It haunts me. Then one night I walk out of my mom and dad's house into the dark and I smell him. I'm stopped in my tracks by the familiar sharp and smoky smell of Tom Ford Tuscan Leather. It isn't one of those nostalgic smells that draws a smile on your face. It's a punch in my gut. Then I see my sister in the darkness.

"Dude, what perfume are you wearing? Is that Tuscan Leather?"

"Oh my gosh, the lady at Sephora told me Gucci Guilty smells like Tuscan Leather. I didn't know what that was," she says laughing and obviously clueless.

"Yeah, well I do. You smell just like Navy's father."

Living in the shadow has become our routine. I do the normal things of a single mother keeping a close eye on her child, and even though that's challenging enough, for me, it's not that simple. The dark clouds feel like they're pressing down on us.

Then one day, as I'm doing dishes and Navy is impersonating a British accent with her little Peppa Pig people on the floor, my phone rings. It's Lancaster Law Firm.

"Hey Lunden, so the DA of Delaware reached out wanting you to answer some of their questions. They're investigating Hunter and think that the financial stuff he sent during the paternity suit can help."

I have no clue what financial information he sent. I never looked at it. Didn't care to.

"Um . . . okay? I mean I guess it's good to comply and do what we are told. Can we avoid them?"

"Yeah, but you can't avoid a subpoena. They'll just come ask you questions, then probably take you in front of a grand jury and ask more questions."

"Oh my gosh. No. Should I tell Hunter? Can I?"

"Uh, I mean it's probably frowned on to tell him, but it isn't illegal. I'll do whatever you want me to do."

"I just think if he knows, he will make it go away. Yes, please contact his attorney and let him pass the word to Hunter." Now I'm relying on Hunter's tactics to keep myself out of a mess.

"You think so?" Clint asks.

"If Hunter knows I'm subpoenaed, it will go away. That's what he does."

Clint has always been on my side. His MAGA ways have him wanting to crush Hunter, but he even says a time or two, "I hope he doesn't go to prison for my client's sake. She wants what's best for her daughter, and that would not be putting Hunter behind bars." It may feel like a stick in Clint's throat to do it, but he does what I ask.

Hours pass and Clint calls back.

"So, you seen the news?"

"No . . . what is it?"

"Well," he begins, and I can hear the "I told you so" in his voice, "after we informed him, he went public to let everyone know he knows he's under investigation and is complying because he has nothing to hide."

I laugh. "Okay? So it'll go away . . ."

"It could. Or it just pissed the DA off who now knows you told him."

"Oh shit."

I talk with Diane that day and tell her about tipping off Hunter. She laughs. "You constantly try to protect him, and he just slaps you in the face with it," she says, but she applauds the grace I give him.

"It'll die down," she says. "But you're not out of this just yet. It'll come back this fall."

She is so candid and gives the best advice. I respect her immensely, and occasionally, she slips in some little hidden prediction that always comes true.

Days, weeks, and months come and go without my hearing anything else from the investigators. Maybe Hunter fixed it, and for once, just maybe Diane is wrong. Not likely, but hopefully.

One day Brie randomly mentions the subpoena. "Hey, so did that all go away? Have you heard anything?"

"Haven't heard anything, but it's September and you know what Diane said."

"Then it's coming." We both laugh knowing Diane doesn't miss.

In June, the laptop gives up its first secret about me, and I find out from a call with Randi. Before I can even say hello, I hear her laughing on the other line.

"Lunnnn," she manages to get out between laughs.

"Remember Jessica? My friend from Little Rock?" Randi continues, "She just called me freaking out saying 'I just saw on the news they've got video of Hunter sneaking Lunden into the Embassy Suites! I barely caught the end of the story, but they've got it on video!' Hahahaha."

"Embassy Suites? I've never stayed at an Embassy Suites in my life."

"No shit. And she don't know that. But what embassy have you stayed at?" she asks.

"Oh," it dawns on me, and we both laugh.

The news got wind of our escapades at the Swedish Embassy, and it just goes to show how people can run with something without having all the information.

As I search around for more articles, I stumble onto a *New York Post* headline: "Hunter Biden: Baby Mama Was 'Basketball Mentor' to Daughter and Sasha Obama."

It turns out emails to Hunter from the House of Sweden, admonishing him for letting people in through the back door, were leaked from his laptop. So Hunter did what he always does when he can't charm his way out. He lied.

But I wasn't the only person the House of Sweden had caught on camera. Their emails also took issue with "a middle aged African American woman who, because of her economic circumstances was dressed [like] an extremely poor person." Bicycles!

Having used his random Obama-connection card on me, he took a different tack with Bicycles, accusing the building manager of prejudice against her race. After a sickly sweet apology email, the building manager responded, "We are very excited and honored to welcome your new colleagues!"

I always wondered why Hunter had his office at the Embassy of Sweden, rather than one of those nice penthouse offices in the city. Maybe it was because Sweden is neutral territory and doesn't extradite for political offenses.

While getting a laugh out of Hunter's ability to smooth talk his way out of anything, the relief fades fast. There's a laptop out there that could have mortifying pictures or video of me, and as I'm staring down the barrel of a grand jury subpoena, I continue to live under the long shadows cast by Hunter and my time in D.C.

Chapter 16

The Circus Just Follows

"Not my circus, not my clowns." I wish I could say that, but my motto is more like, "Do you ever feel like you're the ringleader and the circus just follows?"

Like Paul writes in the Bible, "Let your moderation be known in all things." Even good things can cause problems if we do them too much. Some of the circus of my life might be due to the fact I put others first, but too much. Enabling, protecting, and trying to save people who would probably be better off hitting rock bottom.

I've done that with Hunter, and that circus continues to make headlines. Maybe because when you invite in the demons of addiction and paranoia, the demon of chaos eventually comes along for the ride. But it's not just Hunter. No matter where I go, the clowns come running. So I'm not surprised that at the same time that my circus has been playing out on a national stage over this last year, my attraction to Brock, who's in a ring all his own, has been creating a circus in the background much closer to home.

It was around the time Katie Dodge made me aware of my termination that Randi Jo and Seva take me out for my first night without Navy to an MMA fight. Sweat and blood spray the front rows, and a local favorite catches my eye from the cage. Brock's five o' clock shadow is lined perfectly with his dark hair, and the bright white of his smile in his tan complexion lights up a room.

"He's a looker," my sister says.

"Yeah, I bet he's a whore too." We laugh.

He was a freshman when I was a senior in high school, but I don't know him well. After three rounds, he's unanimously judged the winner, and minutes later his crooked grin and perfect white smile make me blush as his eyes connect with mine from the crowd.

"I saw that," Seva laughs.

"Saw what?" I ask, playing dumb.

"He's always had his scope on you. You've been his dream girl since high school." Apparently he's been telling Seva's husband for a long time that he'd do anything if I would just give him one chance.

I'm shocked and speechless. This good-looking guy considers me his dream girl? After the last few years of being rejected and abandoned, I've lost all confidence. I never want to be heartbroken again, and I'm sure going to protect my daughter's heart at all costs.

"I thought you knew," she says.

I didn't. And I doubt it matters now. I'm a single mom and he's an eligible bachelor.

"He's staring at you," Randi Jo says, looking over my shoulder at Brock talking with Seva.

"Oh shit. What do I do?" Fight-or-flight, I think to myself. But a nudge comes from my backside, and I turn around.

"Uh, so somebody is like in love with you," Seva says. "Like *in love*. Brock just asked why you were wearing a ring on your left hand and if you were tied to your daughter's father. I told him it was your grandmother's diamond, and no, you're not. He said that was good, cause he's about to make you his."

I freeze. My life is in turmoil, there's a massive storm brewing as I'm about to take legal action against Hunter for paternity, and this is my first night away from Navy ever. This is not the time to get a relationship going.

Maybe his personality sucks, I think to myself, and I won't even be tempted. That's more my luck.

"Oh God. He don't want this smoke," I say laughing, but truthful.

Honkytonk throw-down music blasts in the background later that night at our small-town country club, as I catch up with people I haven't seen in a long time over buckets of beer. Then Brock walks through the door. He's not the shirtless fighter now, exposing his insane six-pack; he's wearing a blue button up with dark denim jeans and a pair of Vans. Still just as pretty, I can't help but smile when his eyes meet mine.

He makes a beeline to me. "So, Lunden, what did ya think about the fights tonight?" he asks, drawing out every vowel sound for a country mile.

I laugh before answering and he blushes. He has the most country accent I think I've ever heard, and I'm from the South.

"Uh, well, I don't know how y'all do that," I say. "Takes balls." Did I just say that? The polite thing would've been to say it takes guts. Guts, not balls.

"Yeah, it does," he laughs.

Throughout the night, no matter who Brock talks to or where I wander off to, I keep catching him staring at me.

"Okay, so I'm gonna need you to put your number in here," he drawls, "so if I lose sight of you I don't lose my chance."

I laugh but grab his phone and enter my number.

Every conversation he strikes up with me leads to lots of laughs. He does have a personality. Fuck.

At the end of the night, Brock walks me to my car. He seems like one of the good ol' boys, not like some guy who wants a one-night stand, although I'm sure he's had plenty.

"Well, it's been a lot of fun, but I have to get back to my daughter," I say. "The thought of her waking up and me not being there is driving me insane."

"Sure, I totally get that. But before you go, can I ask you a question?"

Oh, Lord. "Sure."

"So would you be open to maybe . . . like," he hesitates, fear of rejection written on his face, ". . . maybe um, going on a date with me sometime. I'd really like to get to know you."

"Oh, Brock, you don't want to date me." A lump forms in my throat. A decent guy who I'm attracted to is persistent in wanting to know me, and I'm fixing to push him away with the truth that comes with me.

"Yes, I do. I know what I want," he says.

"It's complicated."

"Well shouldn't I be the judge of that? I've wanted a date with you for years."

I order him to get in the car, throwing him off guard. He opens the passenger door and slides in next to me.

"You know I have a newborn baby, right?"

"Yeah, I know. I'm okay with that."

"What you don't know is the chaos that comes with that. A shitstorm is heading my way, and you should steer far from me."

"It can't be that bad."

"It will be, and I wouldn't want to put anyone else through what I'm about to go through. You're young and have so much going for you, don't waste your time on me."

"Look, I ain't no pushover. My life was a shitstorm growin' up. I can handle it."

I pull out my phone, showing him a picture of Hunter. It's one I found on Google and planned on putting in Navy's baby scrapbook to fill the place asking for a picture of her dad. He's wearing a black suit with a white button up, smiling from ear to ear. He seems happy, which is why I chose it for her.

"You know this guy?" I ask.

"Uh, he kinda looks familiar."

"His father is the former vice president and probably going to be the next president. Have you heard of Joe Biden?"

"Uh, yeah. What's that got to do with anything?" he asks, confused.

"Joe Biden is his dad. And he, well," I hesitate, knowing once the words come out, I can't take them back, "this guy in this picture is Navy's dad, Hunter Biden."

"That don't mean shit to me and damn sure ain't gonna make me not wanna take you on a date." He's simple and oblivious, and I appreciate that about him.

"If his father runs for president, I will be a scandal. It will be publicized heavily, and I will be criticized, possibly anyone that has anything to do with me too. It gives me anxiety, and I don't want to put you through it."

"Don't scare me one bit," he grins.

I've warned him of the demon of chaos following me, and he wants to be a part of it. It's my first official red flag; he's crazy. But he wears me down, and before driving off I agree to go on a date.

A week later, my sister watches Navy, and I fall in love with the goodness I see in Brock over dinner and a bonfire with friends. We just jibe. He's been leading a youth group for the last few years, picking up kids three times a week and bringing them to church for a home-cooked meal and a lesson about the Bible, and I love how simple and honest he is. With Hunter, everything was so complex, but with Brock, what you see is what you get. At least at first.

He wants to see me again, and I want to see him too, but I'm a package deal. So he babyproofs his house, buys a baby swing and diapers, and dotes on my daughter as she takes her first steps. For five months it's perfect. We're in church every week, and even the pastor loves him. Brock's best friend Dustin is married to my best friend Seva, and their daughter and Navy are best friends too, so we hang out with them every Friday night. I couldn't be happier. Finally, things just fit.

In April 2019, I tell him I'm filing for paternity. We both know it's been coming, but Brock sort of freaks out, thinking he needs to do something, as though he's going to lose me. One day, out of the blue, while I'm doing a mother/daughter photo shoot in a field of flowers with Navy, he shows up with a ring.

"Uh, do my mom and dad know?" I ask in shock, as I turn to see him on one knee.

"Yeah," he smiles up at me.

"Did they say it was okay?" I'm reeling.

"Yeah." He nods, finally standing because I've taken so long to answer. The longer I take, the more nervous he gets.

Maybe it's because I don't like titles, or maybe it's because I know what's fixin' to happen in my life, but I'm more than a little hesitant when I say, "Okay. Yes."

It turns out my dad had given his blessing after all, but also said that with everything going to shit, he doesn't think now is the right time. But Brock seems to feel like he needs to nail me down, like somehow he's going to lose me to Hunter during the paternity suit. I'm the biggest crush of his life. He was just a country boy who never thought he could be with someone like me. Even in my gym clothes in high school, he thought I was the most beautiful thing he had ever seen.

But the whole time he has me on this huge pedestal thinking I am so much better than him, I'm thinking just the opposite. After the ordeal of being rejected and abandoned, I don't feel worthy. I feel flawed, and while I'm amazed that Brock wants to be with me, the stuff from the past has me really down on myself.

We both have our insecurities, I guess, and insecurity has a way of getting out of hand when it's not dealt with. For Brock, first it's the fear of Hunter. I never tell him about my relationship with Hunter or talk about him at all. It's clear it makes him feel insecure. Then there's the fear of me meeting his parents. He seems to be ashamed of where he came from. Maybe it's those insecurities that make things take a turn, or maybe it's the demons that still haunt me, but for as good as things are in the beginning, the chaos that's coming makes my previous circus seem tame.

The paternity suit hits the media in June 2019, with Page Six trumpeting "Hunter Biden sued by woman claiming to have had his love child." That's when I start to see the change. Navy and I are spending more time at Brock's house than Mom and Dad's, and one Friday we're spending the night there when Dustin and Seva bring over a bottle of Fireball.

"What about Fireball Friday?" they ask, and we all laugh.

No one seems too drunk, but when our friends leave, a switch flips.

"You know it's really stupid that you're a Democrat," Brock spits as I walk back into the kitchen after putting Navy to bed. "You do some really dumb things."

"What?" I ask, irritation masking my surprise at the out-of-the-blue insult. But I shake it off. I know that's not him; he's just had a little too much to drink.

The next day he's mortified when I tell him what happened but can't remember a thing.

"We didn't even drink a whole lot and you can't remember." I'm surprised. But if you drink and don't remember, it's a sign of an alcoholic, I always heard. A few weeks later it happens again, and a few weeks after that. The insults get worse each time. It's as if drinking and degrading who I am is now his go-to. But it always happens when Navy is asleep. First, it's Coors Light, then whatever alcohol happens to be available.

Just as the late-night drinking and insults grow worse, so do the stories being "reported" about me. The story of Hunter meeting me at a strip club he frequented comes out, and now I'm a "prostitute" in Brock's eyes. But he never once cares to ask me for the truth. He would believe whatever story was written about me then make it worse with his exaggerations of the false stories.

Brock must have a Google alert set for my name, because any time I pop up in the media, he's all over it. He latches on to the story, and one night he gets drunk and starts calling me a whore. In the morning, he claims it never happened, so I start recording him. Even though sober Brock and intoxicated Brock are two different people, it's time they met.

Even on his worst cocaine bender, Hunter never made me fear for my safety. He was a happy, if manic, addict. Brock is different. On nights when we get into fights, even when I stay at his house, I lock Navy and myself in the bedroom, slide a dresser in front of the door, and sleep with a pistol under the pillow. The look in his eyes gives me nightmares for years to come. In his sane mind, Brock would never hurt us, but with the way he talks about me and Hunter when he's drinking, I could see him kill us and wake up in a jail cell not knowing he had done it.

One night it gets so bad that he drags on for two hours, dogging Hunter, bringing up politics, telling me I'm stupid.

"Dude, shut up and leave it alone," I say, but he can't. I never allow anyone to talk bad about Navy's family, but he's fixated. At 1:00 a.m., while he's going off, I wrap a sleeping Navy in a blanket and leave for a hotel. My relationships are private, and I don't want my parents to know—especially Dad. It wouldn't go well for Brock if he did.

"Look, we're not married," I tell him when he apologizes profusely the next day, "and if you continue down this road, we won't be married. Navy and I need a home of our own because when you throw your tantrums in the middle of the night, where are we supposed to go? This is your house, and I shouldn't have to wrap her in a blanket and travel across town so we get a safe night's sleep." He's not happy about it, but I'm an adult, and not yet married, and I don't need to be bouncing between my parents' home and his. Navy and I need a place of our own, and if it provides some space from Brock, that's even better.

By February 2020, the paternity suit is finally settled thanks to Clint and the downright heroic Holly Meyers. Despite what the U.S. version of Britain's *Sun* tabloid reports months later ("Scandal-hit Hunter Biden 'agreed to pay baby mama $2.5 million to settle paternity case despite claiming to be broke'"), Hunter doesn't pay $2.5 million to settle the case. More crack reporting from the media.

The national ring of my circus quiets down, while the circus ring at home becomes the main attraction. Brock is up and down. Some weeks he's clean and wonderful, others are full of verbal abuse and raging benders. Despite that, he's always good to Navy, loving her as if she were his own, and the love she shows back to him is obvious. I stick around because that's how I am, for better or worse, and I already feel like I've failed Navy in the fatherhood department. In his sane mind, Brock is an amazing dad to her. I keep hoping if he can get it together, she won't have to live without a father figure in her life. But his sane mind has control less and less.

By August 2020, we've been engaged for over a year, and I haven't made a single wedding plan. But I do make a plan to take Brock to Hot Springs for his birthday. He's currently clean, so things are perfect, and he claims he wants to do what it takes to build the future we planned.

After an alligator farm visit and a horse drawn-carriage ride, we stay at the Arlington Hotel, where gangsters like Al Capone vacationed in the prohibition days. It has that old-time feel, and two-year-old Navy bounces around the table to the live band in the lobby. Picking her up, Brock sways to the music and she explodes with delighted giggles. They make their way through the spotlight of older couples' gazes as an elderly lady lays her hand on my shoulder. "You have such a beautiful family," she says.

The moment is perfect, but the demons are lurking.

"I'm going to stay down here for a little bit," Brock says as I start to head for the room to put Navy to bed. "It's my birthday. One or two beers won't hurt. I've been doing good."

But it's never one or two, I think as I cuddle Navy upstairs, singing "You Are My Sunshine." Her big blue eyes get heavy, as do mine, and I nod off next to her in the hotel bed.

Wrenched from deep sleep by cold water pouring over me and my baby girl, I snap my eyes open as it hits me in the face and Navy lets out a cry.

"You are so fuckin' corrupt," Brock's voice booms in the darkness. "You had sex with some old nasty man for money. You hooker!"

He's insane, standing over us with an empty ice bucket.

"I'm a prophet and I might not always do everything right, but God sent me here for Navy because you're fuckin' corrupt."

"Yeah? God sent you here in a drunken stupor for Navy," I shoot back while grabbing a towel from the floor and drying Navy off. "That doesn't sound like the God I serve." Navy's startled face tries to make sense of what's happening as Brock yells, "Moses was a drunk!"

In that moment, it occurs to me that he might be thinking of Noah, but what do I know? After all, I'm not a prophet, just a whore.

Navy starts crying. For her, Brock is the only dad she's known, and she's never seen this side of him. She collapses into tears, and I scoop her into one arm while packing our things and hoping my comforting her drowns out his insanity.

"Lord, I pray you have mercy on this whore's soul," Brock cries out in his delusion. "This poor child has to live through this life she made her. She laid with a fifty-year-old Biden for money. The Lord knows, he told me. You know too."

But when he sees I'm not buyin' the nonsense and fixin' to leave, he begs me to stay. Navy clings to my leg crying when I set her on the ground to sling the straps of her backpack over my shoulders. But before I can pick her back up, Brock grabs the handle on the top of the backpack and throws me to the ground.

"Mama!" Navy explodes, her haunting cry filled with fear.

In a decade of basketball, I never moved so fast. Jumping to my feet, I swing a right hook in Brock's face, screaming for him to keep his distance. Navy clings to my leg terrified and I yell not to come any closer. Then a fist pounds on the door.

Perfect. Someone's heard the redneck fight going on and come to ask us to quiet down. Scooping Navy up, I open the door, embarrassed but relieved. Two men in black suits stand in the door. "If you don't leave now, she's coming with us," they say, pointing at Navy. I stare back in shock, mouth agape.

"I'm getting out now actually," I assure them, thankful they've intervened.

"That's fine, we will wait." They stand firm in place like statues staring holes in a confused but fortunately quieter Brock as I grab my last bag.

With Navy in my arms, we walk down the hall and wait for the elevator, men in black close behind. Turning around once inside, I watch them return down the hall as the doors close, wondering where they are going and if I should say thank you or something.

At the front desk I ask about the men in black suits. They aren't employees. Again, at the valet I ask if they saw them arrive. They have no clue who they are. Are they angels? Did Hunter hire private security to follow us? Is the Secret Service on our tail as the campaign gears up? As I'm trying to figure it out, the lobby elevator doors open back up, and Brock stands on the other side.

"They're searching the room, Lunden," he whines in his country drawl. "They're coming to get me!"

"Who Brock? Who's after you now?"

"Hunter Biden! He's trying to assassinate me. His hit men are in there right now!"

I pack Navy and the bags into my new Tahoe, only to find Brock's gathered his things and snuck into the passenger seat without me seeing.

"What the hell are you doing?"

"I'm sorry," he drawls, "I won't say a word the whole ride back to Batesville."

I sit for a moment, then do the stupid thing I always do.

"Not a fucking word," I hiss, pulling out of the parking garage. But by the time we hit the interstate, where there's no turning back, he's set in on me again.

For the next few weeks, every day Brock shows up at Mom and Dad's house, but I'm not ready to see him. "This will never work unless you get help," I say when I finally let him in, and I place his ring back in his hand. Misery and desperation are painted on his face, and he's ready to do anything to get us back. "Look, maybe having some space is good," I say, as I think about moving into the home I'm about to close on. "Maybe if it's meant to be, we can rekindle the flame."

But space isn't something Brock is ready to give. Immediately rekindling becomes the only thing on his mind. He's constantly knocking on my door, trying to talk to me, sometimes in a good state, sometimes not. I don't cut Brock out of my life the way I probably should, and because I put others first, I keep taking him back. He knows how to manipulate me. He blames the outbursts and addictions on the paternity suit, knowing I will feel guilty for bringing it into his life. That's why I keep enduring the nightmare, praying it won't get any worse.

Chapter 17
Sharing a Jail Cell

But it wouldn't be my life if it wasn't one thing after another. I'm in the car when the phone rings with a number I don't recognize.

"Hey Lunden, its Clint. This is my personal cell. I don't normally give it out to female clients, but I figure it's okay since we might be sharing a jail cell," he laughs.

I respect Clint and Jennifer's marriage and the boundaries they set, but my mind starts racing about the jail cell.

"Oh gosh, what did I do now?"

"Remember those depositions you hoped Hunter would make go away?" he asks, almost laughing at the possibility of that. "The assistant U.S. attorney wants to ask you some questions."

It never ends.

"Do I have to?" I ask, hopeful he can just tell them to get lost.

"Well, yeah, it's a subpoena, so you don't really have a choice."

Great. Diane was right all those months ago. The AUSA went away in the spring and came back around in the fall. And it's not the only thing she's right about.

A couple weeks before the dreaded testimony, Brie and I are at Lowe's when my phone buzzes with a text.

"You know I love you like a daughter," Diane's message reads, "and I always want you to know when I'm thinking about you. This morning during my prayers I felt a strong energy of a baby around you. Be careful who you're with, Lunden, because the father of that baby will be the man you spend the rest of your life with."

If a pallet full of cinder blocks fell on me at that very instant, it couldn't hit harder than this pile of emotional bricks.

The only man I've been around is Brock on and off, depending on what state of mind he's in, and I can't speak.

Brie reads the message, her eyes growing big. "Noooooooooooo," she exclaims in astonishment. "There's no way this is happening!"

We grab a box of tests at Walgreens, then beeline for Brie's house where I rip open the package and place three tests on the bathroom counter. PTSD sets in. But as one blue line becomes visible, I take my first real breath since I opened Diane's message. Maybe it was just a warning. But one thing's for sure, I'm not ever having sex again because she has scared me half to death.

The next few days I spend mentally preparing myself for the coming deposition, but I can't shake Diane's prediction. Pregnancy tests can be wrong, so I decide to take another test, just to be sure.

As the PTSD comes back to me again, I pray to God to clear my mind and let this be negative. Time has been taking a toll, so as I wait, I grab the bottle of moisturizer and rub it under my eyes, trying to brighten the dark circles. But it doesn't take long for my eyes to shift to the two blue lines looking up at me.

"No no no no no no no . . ." I repeat to myself in disbelief, my legs going limp. The moisturizer was a waste because tears instantly wash it away. How could this happen? I was on birth control.

I start trying to tell myself God has a plan. He always comes through. "All things work together for good . . ." right?

How do I tell my family I'm pregnant again?

Tears stream down my face as I sit on the toilet, and I remember when I was pregnant with Navy, a nurse told me everything I feel the baby feels. So I dry my eyes and gather myself. I've done this before. I don't want to always have to be strong, but I've grown accustomed to it. Instead of living, I'm surviving due to my own choices in life.

Within minutes I hear a diesel engine in the driveway followed by a knock at the door. It's Brock. I know at first glance that he's sober today, as I open the door.

"Hey, can I get that box of my things from the closet?" he asks.

"Sure," I say pulling the door back further to let him in.

"Navy Shark still awake?" he asks.

"No, I just put her to bed." I'm still not in my right mind, but trying to play it off. Then my absentmindedness comes floating to the surface.

"Uh, what's this?" he asks, walking from my room with the positive pregnancy test in hand.

How could I be so stupid? I knew he had to go through my bathroom to get to the closet. Immediately tears well up and stream down my face as I slide back against the wall and down to my knees. Brock runs over and puts his arms around me.

"What's wrong . . . this is a good thing, right? A baby," he says.

How can he think it's such a good thing when I'm so mortified? "I don't know," I choke out. "I've been down this road before."

"What do you mean? You went through a pregnancy alone. You're the strongest woman I know. But this pregnancy you won't go through alone. I'm here. Hell, I'm fucking happy!"

This is him sober. But I know the sobriety won't last, and when he's under the influence, he'll be saying just the opposite. And when the sober days become shorter, his absence will prevail, leaving me pregnant and alone, again.

"It's . . . me, isn't it?" he asks, as his happiness fades to remorse.

I want to tell him it has nothing to do with the sober him and that it's his alter ego I'm worried about.

"You're upset 'cause it's my child? I bet you'd be happy if it were Hunter's baby, not mine!"

Okay, not what I was expecting, but there goes his sanity and here come his insecurities about Navy's father. Brock stands, looking down like he might spit on me. I don't get up.

"You can't be serious," I burst out. "You think I'm upset because I want to have Hunter's baby and not yours? Where the fuck is your reality?"

"Well, that's gotta be it! I knew it!"

"No, your insecurities and conspiracies never make sense. If you must know, I'm upset because I feel I'm in the same position I've been in before, dealing with an addict who will not step up for me and my children."

"I'll step up. I'll be the sole parent in this baby's life," he retorts as he slams the door. I peel myself off the floor and check on Navy. She's still sound asleep, and I lay beside her, watching her breathe, trying to process what's happened in the last hour.

As the date of the deposition grows closer, the fights with Brock grow worse. I'm caught in a vise between Hunter and a grand jury on one side and Brock and a new baby on the other, and the stress is breaking me.

The familiar diesel engine roars in the driveway one night while Navy sleeps. I contemplate just continuing to wash dishes, but I don't want his knocking to wake Navy up, or the neighbors.

I can tell by the sway in his stance he's had a lot to drink as he barges through the door.

"How ya feelin'?" he asks, but based off the look of disgust on his face I can see he doesn't care.

"A little sick, but I'll manage," I tell him, sitting on the couch trying to settle the motion sickness. I didn't get sick much when I was pregnant with Navy, but lately anytime I move my head too fast I throw up.

"Well, it ain't like you got anything else to do," he says, insinuating that working for my dad's company isn't work and I do nothing.

"Actually, I have a deposition in couple days I should be preparing for," I spit back.

"A deposition? What are you talking about?"

"Some assistant U.S. attorney called. They're coming down to ask some questions."

"About Hunter?"

"I guess. I don't know what it will consist of honestly." I still never tell Brock anything about Hunter; he only knows what tabloids release and quite frankly he believes every bit of it.

"So you're goin' down to spend a day talkin' 'bout your ol' baby daddy," he says with a snide grin. I can see the alter ego sparking up; here we go.

"Uh, whatever that means, I guess." I brush it off, not entertaining his stupidity.

"Well, I'm tellin' ya right now my child ain't gonna have nothin' to do with Hunter Biden and that fuckin' mess." The anger in his voice starts boiling over.

"Okay." I'm in no mood to argue.

"I'm gonna raise my child on my own, and I'll make sure you ain't around it."

I laugh. "Then you better kill me, because you do realize no judge in any of the states will take a child from a mother's arms unless they can claim she is unfit. I may not be a lot of things, but I'm a damn good mother and you know that."

"Yeah, but the court's gonna think otherwise once you get pulled over and they get evidence of your fingerprints on a cocaine bag, then you're sufferin' possession charges," he explains as if he makes sense.

"What the hell are you talking about? You won't find a cocaine bag with my fingerprints on it I can assure you."

"There will be," he says, acting like he's fixing to one-up me, "I got your fingerprints. Me and Dad got 'em and we're gonna put 'em on a cocaine bag in your car. Then when you have that baby, those possession charges are gonna make ya an unfit mother and I'll be the only parent." His chest pokes out with pride, oblivious to the idiot he actually is.

"Ohh, is that right? How did you capture my prints?"

"What do you mean? Don't worry 'bout it. I got it," he says, a hint of confusion showing, but still not realizing the stupidity that consumes him.

"Oh, so you have a dust print lifter and know how to lift prints?" I nearly laugh in his face.

"A what?" He's confused.

"I went to CSI school, dumbass. I know how to lift and transfer prints. You obviously don't. Get the fuck out of my house and don't ever threaten me again."

When he's gone, I slam the door and flop onto the couch. My stomach has been cramping the last couple of days. I assume it is the anxiety leading up to the deposition, but I'm wrong.

Later that night, just two days before I'm due to testify in Little Rock, I wake up in a cold sweat, sharp pains piercing my abdomen. Something isn't right. As I get out of bed, I feel it. I'm bleeding.

I bled when I was pregnant with Navy, but there were never any cramps. Lying on towels in the bathroom or sitting on the toilet until my legs go to sleep, I somehow make it through the night, then Dr. Chang's office tells me in the morning what I expect to hear. Take it easy, rest, no stress. I'm having a miscarriage and it will pass on its own. It's too early for them to do anything, but if the blood loss becomes too severe, go to the ER.

The bleeding doesn't get too bad, but the contraction-like cramps continue. And through the pain I still have to be a mom. I'm up making Navy breakfast with the little energy I have. The deposition is tomorrow, and Navy is expected to be with my mom for the day. What isn't expected is having to pass a baby in the midst of all the other stress I'm carrying. But I manage to hold it together.

After telling Brie everything, she's in the car and headed my way, only stopping to get some women's diapers at Walmart. Miscarrying a baby isn't very peaceful, but I'm able get as much rest as possible before the deposition, while Brie takes care of Navy.

The next morning finds me too soon, and as I pull into my attorney's parking lot, I feel like I'm heading into an interrogation. Sitting in my white Tahoe, I scan for media from under my Bvlgari sunglasses. No one is supposed to know, but I've heard that before. I know one thing though, I will not show any signs of being shaken, scared, or intimidated.

Clint meets me at the elevator. "Hey, so come on up, I'd like to talk to you in my office before we begin."

"Okay, should I be nervous, Clint?" I ask as the familiar anxiety creeps in.

"You're not the one being investigated," he says as the elevator dings. "You just have to answer questions."

My crème stilettos click on the hallway floor.

"Okay," he says when we get behind closed doors. "Don't be intimidated. There are a few federal agents in there too."

"Do you know who my child's father is?" I blurt, caught off guard. "I'm not intimidated, I don't want to do this."

"I understand. Answer honestly, and it's okay to say you don't recall if you don't remember things. Just don't lie. And only answer the questions they ask. Be brief. Do not give more information than what is asked. I think that's our prep. You ready?"

My mental preparation fades when I see the people seated at the round hardwood table. Men in ties shake my hand, and all I focus on is the one claiming to be an IRS agent.

As I fix my conservative silk top and black pencil skirt and set my Louis Vuitton on the table, a small, attractive lady with dark hair down to her shoulders stands to shake my hand. I don't know who she is, but I can tell she is in charge. She introduces herself as the district attorney, and seems nice, but as soon as she speaks, she's all business.

"Now Ms. Roberts, we have some questions for you, but I want to make you very aware that it is a felony to lie to any federal officer, and the consequences for that are very real."

At first, I wonder if I am the one under investigation, but then the questions shift to the paternity suit and Hunter's character. I want to tell them he's a great guy, he's kind, humble, charming, intelligent, generous, the list goes on; but based on the facts of the paternity suit, the abandonment during the pregnancy, and his lack of acknowledgment of our child, they have a different perception. To be honest, I don't know what the investigation is truly about. I've stopped watching the news because it gives me anxiety and breaks my heart to see Navy be excluded from the first family, so I don't know how I can help them, or Hunter. But the questions go on and on. At times, I don't know if the pain in my stomach is from the miscarriage, or just nerves.

"You did great," Clint reassures me as we step in his office. "How do you feel?"

A lot of things come to mind, but I shrug and just say, "Drained." As I smooth my pencil skirt, I'm reminded of what's underneath.

"Okay, they will let me know if further questions are needed, so I will keep you updated."

I walk back down the long hallway, ready to get home to my child. Someday, if Hunter decides to step up and be a present father to our daughter, I never want her to have to visit him in a prison. I'd never intentionally try to put him away, nor do I feel I have the information they're looking for. Between the weight of that, the emotional trauma, and the contractions tightening my stomach, I just want to leave this day behind me.

One thing about trauma is that your brain pushes a lot of information to the back, and you don't remember things, especially when it comes to paperwork and business. So I don't recall a lot of things. I don't forget people, like Hunter might, but some details slip.

I've heard about a treatment called brainspotting that's used to retrain your brain. I hadn't exactly returned from war with PTSD, but going through such a dark time during pregnancy, mixed with the public attention and extreme interest in my daughter, along with life's current events, I consider myself needing help with trauma.

Brainspotting is a form of hypnosis where you focus your eyes on a tiny ball at the end of a stick while a therapist moves it around. Certain emotions are supposed to arise and allow your brain to compartmentalize the right emotions with the right memories.

"Have you heard of the fight-or-flight instinct?" the woman asks, as my palms start sweating and my eyes try to close.

"Sure, when you're in danger your body has to make a quick decision about whether to run away or stand your ground and fight back."

"That's right. I'm not real clear on how to get through to you. It seems your fight-or-flight is very strong and appears to be in the 'on' position. I'm not sure if we can help."

That's reassuring. My baby mama drama has traumatized me to the point that my brain can't turn off. My instincts override everything else. And it's about to get worse.

In an attempt to distract myself from the chaos of the last few days, I invite Brie for a girls' night. After wrangling Navy off to bed, I pour a glass of wine for me and Brie, and we pass the night laughing and telling old stories.

The next morning I'm jolted from a very nice dream featuring me, Johnny Depp, and a deserted island, when Brie violently shakes my shoulder.

"What the hell?" I exclaim, as Johnny fades and the alarm in Brie's eyes registers.

"The doors," she gasps breathlessly. "They were open all night!"

"Brie, you were dreaming. ADT would have gone nuts if anybody tried coming in."

"No! Lunden, they're wide open, get up!"

The Colt 1911 from the bedside table feels heavy in my hand as I walk out of the bedroom. Feeling the cool morning breeze on my legs, I take in the sight. Every door in the house—front, side, and back—stands wide open.

Frantically I look around to see if anything or anyone is not where it should be, thankful Navy slept in my bed last night. Rushing back into the living room, my eyes spot a hunk of metal lying on the floor. It's the deadbolt and all its screws, taken smoothly out of the door.

Every single chair at the breakfast table has been moved back about ten feet. The bar chairs are all turned around, and little lines on the floor mark their nocturnal adventures. And large boot prints are scattered across dark wooden floors.

After securing the house the way Dad always taught me, I whip out my phone and open the ADT app. My jaw hits the floor when every bit of video from the last twenty-four hours is missing.

As we try to get our blood pressure under control, we replay the night before in our minds. Everything is crystal clear up until the wine. We both can hold our liquor, so why did we pass out and not hear anything. We're both very light sleepers. Slowly our eyes meet and in unison we exclaim, "Were we drugged?"

In July 2022, British tabloids release text messages between me and Hunter that they've found on his laptop. The US edition of *The Sun* ran the headline "Hunter Biden's baby mama sent him message begging him to see their love child—before being removed from his payroll."

Brock sees the texts and in his paranoia, he explodes, "You cheated on me with Hunter!"

"Brock, those texts are from September of 2018. I didn't even meet you until November." But he can't get that to make sense in the delusional realms he's created.

The next day he messages me saying he's going to take out a restraining order against me, despite him being the one to constantly reach out. After I told him about the miscarriage, his harassment just spiraled. Baffled, I bring Clint up to speed.

"I don't get it, Clint. He didn't used to be like this."

"Well, Lunden, that would be drugs. Let me see if I can do any good here. Send me his cell number."

Ten minutes later he forwards me a message. "Mr. Stanford," he calls Brock, "this is Lunden's attorney, Clint Lancaster. My client wants nothing more to do with you. Consider this your warning. If you reach out to her again, we will file a restraining order and I will ask local authorities to search your vehicle, house, and property for methamphetamines, and any other drugs you might possess. Unlike your many conspiracy theories, I am very real."

Brock doesn't take it well, resorting to parking his truck in my driveway at all hours of the night, revving his loud diesel engine, throwing beer cans at my house, and speeding off as Navy wakes up crying. It's months of terror and nightmares, but slowly, over time, it lessens enough that my life almost seems normal.

It's a beautiful fall day when I put on my python cowboy boots and take my younger cousins to a Morgan Wallen concert in Little Rock. We're having a good time, enjoying the music when my phone rings. It's Brock's Aunt Paulette. I've blocked him on my phone, but I'm his family's go-to when he's out of hand. Ignoring the call, I hope it's a butt dial. But she immediately calls again.

"Lunden, are you at the concert with Brock?" I can hear the desperation in her voice.

"What? No," I say, heading straight for the lobby so I can hear her better.

"Something bad has happened," she says. "He's apparently gotten kicked out of the concert and some people jumped him or something. I think he's in bad shape."

"What the hell? He's at this concert? Let me see what I can find out." I go to the area where they take people who get kicked out of the concert and see Brock through a glass door. He's planking on the sidewalk with his nose to the concrete. As I open the door, a security guard stops me. "If you go out, you can't come back in."

"Screw it," I shoot back, desperate to check if he's okay.

Grabbing his shoulder, I pull him back to see his face. He drops to one side, definitely alive, but he's crying. I can't make out what he's saying, other than "I promise I didn't do anything."

As Paulette shouts from the speaker phone that his little cousin should be with him, I decide to call him instead to get more insight on what is going on.

"Are you with him?" his nephew yells when he answers. "Are you with that stupid motherfucker?"

"Dalton, what's going on?"

"Ask him," he shouts.

"Brock, you have to tell me what happened. I'm here to help." I let Dalton linger on the phone, hoping someone will tell me what is going on.

"Okay," Brock sobs, "but you're not gonna believe it . . . I didn't do nothin'. I got here late and when I got to my seat this security guard comes up and says, 'Are you Brock Stanford?' And when I said, 'Yeah,' he said, 'This is for Hunter Biden.' Then he threw me down and they started kickin' me." He sobs into his hands.

My jaw has fallen open when I hear Dalton scream from the phone's speaker, "Oh my God! You don't believe that, Lunden! He's a fucking liar!"

Taking Dalton off speaker, I stand and take a few steps back. Brock's delusions are at an all-time high.

"So, when we got to our seats, a lady informed us we were in the wrong ones and ours were just a couple over," Dalton says "Brock was so drunk he threw a beer in her face, so security threw him out! He's out of his damn mind. He drank a whole thirty pack on the way to the arena, then stopped and chugged a little bottle of whiskey in the parking lot. And that's only what I've seen him drink in the past couple hours. He was shit-faced before I even got to him to leave for the concert!"

"I'll take him to Paulette's house. It's not far from here. I can't just leave him out here like this, please let me know when you make it home." I can't imagine taking my underage cousins to a concert just for them to have to take care of me.

"You should leave his ass," Dalton yells before hanging up the phone, but I have my cousins meet me outside and haul his muscular deadweight to the car.

"What happened?" They're shocked by the state Brock is in.

"Hunter tried to kill me," he tells them in his whining drawl. "You don't believe me, do you?" He tries to make out my face through his drunken haze, but I'm too busy watching my cousins try to contain their laughter from the insanity. "This ain't the first assassination attempt he's put on me! And you're too dumb to see it happenin' right in front of you! He's corrupt, and he is tryin' to kill me!"

"Brock, I've had it! Shut up," I yell, dropping his arm from my shoulder and facing him. "Do you realize what you're saying? I would believe a grizzly bear waltzed inside the arena and drug you out before I'd believe the first son of the United States put a hit on you at a sold-out Morgan Wallen concert, then failed! You're fucking crazy! You need to shut the hell up before you end up under the damn Pentagon and labeled a damn terrorist!"

Anger turns to sadness as he hears me taking Hunter's side again. But at this point, let's call a spade a spade.

Brock cries from the third row of the Tahoe, and my cousins think I'm crazy for giving him a ride, but find his insanity pure entertainment, possibly better than the show Morgan Wallen was putting on.

Before we pull into his aunt's neighborhood, a phone call pops up on my CarPlay. It's Brock's dad. I answer for everyone to hear.

"Lunden," he says.

"Yes, sir?"

"You got my boy?"

"I do."

"I want you to take him to the worst neighborhood in Little Rock and drop his ungrateful ass off on a damn corner." I can hear the anger in his voice.

"You know I can't do that," I respond.

"I know, but hell, that's what he deserves."

Brock never says a word, he just sobs.

At Paulette's, he storms into the house, probably headed to the refrigerator in hopes of another beverage. Paulette meets me on the front porch.

"Did he tell you what happened?" I ask.

She nods. "You think it's true?"

"Hell no," I laugh. "It isn't true! Nobody in their right damn mind would believe that."

"Now Lunden, he's told me he has bags of letters from Hunter that prove every attempt to kill him . . . he even told me about the man that lives in your attic that Hunter has there to watch over y'all."

"What?" Just when I thought it couldn't get any crazier.

How did it come to this? If there had still been a glimmer of hope that I could save Brock from what he is battling, this night proves to me I can't. I warned him about the chaos in my life, and the paternity suit didn't cause his addictions; he's responsible for them. I didn't ruin a good man. These choices are his.

It takes a lot of healing and reflecting to really own the fact that it was never me, but something Hunter told me one time helps. "This is my addiction, Lunden. It's not yours or anyone else's. I own this." Back when he said it, I thought maybe he was owning it in a way to flaunt it somehow, but I realize over time that he owned it because he wasn't blaming anyone else for it. That's the difference in someone's character. Brock blames me for what he does, while Hunter took accountability for his addiction, even in the midst of it.

Within an hour of the car ride home, Paulette calls. "Hey, Brock is calling cab companies, saying he has to get back to Batesville. He's saying some things that scare me. If he leaves here, you don't need to be at your house tonight, or alone."

At bedtime, I barricade myself in my room, thankful Navy is at Pappy and Yaya's for the night, and sleep with a two-toned Glock under my pillow, a Sig Sauer under the nightstand, and a shotgun behind the head-board. I jam Guard Dog sticks (the things that are like putting a chairback under your doorknob) on every door, and set booby traps at every entry. It's not just Brock, it's the media, election crazies, political operatives. I can never deal with just one thing at a time. I want to hear any intruders before they can make it to me.

Filing a police report is the reasonable thing to do. Hell, at this point even my neighbors talk about putting up gates to our community, and it's humiliating because I know why. They've all witnessed Brock's actions outside my home. But I can only imagine the headlines about the president's granddaughter being in danger, and the thought of that makes me sick to my stomach. I keep hoping it will just go away.

Two months pass with barely any contact. Then as my luck has it, at 4:00 a.m., Brock pounds on the door. It's Christmas morning, and I bolt out of bed, seeing the neighbors' lights flicking on through a window. I crack the door, backstopping it with my foot, to try to quiet him down. He barges through my foot stop, babbling about needing to see my phone. I feel like pulling my hair out. There is no reasoning with crazy.

Somehow managing to force him out, I spend a sweet Christmas with Navy. She is three, and loving that Santa brought everything she asked for, including a French Bulldog named Kobe. However, that evening, Brock shows up at the door again.

"Brock," Navy cries, as she sees him through the glass. He's drenched in sweat, but in his sane mind.

"I promise I'm sober, I haven't done anything since this morning," he tells me, looking sick. I open the door and offer him a seat on my sofa, while telling Navy it was time to go pick up toys and start getting ready for bed. Once she walks around the corner, Brock confesses that for months he's been drinking alcohol and mixing it with multiple types of drugs.

I don't know how he isn't dead, but I'm relieved that I'm not losing my mind. Relief is temporary, though, and I fight back the unreasonable yet intense sense of guilt that I'm the one who pushed him off the edge.

After everything is off his chest, Navy comes back into the room wanting to show him all her new toys. In his destroyed, detoxing state, he slides to the floor and picks up a pink crown.

After watching them for a few minutes, I interrupt to tell Navy it's time for bed. She's brokenhearted, not ready to end the play session with Brock.

"Bye, Shark . . . I love you," he says slowly, sadly taking off the jewelry. He gives Navy a kiss on the forehead and walks out of her life.

Chapter 18

The Mole

After Christmas, I foolishly hope the national circus is winding down, thinking maybe I wasn't helpful to the investigation and truly hope whatever the investigation pertains to, Hunter gets off. He is my child's father and I always want the best outcome for him.

But mid-January comes, and I get a call.

"Hey Clint, everything okay?" I've grown accustomed to seeing Clint's name pop up on my phone and knowing it will be followed by legal dramedy.

"Well, the AUSA reached out and wants you to testify to the grand jury."

"What? Why?" I ask, sitting down on my couch as Navy plays, not a care in the world.

"I'm not sure. I think you're probably just a character witness now, because of the acknowledgment of Navy and how the paternity suit was handled. But the AUSA's secretary will reach out and be in touch."

"Great, looking forward to it," I reply with sarcasm.

Laying back on the couch, I watch as Navy calls her LOL dolls "honey" and tells them to be respectful and kind to each other. Through all the chaos and turmoil that surrounds her, Hunter and I really did create something magical. She's perfection, and I'm so thankful God chose me to be her mama, even if it means I have to go through hell for her father.

Just a few days after talking to Clint, my phone rings with an unknown number. When the *Daily Mail* leaked our texts from Hunter's laptop, they failed to redact my cell number from the screenshot. After that, my phone explodes. This time it's not dozens or even hundreds of messages; now we're talking thousands of hate texts from MAGA supporters, and voicemails about how I'm worthless, disgusting, and a whore, and I should suicide myself. Thanks, *Daily Mail*. However, this isn't one of those calls.

"Hi, Ms. Roberts. This is Evelyn Smith with the AUSA's office. How are you today?" she says in a soft voice.

"Hi Ms. Smith, I'm fine," I reply, thinking how much better I'd be if she weren't reaching out.

"Can you hear me?" she asks over the shouts coming from my living room.

I walk around the corner to see Navy riding her Radio Flyer horse, Speckles, belting out "Should've Been a Cowboy" by Toby Keith.

"Yes, sorry. My daughter has a newfound love for horses and Toby Keith," I laugh, proud of my little country girl.

Evelyn laughs, probably wondering what Navy's paternal side would think of that, but she continues. "I'm just calling to let you know the AUSA wants your testimony for the grand jury on the 15th of February. I will send you a list of the information we will need, such as the closest airport and all your personal information to book your flight. We will want you to fly up on the 14th, is that a problem?"

Of course. Most people spend February 14th with their kids or lovers. Nope, I will be in my ex-lover's home state testifying on his dealings. It looks like Hunter is my Valentine and doesn't even know it.

The last time I was in Wilmington I was pregnant with his child and neither of us knew it, I think as I board the plane when the day arrives. I look around at all the people under their COVID-19 masks, and doubt any of them have a federal jury to tend to. How do I always get myself into these situations? I fidget in my seat, thankful for the anxiety meds I took before takeoff.

The woman who checks me in at the Wilmington DoubleTree is very polite, and after telling her my name she gives me a sympathetic smile. I'm sure she knows, and I wonder who else is boarding here with me to testify tomorrow. But I head to my room, hoping not to run into any familiar faces, and when the elevator dings at my floor, I call my sister.

"Well, just wanted to let you know I made it," I say, knowing my family is worried.

"Good. Now go to your room and lock the door," she laughs.

"You know it wouldn't be me if I didn't lock the door then set an entire booby trap up in front of it." We both laugh. "Umm, looks like they have cookies for me."

"What? Like homemade?" she asks. "What kind of package are they in?"

"Just a clear package, looks homemade, but probably store-bought."

"Probably made with rat poison! Do not eat those," she yells.

I laugh at her paranoia, but throw the cookies in the trash, because she has a point and I'm not taking any chances.

After a hot shower, I text my mom to check on Navy. She replies back with several pictures of her having the time of her life at Pappy and Yaya's house.

As the sun fades through the window, my stomach growls, reminding me it's dinnertime. Most people are probably enjoying a romantic date with their significant other about now, but my life and choices make it hard to celebrate this day of love. So I decide to throw on some clothes and feed myself at a popular sports bar a couple of blocks away.

"What can I get you?" the bartender greets me.

"A beer and a menu," I reply with a smile.

He brings me back a Bud Light, even though I'd prefer a Michelob Ultra, and as I skim the menu, there is my child's father's face on the TV screen above the bar.

"Do you mind if we turn on sports or something?" I ask the bartender.

"Absolutely. Any requests?"

"Just anything but this," I say, handing him my empty bottle.

Wilmington is a small town, and while I eat my food, I wonder how many of these people know Hunter. Did they attend school with him, know his family, or maybe they're his cousins? In my hometown, if he went to a restaurant, he'd find at least a few people there, if not all, who know my family.

My thoughts are interrupted by a man's voice. "You running from someone?" he asks with a smile, running his hand through his short red hair.

"I'm sorry?" I say.

"You keep looking behind you like you're running from someone." His pale face looks puzzled, as if he was sure I'd understand the question without an explanation.

"Oh, I don't guess I didn't realize I was doing that."

"Maybe it's a habit," he laughs.

I laugh back. Paranoia has become such a habit that I don't realize it.

Throwing on my pea coat, I head back down the street. This time, whenever I turn around to look behind me, I notice it—eleven times in a ten-minute walk. I set my booby traps with an office chair in front of the doorknob and a towel under the door. Now that I think about it, Hunter always put a towel under the door. I don't know if it was a booby trap, or so people couldn't smell what he was doing on the other side.

Morning comes too soon, but I can't sleep any longer. I dress in an elegant white romper and tan blazer, and style my hair in loose waves.

At the courthouse, security directs me where to go, and a lady greets me outside the room. It's Ms. Evelyn Smith. She's a frail older lady, but very sweet.

"How are you this morning, Ms. Roberts?"

"I'm well, thank you. How are you?"

"Just fine. How's that little girl of yours?" she asks as she walks me to the room where I'll wait until it's my time to testify.

"Oh, she's great. Growing too fast." I show her the photo of Navy I use as my phone's wallpaper.

"Oh my. How beautiful. She favors her father, doesn't she? You know, I actually worked for Beau when he was attorney general. He was a remarkable man," she says with pride.

She opens a door to a small conference room. "I think you're the first one up today. The AUSA will give a small background to the jury on you, then she will come get you when it's your time."

I wait for about thirty minutes, and my nerves start coming back. Is it too late to run? Then the door opens and Ms. Smith points me in the direction of the assistant U.S. attorney I met in Little Rock, Ms. Lesley Wolf.

"Good morning, Ms. Roberts," she says. "Any questions as to the process before we go in?"

"I don't think so," I say, following her down the hall.

She opens a door and invites me in. I had assumed testifying to a jury would be like ten people, but the room is full. It seems like a hundred people sitting, waiting for my testimony. Immediately, I just want this to be over. Making my way to the front of the room, I sit in the seat designated for me, with a microphone just inches from my face.

I hate being the center of attention, and I have everyone's in the room.

"Ms. Roberts, when I ask you these questions, I ask that you speak into the microphone very clearly," Ms. Wolf says from her podium.

I'd rather not, I think to myself. But I nod and say "Yes, ma'am."

The jury sits at desks like a classroom, except larger, all of them with notepads and pencils. I can't make eye contact; I feel so awkward. Everyone's wearing casual clothes, I notice. The only ones dressed up are me and Ms. Wolf, and I maintain eye contact with her.

"Let's get started," she says.

Over the next few hours, I'm questioned every which way and told to speak into the microphone at least a dozen times.

Ms. Wolf lets me go but asks that I wait outside the courtroom in case the jury has any questions. Making friends with the guard, I ask, "Do they normally call people back in?"

"No, they never bother with that," he reassures me.

"My luck, they will."

Moments after that the courtroom door swings open, Ms. Wolf peeks her head out, and tells me to come back in.

I flash a smile at the security guard while he chuckles. "Good luck."

After another hour of questions and more demands that I speak into the mic, she finally lets me go.

"Brie," I say when she picks up my call, "It's over." I push the glass door open, relieved to feel the sun when, ". . . Wait. . . . Brie, the media is here. There's photographers taking pics of me."

"What! Are your sunglasses on?" she snaps.

"Shit, no. Hold on," I say, pulling them from my bag. I should have left my COVID-19 mask on to cover up the rest, but I'm too caught off guard.

"Lunden Roberts?" someone says behind me. I turn see a familiar man, but I can't place his face. Brie lingers on the phone pressed to my ear.

"I'm Ben Ashford with the *Daily Mail*, perhaps you knew I'd be here."

"Excuse me?" I say, shocked.

"I'm sorry. I assumed it was you that told me."

"Me? Told you what? I'm confused." The AUSA had assured me no media would be there.

"I received a message from someone telling me you'd be here. I've received a lot of tips from this number actually, about you. The truth, I'd like to think. Do you have a minute?"

"Umm . . . let me go back inside real quick. I forgot something."

Back in the courthouse, I head to where Ms. Smith met me when I first arrived. She hops up from her desk and runs over to shut another witness's door. I immediately wonder who is on the other side.

Turns out it's WeedSlut420. The media does an article on her in the next few days, and it looks to me like she's shared a ton of pictures with them, and dished dirt on Hunter. I've seen this name before. That's who's been sending me the follow requests on Instagram. Between her story and the media's portrayal, she's painted as the person who somehow saved Hunter. Not his children, not his wife, not even Hunter himself. No, WeedSlut420 saved him and helped him find his love for art. Sure.

But for now, Ms. Smith is asking, "Ms. Roberts, you're back. Everything okay?"

"Uh no, so I just walked outside and noticed a guy taking pictures of me. Then another man walked up saying he's with the *Daily Mail*. I was told there would not be media here." I'm starting to wonder if they set me up, or if my presence here is some hidden agenda.

She runs to look out a big window and down to the street. The *Daily Mail* reporter and the photographer are still standing there.

"Oh my. I'm so sorry. I will contact Ms. Wolf, but I don't know how soon she can handle this. She's already questioning the next person. Let me send her a message!" She grabs her cell and frantically sends a message. Within a couple minutes, the door swings open and an out of breath Attorney Wolf comes hustling out, mask off to the side.

"What is going on?" she says, going straight to the window to see the commotion.

"They approached me when I walked out. They say they're with the *Daily Mail*. I didn't think any news source was supposed to be here." I'm still suspicious that this is a setup.

"No, they're not supposed to be. Who could have told them? I will contact the marshals. They'll get you back to your hotel. I'm so sorry."

But it's too late. The *Daily Mail* already has pictures and posts them to let everyone know I'm testifying to a grand jury about Hunter's affairs.

I walk with the marshals back to my hotel, looking over my shoulder every second. In the lobby, I get my phone out to text Brie. With my head still down, I press the elevator button, and the familiar voice comes back.

"Can you spare a few minutes to talk?" It's Ben, again. He's sitting in the chairs beside the elevator.

"How did you know where to find me?"

"Well, the trick is," he says in his British accent, "we called this morning to the nearby hotels asking to be transferred to your room. When we called here, they transferred us to a room, so we knew where you were."

"Clever." But I won't talk to any journalists.

I've made that mistake before. A *New York Post* journalist texted me one day asking why I felt Hunter would be indicted. I texted back letting him know I never said I thought Hunter would be indicted—my attorney did, unbeknownst to me, and he has a right to his own opinions. I also let it be known that despite what they think, I have never opined on Hunter's financial affairs to anyone, nor anticipated doing so. I was solely focused on the well-being of our child and asked for privacy. That same day, Jack Morphet from the *New York Post* wrote an article with the headline, "Lunden Roberts finally breaks silence on Hunter Biden." Who knew one little text would break the internet? I don't trust journalists.

"Please," Ben says, his British accent making it hard to turn him down. The *Daily Mail* knew what they were doing when they hired him. "You don't have to say anything. However, if you had no clue I'd be here today, then I think you might want to hear what I know. There must be a mole near you."

"A mole?"

"Please have a seat."

Taking a seat in a wingback chair, I'm curious as to what the hell he thinks he knows. Turns out he knows more than I thought most did. I listen, careful not to confirm or deny anything.

He tells me stories of me and Hunter that I had never even told my friends. Not only does the mole spike my interest, but I also wonder why Ben's never released all this information.

"Well, I did release the article that you meeting Hunter at a strip club and being a one-night stand could be a red herring," Ben says, "because we could confirm that you actually worked at Rosemont Seneca as his assistant and were on payroll there."

"Oh, that was you? How'd you find that out?"

"The mole told me. They told me that they hated the way the media treated you. I was told what a great mom you are and how you actually did love Hunter, and how fiercely you protect him from afar. It's admirable. But when the mole let it slip that you actually worked as his executive assistant and knew Hallie too, I took my anonymous tip to someone who could prove and fact-check that. They did. So I wrote the story."

"Interesting. Can you give me the phone number of this mole?"

"Well, no, it's anonymous. Plus it seems to be a burner phone. It was so close to the truth I thought it was you. I will tell you this, whoever it is loathes Hunter, but respects how much you don't."

I'm intrigued. It's definitely someone close to me, however, some stories he knows I've never told anyone about. The only other person who would know them would be Hunter, if he recalled. And we all know no one loathes Hunter like Hunter does.

On my way back to Arkansas, two thoughts keep running through my head. First, I can't wait to see my little girl. Second, could Hunter be the mole?

Chapter 19

Slashed Tires, Cut Wires

Putting the Delaware depositions behind me lowers my stress level a little bit, but the chaos demon is still holding court in the circus of my mind.

The week before Easter, my cleaning lady lets herself into my house and finds me on the floor in the dark, completely cried out. "Oh honey," she gasps, "something just told me to stop by and check on you. You're going to lose your mind trying to understand insanity. This is not your fault."

Christmas didn't change anything. Brock is back to harassing us, and I plead with her, "If I'm a good person, how could I come into someone's life who is good and turn him into a monster?"

"You can't take that on yourself," she says, helping me to a chair. "Those are his choices, not yours."

She's right. I may have brought my chaos with me into Brock's life, but I warned him, and he still chose to get in the ring. So I make a decision.

On Easter Sunday I tell Mom and Dad that I'm taking Navy on her first road trip. We need to get away, and what better place to go than my second home, D.C.? They're worried for our safety there. Little do they know how much safer we'll be than when we're at home. They know about the concert chaos, and a few other details, but they don't know Brock regularly throws beer cans at the house, beats on the front door, or drives by revving his diesel engine. If Dad knew, MMA fighter or not, Brock wouldn't stand a chance.

Before rolling out, I do as much work at the gun shop as I can so that things don't bog down on my end while I'm gone. Dad can tell I'm in a place where if I stay, I'm not going to be much good anyway.

After a two-day drive we find ourselves at a little cottage on the Chesapeake Bay, about forty-five minutes from D.C. Kelsey meets me there. As the sun and breeze hit my skin, I watch my daughter dance around with a dandelion in the backyard. "Mama, I love it here," she shouts. For the first time in a long time, I'm in my happy place.

Peyton visits with her two daughters, close in age to Navy. For a few days I get a glimpse of what my life could become—the best parts of my old friends and old life coming together with my new one, without any of the bad from either. I don't know how I feel about taking Navy near my old haunts, but it's rewarding to see how far I've come. Here, away from all the turmoil of the demons, I'm starting to feel proud of who I am becoming.

In Arlington one day, we run into Brad Sanders, the father of one of Maisy Biden's classmates. He's a member of a club for successful black men that Hunter claimed he wanted to join. Over lunch he is astonished by how much Navy reminds him of Maisy. He even calls her Maisy's name by mistake.

Diane comes to stay a couple nights as well. As Navy's fairy godmother, she brings her plenty of treats, and even though I'm far from Arkansas, this feels like home.

Diane and I take Navy into D.C. itself on a beautiful spring day. Parking in the city, we stroll through the National Mall to see the monuments. I want her to see it all, but a part of me dreads it. I decide to stop at the White House. Once that one is out of the way, I might actually be able to enjoy showing her the other sights.

Holding my breath, I approach the gates, fearing Navy will ask what purpose this building serves, or worse, that she would realize who might be inside and ask if she could visit her grandpa. She's only three, but even the small chance of that happening leaves a pit in my stomach.

Like every other American, I grab my phone to capture a picture of my child in front of our nation's historic home. The emerald green grass and bright blue sky frame the big white building, as Navy presses her face close to peer through the bars. This would have to be the first time in U.S. history a granddaughter of the first family isn't allowed inside those gates. The sight is etched into my brain forever.

Diane grabs Navy's hand to continue our walk while I tread behind lightly, focusing on breathing and swallowing the lump in my throat that feels more like a boulder. On the other side of the street, Navy spots the one thing she loves more than anything, the thing she tries to sneak at least eight times a day—ice cream. She gets that obsessive love from her father and his father. We sit on a bench and enjoy the views of the U.S. monuments, while a little girl licks away, having no clue what's around her.

Navy enjoys the people-watching and all the big monuments as we walk along the mall. Then the unexpected happens. She may take after her father in a lot of ways, but deep-down Navy is an Arkansas girl like her mama, and sometimes that wild country girl comes out. Before I know what's happening, Diane is laughing. "Oh my goodness, if only these people knew who her grandfather was!"

I turn to see Navy wading in the reflection pool in the middle of the nation's capital as if it's a bayou back home in Arkansas. Her cute satin bell bottoms are drenched from the knees down as she yells, "Hey Mama, they have gators in here?"

Diane and I join the many others around us laughing and taking pictures. Her grandfather might be the man who sits behind a desk and makes decisions for our country as the leader of the free world, but right now her other grandfather, Pappy, is showing in her through and through. A sense of pride swells in me.

We spend four weeks exploring the east coast, going to the Eastern Shore, and even to Assateague Island where the wild horses roam. As we near the end of the trip I ask, "Navy what was your favorite place?"

"Umm . . . I like D.C.," she says. And there it is, her mama coming through in her again.

"You did?" I ask with excitement. "Why D.C.?"

"Because of the free ice cream," she shouts without hesitation. And there's her daddy, coming through in her too.

With all the excitement and beautiful architecture the illustrious city has to offer, the "free" ice cream is her favorite. It's a trip she may be too young to remember, but it's one I will never forget—spending time with my favorite human in my favorite place.

Nearly four years earlier, when everything was so dark, I started praying in a way I never had before just to survive. The relationship God brought me into then has carried forward, and I can see how the entire time He was leading me and preparing me to be Navy's mother.

On the drive home, I compare my life in D.C. to the time I just spent there with my daughter, and I realize just how much more it means to me now. The parties, connections, and Hunter were all intoxicating, and at the time, the richest life I thought possible. But as Navy and I cross the Tennessee-Arkansas state line, I realize that it was an illusion. Real riches could never be found living the life I had chosen. What looked glamourous was all so fleeting. One big life challenge, and it vanished before my eyes like a breath on a mirror. Now I have the truest riches life has to offer—riches that make everything else I've ever experienced pale in comparison. And those riches are sitting in the car seat behind me as we drive west into the sunset.

I probably would have stayed longer if Navy wasn't starting T-ball and I wasn't the coach. But after the first practice, she asks to stay the night at Pappy and Yaya's house to swim in the pool.

Brie is on a cleanse this month so I can't drink alcohol, but we have a kid-free night and head out to the country club for a nice dinner. It's really a bar that's barely disguised as a country club, because in a dry county like ours, alcohol can only be served at a private club.

"Shit," I hear Brie say from her side of the booth where she can see the bar. "Don't look now, but Brock is here."

I try to act as casual as she is. "Um okay . . . are you sure?"

"I don't think he knows we're here. Maybe he won't notice us," she laughs. This is a go-to place in my hometown, but it's not big.

"Okay, well, we'll just keep our distance. I don't think he would ever do anything in public, right?" I ask needing reassurance.

A few people stop by our table, and then Brie looks me straight in the eye and says, "Brock definitely spotted you. I saw his face change when he looked over here, then he just grabbed some girl to dance."

I laugh with her. Great, so he wants me to see him, obviously moving into my sights. But we focus on our food and not the fool on the dance floor.

We are deep in conversation when we hear a loud thwack! Apparently, Brock didn't like being ignored. While passing the table next to ours, he smashed his hand down as hard as he could and kept going, slamming the door as he walked outside.

"What the hell," Brie laughs at his foolishness.

"How embarrassing."

Within seconds, "No Caller ID" pops up on my phone as it rings. Then again. And again . . . and again. Sixty-some times he calls, demanding my attention.

A friend of my cousins named Ricardo walks by. It's been a long time since I've seen him, and he sits down to chat. Suddenly, the door to the club nearly flies off its hinges. A rain-soaked man stands in the doorway, silhouetted by a crazy well-timed lightning bolt. As the flash subsides, I catch the look in his eyes—it's one I'd feared many nights. Brock's back.

He stomps up to our booth.

"Where the fuck is my daughter, you fuckin' bitch! And who the fuck are you?" he yells, bumping up to Ricardo who's sitting clueless in the booth and now quite scared. A few nearby cowboys intervene and push Brock back. A barrel-chested beast of a man stands directly in front of our booth. "I've heard of this guy and what he's doing. He ain't getting past me," he says. But it doesn't quiet down Brock's yells.

"I'm gonna get Navy," he shouts. "You can't do this, you bitch, I'm comin'!" He screams until my cowboy boot–wearing guardian angels finally push him out the door and into the parking lot.

The country club is the quietest I've ever heard, and all eyes are on our booth. If I didn't already have social anxiety from the media and who my child's father is, then I do now.

"Oh my God," Brie says as she finally turns her head from the door to me.

"We've got to go," I say, mortified.

A security guard approaches our table. "Ma'am, I'm gonna ask that y'all don't leave until he is good and gone. We are making him leave now."

"Thank you! I'm so sorry this is happening. Please let me know, and we'll leave so y'all can get some peace."

Two hours and another thirty-something "No Caller ID" calls later, we pay our ticket and finally get the all clear.

"Sorry ma'am, he came back three more times. One time he parked down the road and snuck through the woods trying to get back in."

It's not your normal moms' night out, and Brie and I get back to the house exhausted. We wash off the cigarette smoke from the club and throw on some PJs, heading for the couch to watch *Soul Surfer*. Maybe a sweet movie will wash the earlier part of the night off our minds.

As soon as we plop down on the couch, Brie shoots right back up, terror spreading across her face. "Oh my God. He's calling me," she gasps. She doesn't answer, so he sends creepy text messages, telling her he's the Joker, and he's coming for his Harley Quinn. He says he's coming to the house and has no intention of leaving without me and Navy.

Delusionally, he accuses us of having men in the house and promises he's going to literally scalp them. And in between texting pictures of the Joker, he writes that he's on his way to pick up an MMA friend, and they're coming to "take our souls."

I'm always the calm friend in the chaos, or at least I am on the outside. So while Brie freaks out, I grab my phone and dial 911. The cops show up and read the messages. They tell me they can patrol the area, but there's only so much they can do unless I file a report.

"I can't," I say. "Y'all are local PD. Hell, you and I went to high school together," I tell the taller officer. "I'm sure you know who my child's grandfather is. I can't file a police report about someone being a threat to the president's grandchild. The media will destroy me and him."

"We understand, but you need to consider it. Until you've made your mind up, we'll try to keep a unit in the area to look out for his vehicle."

Back inside, fight-or-flight kicks in. I've been a hunter my whole life, and Dad has taught me how to stalk prey. Now I'm the one being preyed on, but no matter how good the hunter is, he can't kill what he can't see.

"Okay, turn off all the lights inside and turn on all the outside lights," I say. "We want it to be pitch dark in here so he can't see us, and bright as day outside so we can see him. There's plenty of guns and ammo in my room. If he wants to show up acting crazy, we will put an end to this."

"Call your dad," Brie screams as she flips every light switch she can find.

"Hell no, if he knew what's going on he'd spend the rest of his life behind bars," I shout as I turn a dead bolt.

Barricaded in my room, we sit on the bed in pitch dark and absolute silence. Minutes pass with no calls from "No Caller ID," and no messages from him to Brie. Our heads rest against the headboard and Brie's foot nervously taps the blanket over and over, as I drift off into my own thoughts. This has to be what men in the army feel like keeping watch, knowing an attack is coming.

Suddenly, we both jolt upright. BANG, BANG, BANG. Each time his fist smashes against the front door, the house shakes.

"Get behind the bed," I whisper to Brie, pushing her off the side with urgency. I jump down and lie in sniper position, stomach on the floor, gun in hands. I stare across the floor from under my bedroom door as far as I can see. His shadow casts into the living room, amid the lights from the porch.

"He's here," Brie whispers to the cop she's just gotten on the phone.

Then suddenly a huge bang, louder than any of the others rolls across the entire house and the light grows brighter under the door. Did he just knock the front door down? Is that the porch light shining through?

"I think he's in the house. Stay down," I whisper.

My hands shake, ready to defend myself, but hesitant to pull the trigger on someone I once cared about.

"AHAHAHAHAHAHAHAHAHAHAHAHAHA," we hear from outside the bedroom window. He isn't inside, thank God. Only now he knows we are in the bedroom, and he's laughing like the Joker outside.

Suddenly the room fills with blue lights coming in from the window. "Do you have him?" I yell, frantically throwing open the front door.

"We didn't see him."

"He literally just screamed like the Joker in this exact driveway y'all just pulled into," I say as my confusion and fear combine. A police officer jumps in his car to go search, but it's too late.

An eerie feeling creeps over me as I circle the house back to the driveway.

"He's still here. He's around here somewhere. I can feel it," I say, looking at the large fist-shaped dents his hands had left in the front door.

Then Brie's phone buzzes. "I know the cops are here," the message reads.

"Lunden, I'm sorry, but you've got to file a report . . ." one of the officers pleads.

"Uh ma'am, you might wanna take a look at this," another officer says, shining his flashlight in the front yard. Tire tracks. It hits me. It was dark in the house, so he had his MMA friend pull the vehicle into the front yard and shine the lights through the windows. That's why it got so bright.

My mind slips into a daze as people talk around me. What would have happened if he had gotten inside? Somebody wouldn't have made it out alive. Would I have hesitated to shoot and ended up literally scalped, or would I have pulled the trigger and lived the rest of my life knowing that I shot a man I truly loved despite his massive faults.

"Ma'am, you have twenty-four hours. If you want, you can rest on it and file the report tomorrow. But you need to seriously consider it."

I can't think straight, but I know one thing for sure. It's time to get Dad involved. Hopefully I can keep him out of prison.

"We'll patrol the area. We're also gonna search for his vehicles and possibly pay a home visit. I'm sorry this is happening," he says, as the rest of his team heads back to their vehicles.

Brie and I try to wrap our minds around what we've just been through, but it's not until the next morning that reality slaps us in the face. Walking outside to go get breakfast, the daylight makes the damage more visible.

"What the hell!" Brie shouts, examining her new 4Runner. Brock slashed her tires. I hate that my chaos has become hers.

"Did you check yours?" she asks.

I scan my Tahoe and spot a fist-sized dent in the door and half of the door handle missing. But what stands out most is which door he did it to—the door with Navy's car seat on the other side. My heart lurches.

Picking up the phone, I finally call Dad. He's there in what seems like seconds. Inspecting me and then the cars, his eyes stop on something. "What happened to the security system?"

ADT had been sketchy a lot, randomly disconnecting from the Wi-Fi in the middle of the night, or shutting down while I was away from home, then coming back online when I pulled into the driveway. So I had stopped relying on the security system, but Brock didn't know that. I follow Dad's gaze. The wires to my system hang there from the house, cut clean through. While Brie and I were waiting at the club the night before, Brock had cut the wires. It was a premeditated crime by a madman.

"I'm filing a report," I say, finally at the very end of my rope. The demons of drugs, paranoia, and chaos had dug their claws into Brock, and they were doing everything they could to come for me.

After the police report, I file for a protective order, and true to the nature of living in a small town, someone at the courthouse leaks the information to the press. Immediately the story is splattered across the news.

The *Daily Mail* runs a piece titled "Mother of Hunter Biden's lovechild—the only presidential grandchild with no Secret Service detail—files for protective order against ex-fiancé claiming he bombarded her with threats and cut wires of her home security camera."

A few days later it gets back to me that someone has shown Joe the media coverage. I understand that his look went blank, then shifted to disappointment as he stood for a moment looking at the story. Then walked out the door of the Oval Office, sadness written all over his face.

Chapter 20

Who's Your Daddy?

After filling out paperwork with the police, I step out on the back porch and give Clint a call, telling him I've finally pulled the trigger.

"You're doing the right thing," Clint reassures me. "The media will probably get ahold of it, but at this point, it's what you need to do."

"I just don't want to wreck his life. I feel like I've done enough to contribute to that."

"No, he did that when he chose drinking and drugs."

"He also claims he is a prophet sent from God. He told me in one of his drunken stupors that him and Navy would go see Jesus."

"Well, that sounds like meth. You're doing the right thing, Lunden. Go through with it. I'll handle whatever you need me to. Being honest, the best thing you could've done would've been to leave the door unlocked and blast his ass across the street as soon as he stepped in your house," he says.

"I don't think I could've pulled the trigger . . . I just . . . I don't think I could've done it."

"Well, I can guarantee if you wouldn't have, Navy would've woken up this morning without a mother. In that state, he wouldn't have hesitated. You have to protect yourself, and her at all costs."

"Do you think Hunter can use this against me in any way?"

"I don't think he would. If anything, it falls back on them for not protecting the grandchild of the president like they should be doing."

Clint is right. It's time to do it. I have to protect my daughter and myself, and at this point that's what it comes down to. I never thought he would hurt us, but honestly, that night could have turned for the worst if he had entered my home.

I didn't realize the effect the harassment was having on me emotionally and mentally. I had grown accustomed to living in fear. And I damn sure didn't realize the effect it was having on my daughter watching that fear in me. Even though she is so little, her mind comprehends the fear and anxiety around her and absorbs it as well.

One evening I'm sitting on the back porch with Seva. Our little girls are playing in the yard as a truck drives by. Not just your everyday, ordinary truck, but a diesel, the same kind of truck that Brock would drive past my house revving his engine. Suddenly Navy starts screaming and shaking. I run to her trying to console her, but she starts projectile vomiting. The anxiety and fear are too much. Knowing what caused it, I feel like I failed her. Tears stream down my face as I hold her. If I hadn't dragged out the legal action thinking I was protecting her from the media, it wouldn't have had this impact on her.

Brock disappears from our lives after the judge orders a no-contact order for us to abide by. It's not long until Navy tries to gain some form of understanding from it all. For the longest time, Brock has been the only man around in her life, other than my dad, her Pappy. Although he was a bloody nightmare at times, he stepped in and stepped up for her and was always good to her. He was the father figure she had grown to love from the time she was just a few months old.

Once Brock is out of our lives for good, she deserves the truth. She sees her friends and cousins with their moms and dads and begins to question when Brock will be back. It breaks my heart more than anything to break hers. Someone once told me that children are resilient. I'd rather she grow up knowing the truth than living a lie and having her world come crashing down when I finally decide to break the truth to her.

I tuck Navy in for bed one night with our usual routine. She gives her kisses and hugs, grabs her favorite stuffy, Slothy, and nestles in, ready to say our prayers. But before the prayer can start, she quizzes me.

"Mama, when is my daddy coming back?" she asks.

"Well, baby, I know Brock has been very good to you, but sometimes we make mistakes. If we don't learn from our mistakes and change our behavior, then those mistakes become choices. Brock isn't making the best choices. My priority in life is you. I'm your mama before anything else . . ."

"Is Brock a bad guy, Mama?"

"Right now he isn't the best guy, sis. And I won't tolerate that around you. He needs help."

"Can we help him?"

"He needs the kind of help we can't offer. I know he stepped in and was so good to you for so long. I know how much you love him and how much he loves you, but we have to love Brock from a distance." The hurt on her face makes my stomach turn, and I suddenly feel a lump in my throat.

"Can we pray for him?" She never ceases to amaze me. She is the epitome of love.

"Absolutely. I pray for him every night. He could use the prayers."

"Who is gonna be my daddy, Mama?" Those words echo through my mind and crash into me like a tsunami. The question was an inevitable ticking time bomb.

"Well sis, everyone has a mama and a daddy. Even though, Brock has filled this void, he isn't your daddy."

"Do you know my daddy?" She doesn't know just yet how a child is conceived, and the stork story is fine for now.

"I do. His name is Hunter. And he's the reason you have such beautiful eyes." The curiosity in her big blue eyes gleams up at me while she holds onto Slothy, hurt suddenly replaced with hope.

"He is? Why don't I see him?" she asks.

"Well, your daddy is a very busy man. Plus he lives really far away, which makes it very hard to visit. Everyone has a daddy, but sometimes daddies aren't always present in our lives." Telling her that makes me want to drive to California or D.C., wherever Hunter is, and kick him in the nuts. His absence is something he should be held accountable for and answer to, but here I am dealing with it.

"Do you have a picture of him?" She sits up in bed, eager to learn about this man who she just learned is her daddy.

"Um, I do . . ." I grab my phone, searching for a picture on my camera roll. The silence is loud. I can feel my heart beating through my fingers as I click on the same picture I showed Brock before our first date. The picture I planned to put in her baby book in the father section.

She stares at the phone screen and the picture of Hunter. His white-collared shirt under his black blazer is striking, along with his smile. He looks happy. I want her to see the best version of her daddy, to know that version before the media tries to tell her otherwise, exposing any of his mistakes and faults.

A smile creeps across her face.

"That's my dad?"

"It is."

"How far away is he?"

"Well sis, he lives in California, or on the East Coast, both of those places are really far away. But ya know what? He loves you no matter how far away he is."

"He loves me?"

"Well of course he does. He wishes more than anything he could be here, but sometimes life doesn't play out the way we plan. He's a really, really busy man. Remember the stories about the queens and kings? Well in our country we don't have a king or queen, we have a president. Remember when I took you to vote and you cheered for 'Let's Joe, baby'?"

"Yes," she nods.

"Well, that's your grandfather. Your daddy is his son. They're both very important people, and sometimes those people have to help others before they can help themselves." Those words seem to echo in the room as she takes her time, staring at the picture of her father and soaking it all in.

Then, looking up at me she asks, "Can I hear him talk? What does he sound like?"

I think about giving her the same clipped Northeast imitation Kelsey and I do when we talk about Hunter. But I know now isn't the time.

This is the first time Navy will hear her father's voice or see a video of him, so two things come to mind. I show her the video of Hunter giving the eulogy at this brother, Beau's funeral. His love for his family is clear. Watching intently, she never takes her eyes off the screen. The second thing that comes to mind is when he was chairman of the World Food Program that won a Nobel Peace Prize. I pull up a video of him discussing it, after explaining to her the importance of the program and just how amazing a Nobel Peace Prize is. That is the light I want her to view her father in.

"Oh! That's it! He is out helping all the people in the world. Then he can see me. And that's okay, because those people need him more than me right now. Someday I'll see him, right? I'm proud of him." Her little voice is filled with pride as she hands me my phone back and nestles her head into the pillow, holding Slothy extra tight.

". . . Someday . . ." I say, holding back the tears I can feel welling up.

"Can you show me how far away they are?"

The only example I feel I can show is a map, so I pull up a Google map of the United States. Pointing out where Arkansas is on the map, I show her how far it is to California and D.C. "Here we are, and these two places are where your daddy spends his time."

"Oh, that's far away. I see why my daddy can't see me," she says.

I have nothing to say.

"Mama, our prayers?"

"Yes, you're right. Enough for tonight, let's say our prayers and go to bed."

"As I lay me down to sleep, I pray the Lord my soul to keep. May angels watch me through the night and wake me in the morning's light. Dear Lord, tonight I pray for Brock. I hope he's safe. And tonight I want to pray for my dad. I hope he loves me like I love him. And someday I'll see him. Amen."

The lump in my throat bursts as tears slowly roll down my cheeks. I'm thankful the darkness in the room covers my moment of weakness. Kissing her on the forehead, I think about how she absolutely amazes me. I don't know how I ever got so lucky for God to choose me as her mama.

"You are so loved, sis," I say. "I love you so much."

"I love you too, Mama."

I walk out of the room, collapse on the couch and can't stop the tears. My heart aches for a little girl who deserves the world and is treated as if she isn't good enough for her paternal side. A little girl who from this day forward prays for her daddy every night and asks about him over and over again. A little girl who will get rejected publicly by her own family for some time. My little girl. Then anger floods me. How could he do this to her?

Everything changes after my conversation with Navy. She wants to know more and more about her dad, wondering more and more about what traits of his will come out in her over the years. I always hoped she would get the good ones—his kindness, charm, desire to help others, and suppressed thoughts about the bad ones.

I never want her to go down the same road he did. She is so much of him. Her ice cream-loving, "honey"-calling, funny-walking self is truly his mini me. But I never want her to be in the state I saw him in so many times before. The demon of addiction is real, and it's had its claws in Hunter for so long. I don't want it to get its claws in Navy. That's my worst fear. If she gets anything from me, I hope it's the ability to keep anything from taking hold. But I pray she never chooses that road.

With Joe being president, and the alleged laptop shenanigans, Hunter and his dad start showing up on TV more and more. At first it's fun pointing them out to Navy, and she delights in seeing them. But the TV appearances don't last very long because of the constant criticism they're getting from the news outlets, and more than a little is aimed at Hunter himself. I don't allow Navy to hear those things or be exposed to them.

The airtime has an unexpected side effect too. Navy begins to point out whenever she sees Hunter or Joe on TV. And like so many other things, like slurping, walking around barefoot, or showering, pointing out that your grandpa is the leader of the free world is better done in private, or with specific people. Navy, however, enjoys pointing out Joe anytime and anywhere, which leads to some pretty strange looks and hushed conversations in nail salons, doctors' offices, and car mechanics' waiting rooms.

Then one day she points out Joe and Hunter on the news and asks who the kids are that are with them in the picture. Looking up, I see a picture from Joe's inauguration. He's celebrating with all of his grandchildren, minus one.

"Well, those are actually your cousins, and siblings."

"Siblings?" I see the confusion creep onto her face.

"Well yeah, that little boy is your brother. His name is Beau . . . and those three girls are your sisters, Naomi, Finnegan, and Maisy. Those are other children your daddy has."

I can see the wheels turning. Each turn of the wheels in her head shoots a searing pain through my emotions.

"Oh! Look at my brother! He is so cute," she squeals. "Mama, can you find me more pictures so I can see them?"

"Uh, sure." Now the wheels in my head are turning. How do I find personable photos of her own siblings? Searching Instagram, I find Naomi and scroll through her pictures.

"This is your big sister, Naomi."

"Whoa, she's pretty, Mama."

"Yes, she is." I keep scrolling, fortunate enough to find pictures of her other siblings that Naomi posted. "And here is Finnegan."

"Finnegan," she laughs. "That sounds like Cinnamon!"

"It kind of does. And here is Beau."

"He's so cute, Mama. Look at him! My little brother is cute," she says with pride.

On TikTok, Maisy once showed up on my FOR YOU page, so I search her.

"And this is your other big sister, Maisy."

"She's silly." Navy laughs as she watches Maisy doing an infamous TikTok dance. She scrolls down the page to find a TikTok of Maisy with her sisters and little brother Beau.

"Do they live together?" she asks.

"I'm not sure, sis."

"Well, they get to see each other . . . and they get to see my dad, too?"

"Well, yeah, they do."

"Why can they see him, and I don't?" The hurt in her eyes ricochets back into mine.

"They live a lot closer to him than you do, sis," I say, looking for any excuse.

The wheels keep turning but nothing comes from her mouth. I hate this.

"Do they live with their mamas too?"

"Probably. I don't have all those answers for you. I'm not sure."

"One day, I'll see them, won't I?" The hint of hope reappears on her face as she asks.

"I'm sure you will someday," I say, just to get the grin to appear on her face.

"They can't come here?" she asks.

"Well, sis, it's like I said, they live close to where your dad is, so that's pretty far away from here."

That last one turns the wheel just a little too far, and I feel my emotional joints rip from their sockets.

Not long after, Navy and I are in a store and she spots a jigsaw puzzle with a familiar shape—the United States. She goes nuts wanting it, and I know why; she associates that shape with her dad.

That night, as I cook dinner in the kitchen, the quiet startles me. I poke my head in her room because things are never this quiet. The sight I see isn't one for this weak mama heart. There she sits on her floor, legs folded under her, one palm on the ground peering at a completed jigsaw map of the United States, and quietly counting. I take a step closer without her noticing. She is pointing at each state in between Arkansas and D.C. and counting them aloud to herself. She is trying to see just how far away her dad really is.

That scene plays itself out every night afterward. Every night in her room she gets the box out, empties it onto the floor, and puts it all together, counting states between her and her father. A nightly routine she does on her very own.

That thought itself puts a sting through my chest I wouldn't wish on anyone.

Chapter 21

Call Me Trump

It's been five months since the night Brock tried to break in. A hearing is finally held for the no-contact order, but the chaos isn't through just yet.

As I sit on the stand answering questions about why I filed this order, a man enters the courtroom from a door behind me and takes a seat. As I turn my head to look, Brock's attorney yells, "Excuse me, Ms. Roberts, I'm talking to you!" He's been rude and arrogant the entire time, belittling me at every turn.

"Objection, Your Honor." Clint explodes from his chair. "My client has the right to turn and see who is walking up on her!"

As Clint and I exit into a hallway shortly after for a five-minute recess, the man who entered follows us. Up close, I realize who he is: our county clerk and a family friend.

"Uh, Lunden," he says, "I know now probably isn't the time, but I wanted to let you know Hunter just filed a suit against you."

"What?" I say, stunned.

"For what?" Clint asks.

"To lower his child support," the clerk replies, seemingly remorseful that he has to deliver the news. "I'm sorry to bother you, but I figured while you're already here, I'd just give the papers to you."

"Yes, I'll take them," Clint says.

As the man walks off, Clint turns to me. "Okay, one guy at a time. Let me handle this one we are currently against, then I'll take the paperwork and handle Hunter, too."

I take a deep breath and shake my head. I can't seem to catch a break.

"Next time you decide to date someone, your father and I both have to approve," Clint insists as he leads me back into the courtroom. "If nothing else, it will let me get to know the guy before we face off in court."

At this point all we can do is laugh. I don't have the best track record with relationships, and it's cost me more in attorney fees than most people's annual salary. But we're granted a no-contact order against Brock, and breaking it will lead to jail time. I'm happy with that.

After granting the order, the judge looks to me from his stand. "Ms. Roberts, I truly wish you the best . . . and the best for that little girl of yours. I think about you often and pray for the very best for you two girls." His kind words aren't forgotten.

The order finally ends things with Brock for good. He moves off, and life starts getting back to normal, or at least as normal as it can.

Hunter's lawsuit for child support reduction claims his income has changed since that night in 2020 when we settled. Arkansas laws have changed as well. There is now a child support cap, and Hunter has been paying about 15 times that amount.

Thus far, he's been doing his part financially, and I've done my part as a mother. But months prior to getting his motion for child support reduction, I asked Clint to reach out to Hunter's attorney. I needed to get Navy's birth certificate for health insurance purposes and noticed Hunter was not listed. After paternity had been established, I thought his name was to be put on there.

"Uh, yeah, I think so. Let me check with Brent Langdon," Clint says.

"Okay, well also," I say, "if we have to edit her birth certificate, does he want to change her last name? Maybe give him that option so he sees the door is open for him to be a father to her." Maybe it could be a step to mend this divide between them. Maybe he thinks I don't want him in her life and that's why he hasn't reached out to be present in her life. Does he think I'm ashamed of her paternal side and don't want her to have anything to do with them, let alone his last name?

"Sure, I'll get to Brent, and I'll let you know," he says.

Having had absolutely no communication with Hunter over the years, the intrusive thoughts are endless. I don't know what he thinks, how he feels, or what he wants with his daughter. But I do know my priority is a little girl who wonders why her dad never visits, so I will do anything to help her have that relationship she wholeheartedly craves.

I never think too far into the political warfare Clint engages in with Hunter and his people. Clint has a job to do and I think he does a damn good job. He does and says certain things to put pressure on Hunter to do the right thing. Sometimes his words can be a little too strong, and his angles can seem a little off. However, Clint isn't going to let me get run over, and that's why I always put my faith in him.

A few days later, as I'm cooking breakfast, Clint gets back to me with a dreaded response.

"So, I contacted Brent and he talked with Hunter . . . I'll send you Brent's response, but I don't think they took it the way you wanted them to," he says. Hesitating to continue, he takes a breath. "They now claim you are using Navy as a political pawn and giving her his last name would cause her more embarrassment and emotional strain."

It's a punch in my gut. The burning eggs sizzle on the stove.

"Are you serious?" I manage to say.

"I'm afraid so. They even threatened that if you filed to do the birth certificate, they would file to lower child support. I'm sorry," he says.

I rush off the phone, consumed by their response. It definitely isn't what I expected. If the food burns, I don't care. If the house burns down, I don't care. My zombielike state lasts a few minutes before I start gathering my thoughts.

Emotional strain for Navy to have his last name? Since when does he care about Navy's emotional strain?

When I was pregnant, Hunter claimed he could never have a child on this earth and not be a part of its life, but here he is doing just that. Navy has the same missing-limb feeling he claims he had as a child growing up without his mother, and he's causing that. The thoughts consume me for a few days, finally turning into anger.

Without hesitation I send Clint an email, asking him to forward it on to Hunter and his minions. I feel insulted and I feel the need to let them know just how disgusting their point of view is, but I will go about it the way I know might get to Hunter—straight to the heart.

"The real concern Hunter and his attorney should be contemplating is the negative emotional effect his youngest daughter may have by growing up without her father. No daddy-daughter play dates, car rides, or dances with her father there as her friends have their fathers by their sides. Imagine the 'emotional strain' it could put on her to grow up watching and reading about the ENTIRE paternal side of her family pretending as though she does not exist. Imagine the heart ache she may have from watching and reading about her paternal family being very much involved with every child and grandchild, EXCLUDING HER. Now, if they would stop and think about the effects this could have on someone besides themselves, we could possibly get somewhere. So please tell them to save their newly found concerns for our child and direct that energy to the real issue at hand. To be clear, I have NOTHING to personally gain from this. As her mother, my sole priority is her wellbeing . . . Since the whole basis of the Biden platform revolves around family, I was hopeful that her taking his last name would show that the door is wide open for them to step up and be present. However, that was my mistake. . . . Might I also remind you I have been very respectful of Navy's father and his entire family, to my own detriment. I have withstood lies and public humiliation to protect them. As Navy's mother and only parent in her life, I solely want what's best for our daughter—more family, more protection, more love, all to which she is entitled. Surely that's not too much to ask."

No response ever came, but now here we are, months later and he's filing a motion anyway. So be it. When Clint calls asking if I want to continue with the birth certificate and last name change, I respond without hesitation, "Sure." At this point, I've spent years thinking he would reach out to be a dad. I've devoted my life to our daughter, and I'm pissed that he acts as if she doesn't exist.

Months of more political warfare from our attorneys, accusations of contempt, and a perpetual sick feeling in the pit of my stomach brings me to May 1 and a hearing at the county courthouse in Batesville.

Judge Meyer remains on the case, and she is not pleased. A few weeks earlier she put the fear of God into Hunter's team, making clear that she didn't care what his preferences were—if he wanted a hearing, then he was going to come to Independence County, Arkansas.

May 1 dawns bright and fair, like most spring mornings in Arkansas, except this one comes with an unfamiliar feeling. One that's difficult to explain. Although I would normally have anxiety through the roof, I feel indifferent as I throw on my navy-blue blazer.

The sky's blue, the air's clear, and I'm not alone. I've made arrangements for Navy during court; however, my mom and dad are off the table. They plan on coming to court, and as I am sticking bobby pins in my half updo hair, my sister and aunt show up to drive me. The media knows my

Tahoe that still has the dents in the door, and being incognito might help limit my availability to them.

Judge Jeffry is a friend of Randi Jo's husband, and has offered to let us use his office to wait until it's time. He says we can come through the back if we want. "Just as a precaution because we know how your anxiety can get with media," Randi says.

The bright sun isn't the only thing that greets me as we walk out my front door. People in my small community clap and chant from their front porches, "Go get 'em, girl!" My heart swells. It's nice to know people have your back.

We drive around the courthouse twice in our incognito charcoal Yukon, looking for the best entrance. Media scans the streets looking for my Tahoe and Hunter's motorcade. He requested to enter through the back door that I used the last time I was here, and cameras are camped out there. We settle on the front entrance where only one cameraman watches, and see the media come running as we slip through the doors.

My sister ushers me into one of the judge's offices. I'm surprised to see more of my family waiting in this room. There sits my mom, my dad, my aunts, and a few family friends. Again, it's nice to know people have your back. They're here for me.

"How you feeling?" Mom asks once I'm done greeting everyone.

"Fine. I'm still waiting for the call saying Hunter isn't coming and everything has been dropped." I laugh. The nice judge who let us use his office gives me a look of dismay.

"He's here," he says.

You could hear a pin drop in the office. However, the words are ringing in my ears.

"He got here a couple days ago. The bomb dogs have been here all week preparing for his arrival."

My poker face stays firm as I listen, then my phone rings.

"Hey Lunden, we are about ten minutes out," Clint says. "Just checking in on you!"

"Well, I've been doing fine, but now I have anxiety. They said he's here. I just figured he would get out of it. Now I don't know how I feel." My chest is tight.

"It's going to be fine. I'll see you in the courtroom in about twenty minutes!"

As I hang up the phone, I overhear the judge talking with my family, "Yeah, he flew into Newport with his detail . . ."

Newport, Arkansas, isn't famous for much. Locally we know it as rows of farmland, a great place to duck hunt, and George's Liquor Store. When you live in a dry county like we do, the nearest liquor store, and the town hosting it, acquire a special place in your heart. But one thing Newport isn't known for is airports.

The thought of him landing on a crop duster enters my mind and I have to laugh.

"Apparently, they called right before they landed and let the tower know that they were landing and needed rental cars and other accommodations for a Secret Service detail, and the air traffic controller said, 'Now listen, we only got one rig here and it's my GMC Terrain. Y'all are welcome to it, but if you're gonna need some cars, y'all gotta go to Searcy for that.' So they all piled into the Terrain and took off to Searcy."

The room erupts with laughter. I chuckle thinking about Hunter's reaction. He must have been mortified.

I take a moment to myself as my family hugs me, heading off to get their seats in the courtroom closest to my bench, when something catches my eye. The door has a small transom window above it with a view to a part of the staircase leading into the courtroom.

People have passed the window several times, but this one grabs my attention. I catch a glimpse of Hunter's head as he turns toward the window, speaking with his attorney while they walk up the stairs.

The black hole that opens in my stomach sucks everything toward itself—my guts, my heart, my breath. My chest caves in as I realize I'm having a full-blown panic attack, paralyzed by what I've seen. I honestly never thought he would show, even after the Newport story. This isn't his normal move. Is it real?

Trying to catch my breath and gather myself before having to walk up into the courtroom, I'm thankful my family has already left the room and don't witness this moment of weakness.

A familiar voice breaks through my panic. "Hey Lunden, you all right?" Clint asks as he, Jennifer, and a man I don't know walk in the room.

"Yes," I say, eyeing the stranger.

"This is Garret Ziegler, he's the witness I was telling you about that can help on your case," Clint says as the man next to him reaches out to shake my hand.

"Nice to meet you," he says.

"Hi, nice to meet you as well," I say, shaking his hand.

"You ready?" Clint asks.

"I am," I say with the small amount of composure I can muster.

Jennifer shoots me a quick smile and pats my shoulder as I follow Clint out the door and up the stairs to face the inevitable.

At the top of the stairs, I take a deep breath and Clint opens the doors to the courtroom. Both sides have people in every row. It's easy to decipher which bench is mine. My family sits in the front row on the right side, while Hunter's front row is filled with Secret Service agents followed by rows of media taking notes. My heart breaks for him, again. I can't imagine coming to something like this without the support of my family.

The media eyes me as I walk past, following Clint to the front.

Hunter's attorneys turn to meet us as we cross through the gate into the gallery. Clint turns in front of their bench to shake hands in turn, first

Brent, then Abbe Lowell, the world-renowned political problem fixer, then Hunter. I get swept along in the line behind Clint, with Jennifer behind me. The whole handshake line is bad, but it's infinitely worse once we hit the end. I am so distracted that I don't realize Clint has just shaken Hunter's hand and moved forward, which makes it my turn. And there I stand face-to-face with . . . trauma.

Our eyes lock. The same blue eyes I see in my daughter. The last time I looked into these eyes I was pregnant, carrying his child, and everything that's happened since fills my mind like flashbacks.

He looks at me with sympathy, nods his head, and purses his lips as his arm lingers in the air from his handshake with Clint. In this moment, I really don't know if he wants a handshake, a hug, or what. The one thing I'm sure we have in common is just wanting to get through this.

I manage a blink or two before stepping aside, thankful Jennifer is behind me to fill my space. She watches everything like a hawk, and is twice as deadly, so she steps forward shaking his hand and taking the attention off my awkwardness.

I mumble a half-realized thank-you and spend every other ounce of effort trying to keep all of the trauma I've bottled up for years from spilling out into the courtroom all at once.

At our table, Clint and Jennifer prepare, and I keep picturing the Hunter I just saw. I don't look at him. It's too much. I had barely looked at him directly, however what I saw is burned into my brain.

Gone is the thick curly hair I once knew. He's lost much of it, and what's left doesn't seem curly. It's gelled and sort of slicked back. He used to polish his appearance, gladly talking about his spray tans and facials at the Four Seasons, but now he doesn't seem polished at all. The Hunter I had just seen looked much less like the Hunter I once knew than I expected. He seemed defeated, as if he had been through so much and life kept knocking him down. His eyes were still kind and sincere, but the man who was once full of life seems like a shell with the life sucked out of him. I'm in no way a fan of Donald Trump, but in that Independence County courtroom after seeing a Hunter I hardly recognize, I find myself thinking over and over, "Where's Hunter? Where's Hunter? Call me Trump, but . . . where's Hunter?"

Our attorneys rant at each other as the judge mediates. Despite Hunter bringing in the "bigwigs" from the big city, my attorney never lets their intimidation tactics stop him from being the pit bull he is. Chaos and arguments fill the courtroom, but I keep looking at the table in front of me, counting every imperfection in the wooden bench, but one figure remains in my mind, the sight of Hunter. My eyes are on the wooden bench, but I might as well be staring at him.

I pity him. There is so much sympathy I have toward him even though I should hate him. He's missed out on so much. Our beautiful daughter just miles away, the one he's never met, and he doesn't even want to visit her? He can't put aside whatever he has against me to say, "Look, while I'm in town is there a chance I could meet my daughter?" Because, honestly, I would never have kept that from him, or Navy.

As soon as the hearing is dismissed, I stand. "I'll meet y'all in that office," I tell Clint. I hightail it straight out the doors to the room I sat in before, waiting for my family and attorneys, and avoiding media questions. However, as I wait, a small feeling of regret rises in me. Should I have just gone over and talked to Hunter like the long-lost friends we are? Or to save myself embarrassment, should I have played the same game he was playing and acted like I didn't know him either?

As my family enters the office, I find we're all feeling the same thing—empathy for Hunter.

"When he walked in, he wouldn't look at us," my sister tells me. "But if he would have, I probably would've stood and given him a hug."

Even my parents and aunts, who have strongly hated his choice to be absent in Navy's life and the way he has publicly left our daughter unacknowledged, have changed their outlooks after seeing him.

I've always said he could walk into a room of conservatives and when he leaves they might not have the same political views, but they will like Hunter. It's his charm. But this time he doesn't even have to use his silver tongue to win my family over.

On the ride home, I watch out the window as people crowd the downtown area near the courthouse just for a glimpse of the president's son. It's not every day that Batesville, Arkansas, gets to see a motorcade from a First Family member, even though a First Grandchild resides here.

"I really think if you would've went and talked to him, this all would be over," my sister tells me as we pull in my driveway, seeming to read my mind.

"It's weird you say that. It's all I can think about . . ." I say. "I should have spoken to him."

The familiar courthouse flashes on the TV as I walk into my home and see Navy running around with her cousin. I hurry to turn the TV off. One thing I can't let happen is for Navy to run by and see the familiar downtown area and images of her dad leaving it. Never could I let her know her father, who she asks to meet, was just miles away and didn't see her.

That night as I tuck her into bed, her curious eyes look at me as I straighten the blanket.

"Hey Mama," she asks as she pulls Slothy to her. "Did you get to see my daddy today?" She fidgets with the pink heart Slothy holds in his hands.

"What? Why do you ask that?" My mind races. Normally I have some sort of heads up and know how to handle things, but I don't think I'm ready for this.

"Because I heard someone say you went to court, and when you go to court I know it's because of my daddy," she says.

She's a sponge, and as much as I try to protect her from hearing things, it's like a fenced pasture, and a cow always gets through.

"Uh, well sis, just because I go to court doesn't mean I see your daddy."

"Did you see him?" she asks again, demanding an answer and not allowing me to dance around it. She is the fiercest four-year-old I know.

Hesitation sets in and I don't know what to do or what to say. Respectful. Kind. *And honest.* I vowed to never lie to her and tell her the truth even when the truth hurts. But this stings worse than I imagined. How do I tell her the father she believes hasn't seen her due to distance passed by the house she was in today to meet me in court? I can't.

So, like the good mother I am, I lie. "No, I didn't see him," I say.

"Because he lives far away, right? And it would take years for him to get here?" she asks, seeming to perk up a little.

"Yep. Now get some sleep," I say, kissing her on the head. Her little heart has too much on it to even touch on the fact that it just takes hours, not years, so I let that lie.

As I leave the room and walk around the corner I rest my weight on the wall, listening to her say her prayers. And this night my prayer is clear to me.

"Dear Lord, if you can hear me, please give my baby what she whole-heartedly yearns for. I pray that Hunter steps up for her. She needs him. . . . also, please forgive me for lying."

Chapter 22

A Pardon and $250K

Hunter surprised me in May, and I decide to return the favor at his June deposition in Little Rock. I'm not required to be there, but I have a couple things on my agenda. It's the Friday before Father's Day, so I tell Navy we can send her father a gift, since that holiday makes her wonder where her father is, and she usually celebrates her Pappy because her father is a stranger.

Her excitement at finding she can send him something is worth it all. She starts by drawing him a picture for us to frame for him. I write on the paper, "Me and my dad as potato heads." Those are Navy's words, *and* the seemingly orange potatoes favor a former orangish president. I don't want him to get the wrong idea. She also makes him a bracelet with beads of her favorite color, purple, and one blue bead because she has guessed that it is his favorite. Then I print off some of my favorite pictures of her over the last four years. I gather it all in a box and decide to give it to him, personally.

The next trick I have up my sleeve is to sit in on the first few questions of his deposition. My attorney can ask Hunter anything he wants under oath. So I give Clint a few questions for Hunter to answer. I want him to look me in the face while Clint asks him if he remembers me and our encounters, the ones he once publicly denied. I want him to answer to his absence in Navy's life. I want to know why he hasn't stepped up and been a dad to our little girl. And I want him to have to explain everything to my face. I know he can lie and say whatever to anyone else in my absence, however, Hunter won't lie about the truth to my face, especially under oath.

The drive to Little Rock makes an hour seem like five. Over and over again I rehearse the words I will say to the father of my child. The first words I will speak to him since 2018 when I was carrying his child. The anxiety creeps in like a thief in the night.

Pulling onto the block of the Stephens Building, where the deposition will be held, I feel my nerves rising more as I watch the media on the sidewalk. Driving my mother's Cadillac keeps me incognito until I realize the windows aren't tinted and I pull into the parking garage looking like a fish in a fishbowl as they point.

I roll my window down to get a parking pass from the attendant and see a Secret Service agent standing in the box with him. He looks like he's seen a ghost, and as I'm looking for a parking spot, I'm sure he's paging ahead to let Hunter's team know I'm here.

Grabbing the white box full of pictures and presents from the passenger seat, I take a deep breath, stride in my nude heels through the glass doors with confidence and every ounce of strength within me. I have no other choice. I can't seem weak, and this box is holding everything that could make my walls come crumbling down. It holds my daughter's love for her father.

Clint greets me at the elevator. "So um, Hunter's team is shook," he says with a grin. "They didn't expect you to be here. Neither did he."

"Shit. Do I need to leave?" I say, knowing that if it's the last thing I do, I will give this box to him personally and say what I need to say.

Throughout the years I've given grace to Hunter. Even with his absence and the things he's said, I've instilled in Navy how great he is and how much he loves her. A mother who loves her child will never make that child hate her father. That will be his own doing if she ever does. Excluding her from the inauguration was a gut punch, and so was his reaction to the suggested name change. So, although I'm going in today with a peace offering, he may have a fight on his hands. When it comes to my daughter, there's nothing I won't do. Enough is enough.

I follow Clint to the empty conference room where the cameras and recording devices are all set up for the deposition. My heart is beating through my chest as we cross to the opposite side of the table next to the hot seat where Hunter will be. I follow suit sitting next to Clint, with a firm grip on the box.

There is a computer on the table with a man on it. A Zoom call?

"What's that," I ask Clint, pointing to the computer.

"Garret Ziegler, our witness," he tells me.

I've just started learning about this Ziegler guy. Although Clint says he will help us, from everything I've recently learned during my deposition just days prior, I can't say I'm a fan. At one time he tweeted "Somewhere in the world there is a little girl whose mother is a stripper and father is a crackhead, and her grandfather is the president of the United States." Fuck off, Ziegler.

Jennifer comes and sits on the other side of me. She can sense my nervousness. "You look beautiful," she says, offering a smile.

"Thank you. . . . I'm just ready to get this over with," I mutter.

"Well, you are so strong for doing this. Navy is one lucky girl to have a mama like you, you know that?"

Jennifer always has a way of comforting me. "I may need you to call and remind her of that years from now," I say, laughing. Her plan worked. She got my mind off what was happening until it happened.

Hunter walks through the door in his white button up and jeans, carrying his glasses and a water bottle. From the time he enters the doorframe, his eyes meet one person, me.

"Hey," he says giving me his intense furrowed brow stare. "How are you?"

"Hey, uh I'm good. You?" I ask as I watch him enter the hot seat. His attorneys fill the room and the opposite side of the table.

"Good, good," he says, placing the glasses and water down and folding his hands on the table.

Clint starts the deposition by going off the record, which might seem strange at first, but he does that for me, Navy, and Hunter. As interested in political warfare as he is, and as frustrating as I might find it sometimes, Clint always wants what's best for me and Navy above all else.

Looking at Hunter he begins, "My client is here because she has something to say to you." Clint turns, eyes on me, along with everyone else in the room. I feel Hunter's attorneys glaring at me to see what bullshit I have come up with, while the guy in the hot seat eyes me intently and curiously.

Standing, I hold up the white box, my eyes fixed on Hunter.

"This may mean absolutely nothing to you, Hunter, but it means everything to our daughter, and that is why I'm here today," I say. "There are things in here that she has made for you, and I told her I would get them to you. I've also put some pictures in here from over the past four years of her life. If you would like videos or pictures, or anything else, please let me know and I can send you a USB of her, or whatever works."

Hunter's intense furrowed brows start to loosen. His face goes from defensive to sincere, almost like he's wondering why I am being nice to him. He's clearly shocked that I would do this, and it finally hits me—he thinks I hate him.

"Uh, great. Thank you so much," he says as he stands to take the box containing the essence of the child he's never met. He doesn't open it or peek inside. Instead, he finds a little shelf behind him to put it on. Out of sight, out of mind, I think. His attention is back on Clint.

Honestly, I thought he would at least look inside to see those precious tokens of her love. I don't know how I feel about it. Part of me wants to stand back up and say, "Uh, open the box, asshole," but he's back to business.

Clint's voice jars me out of the dark thoughts as he starts the formal part of the deposition. Suddenly I'm hearing words like "Ukraine" and "China," and I'm wondering what this has to do with my little girl. The words "political warfare" cross through my mind, and I can see the frustration in Hunter's eyes as he mouths to me "toxic litigation" and shakes his head.

I'm sweating bullets, trying to count cars out the window and praying God will just let me leave. It started out with a box full of love and good feelings, and now it's about taxes and foreign affairs.

Jennifer can tell I'm weakening and texts, "Don't break! You being here is great!"

I text back, "I just want to leave."

Getting him riled up wasn't my intention. I came here with a peace offering.

And then, as if hearing my thoughts, Hunter cuts in. Turning from Clint and looking directly at me he asks, "Would you be open to talking to me privately?" I'm not opposed.

"Sometimes the parents can get more progress communicating than us attorneys can," Abbe Lowell jumps in.

I'm here for Navy, and if this can be settled to better her life in any way, that's what I want. Maybe if he had communicated with me throughout the pregnancy, or after I had our child, or after the paternity test confirmation, we wouldn't be here. Nor would "toxic litigation" exist. It could have all been solved with communication, but instead I received avoidance, abandonment, and nothing more.

Hunter and his team leave so my attorneys and I can talk. "Hear him out," they say, "but do not agree to anything without talking to us first." I understand and walk into the hallway where Secret Service agents eye me from every angle. Hunter's attorney points to where Hunter is waiting for me, and I take a deep breath and walk down the hall.

It's a small conference room with briefcases on a table along with a Patagonia backpack. Some things never change.

Hunter is on his feet, coming around the table to . . . hug me. I wasn't prepared for that. Every wall I have comes crashing down as he puts his arms around me, and the tears start to flow. It's the same old Hunter I once knew, the one who wanted to know how I was, and greeted me with a hug. Except for one thing—there's no smell of Tuscan Leather.

"Hunter, I'm so mad at you," I choke out as he pulls back to look at me.

"I know. I'm sorry." His tearstained face is sincere.

Stepping back, he pulls out a chair for me to sit in, then sits down next to me.

"Hunter, I hold so much resentment . . . I . . . Navy . . ." I try to talk, but the tears keep flowing. So much has happened since the last time I saw this man. He's been through a lot. We've been through a lot. And we share a daughter in the center of all of that who craves a relationship with her father.

He puts his arm around me again, trying to comfort me. "Lunden, what was I supposed to do? . . . You know me. I have lived with my own guilt and remorse every single day that little girl has been on this earth without me being a part of her life." His lip quivers, and he wipes a tear from his cheek.

"Then why couldn't you just be there for her? Every night, she prays for you. She puts a puzzle together counting the states between Arkansas and D.C—the distance to get to you. She prays for you all the time. It's not fair."

"I know," he replies, filled with emotion. "This toxic litigation is the exact reason I couldn't step in. Your attorneys want to destroy me. It has to stop."

"Will someone bring me the box Lunden gave me?" Hunter asks his attorneys in the hallway. They scurry off and return, and Hunter sets the white box on the table in front of me.

"Why did you not open it when I gave it to you?" I ask. I think about how much work and excitement Navy put into it, and he disregarded it.

"You think I'm going to let your attorneys see me be emotional or vulnerable?" he asks sincerely. "I was not meaning that to be a jab toward Navy. I didn't want to give them the satisfaction of me being weak."

I nod slowly, considering what he's saying.

"I'll share the moment with you. But I won't do it in a room with people like your attorneys."

He lifts the lid and pulls out a pile of pictures. We find ourselves laughing and crying as he sees Navy and I explain the moments in her life. His favorite is picture of Navy with mud on her face, sunglasses upside down, and a Rolex on her wrist. Another has her in a yellow romper with a Biden pin, and I tell him how she went with me to vote for her grandfather that day. A genuine smile spreads on his face.

Picture after picture he sees of his beautiful daughter, with the bright blue eyes she gets from him, an infectious smile and blond curls, and I see him get emotional. "Honey," he says, truly upset, "the hardest thing for me was when I saw in the news what your ex was doing. I had to calm my nerves or I would have gotten into my car and driven to Arkansas to get Navy. I never had any question that you were a good mother and that she was loved, but when I saw that restraining order and what had been going on around her, it just got to me."

Sadness turns to pride when I tell him how she knows she's a Roberts, but that her dad is a Biden, and she will gladly tell anyone that. But then his lips turn down in a frown and his brows furrow again. "Your dad must hate me," he says.

"Actually, my dad defends you. He says without you he wouldn't have one of his greatest blessings, his granddaughter, and out of all the men I've dated, you're probably his favorite."

"That's because your taste in men is horrible," he says laughing.

"It's because he never met you," I shoot back, and we both laugh harder.

"Well, my family was scared for me to even come here," he confides. "They think you and your family want me dead."

"Oh my God, Hunter. No."

"It's because of the litigation, Lunden. It's been toxic and too political. I couldn't even be the dad I wanted to our daughter because your attorney was too busy trying to send me to prison somehow or another. Where did you even find this Lancaster guy?"

"My attorneys may not like you, but my family and I don't hate you. I've been protecting you for years from afar . . . hell, my dad went on a hunt with Trump Jr. and it caused a family dispute. Dad doesn't see anything as political, and I take everything political personal, because of who Navy is."

His eyes flicker just a little. It's finally dawning on him that there's a big gulf between what he thought reality was and what it actually is. I can tell he's beginning to understand, but he also brings up the child support change throughout the conversation. It's hard to tell if he's dropped all pretense and is just being honest, or if he's playing a longer game and trying to save himself money.

By lunch time I'm drained. Fight-or-flight has set in and I just want to lie down on the floor. I can't form complete sentences, let alone make a decision right now.

"He has his claws sunk right down into you where he wants them," Jennifer warns me when I join them for lunch. "Don't give in."

I can't think and I want to sleep, so Clint comes up with a plan. "How about you call Brie," he suggests. "She's an attorney and I can swear her in as part of your legal counsel."

Brie knows me better than I know myself sometimes. I pick up my iPhone and FaceTime her.

Clint swears her in and catches her up. She talks with me about the decisions I have to make until Clint interrupts, "Uh oh, here comes a not-so-happy Hunter."

Through the glass door I see him, phone in hand, coming straight for us. Attorneys on his heels.

"See this! This is your character witness doing this!" Hunter explodes, holding his phone out where I can read the screen.

Tabloids have leaked that Hunter Biden's baby mama surprised him at deposition. Hunter obviously blames Garrett Ziegler for this.

I don't say anything. Looking back at my phone screen so Brie can see my face, she laughs as she recognizes the "gosh damn its always something" face I give her.

"Let's settle this. Come on," he tells me.

"Hunter, this is Brie," Clint says pointing to the phone on the table. "She's been brought onto Lunden's legal team."

Brie waves from the screen.

"Hi Brie," Hunter says, picking her up and nodding for me to follow.

Back in the small conference room he props Brie up on the table, then pulls our chairs into her view.

When Brie sees the two of us, she starts crying. Hunter and I look at each other, not sure what's so emotional for her. But Brie loves Navy, and has watched her suffer from not having her father in her life. Seeing us sitting beside one another and talking is a turning point.

"Gosh, Hunter," Brie says wiping the tears from her face. "You have no clue how amazing your daughter is. I can't even explain it. And she loves you so, so much."

The words hit Hunter.

"Brie, listen, you don't know me. But I promise, I have regretted every day of my absence in her life," his lip quivers as he starts crying. "I've dealt with it every day and it's . . . it's not been easy."

"So what's stopping you?" I ask.

Looking at me he takes a very Hunter tack and says, "Lunden, we have to come together without this litigation, as parents, for Navy. What if we set up child support for a reasonable amount? What I want to pay is $5,000. Work with me here, please."

"Okay, if that sacrifice is made, what does Navy get in return?" I ask.

"Hunter, in settlement, not everybody leaves with everything they want," Brie butts in. "It sounds like you're getting off pretty easy here and Navy is getting ripped off."

"No, I wasn't done . . . two things I love more than anything—my family and art. Those two things get me through every day. I may not be able to financially give what I have been, but my art sells. She will also get a painting from me every month."

Wait, so now my home will be an art gallery? He sees confusion tinged with suspicion creeping across my face.

"The painting will be picked out by her every month," he explains, knowing I'm still not catching on. "As in, we start to build a relationship through my art . . . what better way to start building a relationship with my daughter? And you can sell it or whatever you want to do with it. But it's a starting point to get to know her and for her to get to know me."

Now it's making sense. He wants to build a relationship with our daughter. The one thing she wants more than anything. No money or artwork can compare to having a father.

"You want to start communicating with Navy and be in her life?" I ask.

"Well, yes! I want that more than anything. This will open the door for that. I can start by Zooming her, then we can do a Zoom call like every week, build a relationship, then move forward. I'll iron things out with my family so they don't think this is some trap with you trying to get me killed, that may take some time . . . but this is as good as I can do right now. It's deal or no deal," he says.

"Okay, let me talk to Clint for a second," I say, stunned. This could be the turning point. I would sacrifice any child support amount for Navy to have that void filled.

"Oh, and Lunden? We need to discuss this last name change," he says. I had forgotten all about it.

"Oh yeah, you're right. What's the deal with that?"

"Living in Arkansas, she benefits more from her Pappy's last name than mine. You know that. For her safety, for her privacy, let's allow her to change it when she's ready. That will be her decision. What do you say?"

"Done. Sounds good to me."

The walk down the hallway feels lighter, but also surreal. Is this really happening?

Falling into a chair, I catch up an eager Clint and Jennifer.

"Let's just go back into deposing him," Jennifer says. "Forget this. He's just playing you." She stands with her folder in her hand, ready to put him back on the hot seat and drill him about foreign business deals. Skepticism creeps into my mind, and I wonder if I am being played once again. But for Navy's sake, I'll take being played as long as she gets a dad.

"We work for you, Lunden," Clint says, reining Jennifer in. "If this is what you want, we will support you, whatever decision you make."

"I know" I say. I had never questioned his loyalty.

"Who do you trust and depend on more than anyone in the world?" Clint asks as he scrolls on his laptop that is filled with Hunter's art, all arranged by size and appraised value. Clint really is a shark.

"My dad," I say without missing a beat.

"Call him. Tell him everything."

A minute later I hear my dad's voice. "Hello."

"Hey Dad, you busy?" I ask

"Nope, what's up?"

I bring him to speed the best I can.

"What does Navy get out of this whole deal?" he asks.

"She gets a dad."

"Well, there ya go. That's somethin' you can't put a price tag on. You know you and her will never need for anything financially, I got y'all, always. Give Navy the dad she rightfully deserves. There is no amount of money you can put on family. Family over everything."

His words are nothing I didn't already know and feel, but they confirm what I know I need to do.

"Thanks, Dad."

"You knew the right thing to do before you even called me. You just needed me to reassure you," he says, laughing. "Go handle it."

I hit the end button and look up at Clint.

"Sounds like we know what we're doing," he says with a grin.

"He is so manipulating you. I hate this for you," Jennifer adds.

"Yeah, maybe, but I can walk out of here with my chin up, knowing I sacrificed a whole lot for Navy, and I have never made one sacrifice for her that I've regretted. This Father's Day, Navy gets to celebrate the promise of the dad she's been asking for. I'll sacrifice everything for Navy to have the one thing she's wanted more than anything in this world and that's him."

"I'll let them know," Clint says, heading for Hunter's attorneys in the hallway. Jennifer and I sit in silence.

"Okay, well, I think that's settled," Clint says when he returns, "but one more thing. Hunter wants to add in that he'll pay her Pappy $250K to shoot any bozo that gets near Navy. And then they'll just pardon him," Clint tells me laughing.

"Oh, if any bozo gets near her, I promise Pappy will need that pardon," I say, smiling.

"You can go home now," Clint finally says, "but first Hunter wants to say goodbye."

In the doorway, Hunter stands with open arms to give me another hug.

"Hey, thank you. I'm glad we are moving forward. Everyone won today," he says.

"Yeah, me too." I smile with all the energy left in me.

The person I care about more than anything in the world won today, and that's all that matters.

A couple days later, on the ride home from church, I see the desperation in my little girl's face.

"Mama, did you send my dad his gift I made him?" she asks.

Today is Father's Day.

"I sure did, sis. And he loved it. Guess what?"

"What?" she asks with hope in her voice.

"Your dad wants to start talking to you and build a relationship. Would you like that?"

"He does! Yes, can we call him right now?" She beams with excitement.

"Well, not right now. But here soon he's gonna start calling you and you can talk to him. Does that make you happy?"

"Oh, Mama! It does make me so happy!" she screeches.

I watch as she looks out the window the whole ride home with a smile on her face.

As days go by waiting for a call, Navy doesn't forget. Occasionally she comes to me. "Mom, can we call my dad today?"

"Not today, sis, but I promise it's coming." I reassure her every time, hopeful Hunter will hold up his end of the deal.

One day when she comes needing the reassurance, she follows with, "Well, can I hear what he sounds like again?"

So I pull up Hunter's eulogy speech at Beau's funeral for her again, and watch as Navy beams with pride. Her little eyes dance while she watches her dad, and in his speech when he says, "I love you, I love you, I love you," her little lips quietly say "I love you" to the man on the screen . . . the man she will soon call "Daddy."

Chapter 23

The Last Person You Would Ever Think

M y Tahoe's wipers willfully glide across the windshield a couple of extra times after I turn off the engine. It's been drizzling most of the day and I've pulled into the garage and turn to help Navy unbuckle from the back seat. A metal tin the size of a man's wallet is in her hand, with the president on it, an American flag, and the last name "BIDEN." She used to keep candy in it, but now it holds her bracelets. Some days she carries it everywhere with her. Other days she keeps it hidden in one of her little ratholes where she hides her money and other important things. She doesn't get that from me.

It's mid-2023, and life feels like maybe it's going to be almost sort of normal if I hold my breath and don't make any sudden moves.

There's a knock at the front door. Joanna, a childhood friend, pops in to catch up. Her boy trouble makes me feel better about my own taste in men.

"Joanna!" Navy shouts, running to jump in her arms.

"I'm just putting the groceries away," I say, as Navy drags her to the living room to play. But minutes later, it's clear neither one of them is having fun.

"Here, Navy, why don't you give me that," Joanna demands, opening the trash can lid. "I'll get you another one."

"What's goin' on?" I ask, seeing sadness drenching Navy's face.

"Did you know she had this?" Joanna asks, holding up the little metal box.

"Yes, she got it when we were in D.C. Give it back to her." My voice is calm, but Joanna can see the rage on my face as she starts to backpedal.

"She doesn't know who it is," she says obliviously. "Navy, do you know who this is?"

"Uh . . . yeah . . . it's um . . . the president," Navy replies hesitantly.

"It's okay, sis," I tell her, standing by her side for strength and comfort. "You have no reason to hold anything back." She should never, ever be ashamed of her grandfather, regardless of other people's political opinions.

She looks up at me, confused as to why Joanna would take her little tin box, then says with a little more confidence, "He's my grandpa."

My blood boils but I keep my calm for Navy's sake. "Go play and I'll start fixin' dinner," I say as Joanna returns the bracelet box into Navy's hand.

"I'm sorry, Navy," Joanna says to her, avoiding eye contact with me.

"You will never do something like that to her again," I say, leveling my gaze at Joanna. "You might have different political views, but in this household, politics are taken personally. That's my daughter's family and you are to respect them when she's around."

"Her father is a piece of shit," she spits out.

"Please enlighten me—how do you know him?" I ask. "Have you met him? Did he give you a reason to hate him? Or are you solely going off what you know through media?"

"I mean . . ." she stammers.

I cut her off before she can dig the hole deeper. "If anybody in this house has a reason to hate Hunter Biden, it's me. I actually *do* know him and have had a personal relationship with him. Navy might hate him some day, but, if so, that'll be on him. How she feels about her dad won't be based on you or your political views. I've put everything he's done to me and her in the past for her sake. Mothers who love their kids will never teach them to hate their father, and I love my kid."

She stands there just staring back at me.

"If you can't accept that, then you should get out," I growl, pointing toward the door. And she does, tail tucked like a dog.

About an hour later, Navy climbs into a stool at the kitchen island as I spoon mac and cheese on her plate. It's just the two of us for dinner, but we're happy with that.

As we carb load on a drizzly evening, she puts on a little bracelet fashion show for me from her Biden tin. I think about how Navy may not have been the savior in Hunter's story, but she has saved me in every way. She's given me a grace I never knew I had, strength beyond what I'd imagined, and a purpose to live for.

Six years ago now, I was painting D.C. red most nights—drinking too much, partying, involved with a man who was addicted to incredibly dangerous substances, thinking solely about myself and truly living only for each day—consequences be damned. I left school and my life was spinning out of control without me even realizing it. All I felt was the high of excitement that left me wanting more.

Then Navy came into my life and suddenly all those things that excited me then but could have killed me later just fell away like a husk falls when the thing growing inside finally matures and comes into its own. Without Navy, I don't know that I ever would have shed that old life and the pain that undoubtedly would have come with it.

Navy saved me, and I'm not the only one.

"Do you like the pink or the green one better, Mama?" I snap back into the present for a quick fashion ruling.

"Definitely the pink. It goes better with your shirt."

"I think so too. Let me show you what it looks like if I put all my bracelets on . . .."

As Navy throws the "less is more" fashion advice to the wind, I think about what else she's changed.

Our family was loyal and tight when I was growing up, but we weren't affectionate or the type to express our love vocally. Mom was always going to be hard, exacting, and sometimes too strict, but a few "I love yous" may have been really good for our relationship. But I can count on one hand the number of times anyone in my family told each other they loved them.

Then, five years ago, this little blonde tornado of confidence, charm, and persuasive ability showed up, bringing one of Hunter's phrases with her from her earliest days, "I love you."

Kelsey, Savanah, and I used to impersonate Hunter in his clipped northeast accent saying, "Honey, I told you that was a bad idea . . . are you mad at me? I love you!" Those words must be in Navy's DNA, because she didn't pick that up from me. Of course, I tell her that I love her, but she never heard me say it to other people. Hunter's mini me, on the other hand, showers people with her charisma, calling them "honey" and telling them she loves them.

She is the only explanation for what has begun to happen in our family, and why my parents now say "I love you" so much. We went from the least openly loving family out there to possibly the most in just a few short years. Navy injected that in us. Her shocking ability to help those around her express love has drawn us closer together and saved us from the knowledge we were loved, but never hearing or saying it.

The fashion show is over, her Barbies are calling her to play, and as I wash slowly hardening elbows off the cheese-coated plates, my mind drifts back to the early thoughts of her saving Hunter.

It seems like not long ago I came to the realization that Navy wouldn't be what saved Hunter. But hope is a funny thing—it can sprout from the most unexpected places and under the most inhospitable conditions.

A month after the child support lawsuit is settled, Hunter rents a $15,800/ per month mansion in Malibu. I gave up $15,000 per month in child support because he said he didn't have the money, and because he said he would try to be a dad to Navy.

There's no price you can put on having a relationship with your father, I keep telling myself as I wait for Hunter to reach out.

"If you don't hear anything within the next couple of weeks," Brie says one day, "why don't you message him and set up a schedule?"

But I've waited for four years already, so waiting another couple of months is nothing. This is something I want him to initiate. I'm not going to pressure him into it.

But a couple of weeks before her birthday he sends a text. "Hey, let's plan a call for the first week of September. I'll send a Zoom link." I'm relieved but cautious, not sure if he'll back out. So I don't tell Navy a thing.

On Friday, September 8, I pick Navy up from school early. My excuse is we are going for lunch and ice cream. Hunter wants to do a call at 2:00 p.m., and at 1:00, after the Zoom link arrives, I finally tell Navy that today is the day she gets to talk with her dad. She's ecstatic, and changes into a top with frilly sleeves, and lets me do her hair, while chatting about all the things she wants to learn about him.

Seconds after setting up the iPad on the kitchen island, I hear a chair scoot back and some gentle clambering. Looking over I see Navy, chin resting on the countertop, staring at the iPad, still as can be.

"Sis, you still have forty-five minutes until your dad calls. You can go play; I promise I won't let you miss it."

"No Mama, I want to sit here and wait. I don't want to miss him."

Weeks ago that would have shot pure pain straight to my heart. But now the emotions are a mix of sadness for what she has been through, hope that things are changing for the better, excitement to see her face when she first sees her dad on the screen, and fear that he won't follow through. He's convinced me before that he would do the right thing, only to pull the rug out from under me. Dear God, do not let him do this to his little girl.

"Navy, do you know what you want to say to him?" I ask her, trying to prep.

"Yep, I want to know what his favorite color is . . . and I want to know when I can see him," she says with confidence.

"Okay sis, you can say or ask him anything you want, or tell him anything you want."

"Mama, I'm nervous." Her little face looks up at me as she fidgets with her hands in the chair, and my heart melts.

"Don't be nervous. He's your dad. There is no way this can go wrong. You can't do anything wrong."

"I just want him to like me."

A shot of pain to my heart.

"Baby, he already loves you! You just be yourself. And ya know what? You'll see he's a pretty cool guy, very easy to get along with."

"Do I call him Dad?"

"You call him whatever you're comfortable with. You can call him Dad or Hunter, and I promise either way will be okay with him."

She nods.

Finally, the ringtone fills the kitchen, and butterflies fill my stomach. Navy's little body stiffens in anticipation as she slowly slides her tiny finger across the screen.

"Hi Navy!" I hear from the speaker.

"Hi Daddy," she says shyly, as the glow of the screen pales compared to the radiance of her growing smile. She chose to call him "Daddy."

Where did that come from? I capture a picture of pure delight as my little girl meets her father for the first time.

"How are you?" Hunter asks, and I peek around to see the same grin on his face.

I could cry, hug her—hell, even hug him. I'm just so happy for her to finally fill a void she had been yearning for, even if it's over the phone. And in that moment I consider what this must be like for him. How it feels to talk for first time to his youngest daughter.

"Navy, I love your pink bow, you look so beautiful," Hunter says, and she smiles. But he doesn't have to take the lead for long. Soon Navy takes over.

"Hey Dad, what's your favorite color?"

"Uh, Blue," he tells her.

"How is my brother Beau?" she asks.

"Well, he's good," he says with a bit of surprise. "He's actually at a thing he goes to for a couple hours a week, kind of like school for you."

"What about Naomi?" His face brightens, realizing she already cares about a family she hasn't even met.

"Uh, well she's good. She just got married."

"And Finnegan?" she asks.

He laughs and tells her how they are looking for a job for Finnegan now that she is out of college.

"And I'll tell you about Maisy, too," he smiles, "since I know where this is going."

After chatting about all her siblings, the question lingers.

"Daddy, when can I see you?"

There are some hard questions Navy will have for Hunter throughout his life. This is one.

"Honey, I promise you, me and your mommy are going to work out the details and get something scheduled as soon as we can, okay? I want to see you so much!"

"Okay," she says with hope.

A blissful forty-five minutes of taking her father all over the house, showing him magic tricks that consist of making something disappear by taking it out of the view of the screen, and making him several ice cream cones of Play-Doh, come to an end and they tell each other goodbye.

Navy looks at me, eyes starting to water.

"Navy! What's wrong baby?" I say as she collapses into tears. "Aren't you happy?"

Between sniffles she manages to say, " I . . . I just . . . I thought it would be longer. I didn't want it to end."

There's the pain again. But hope begins to replace the fear.

Instead of calling just once a month for Navy to pick a painting as the court ordered, Hunter Zooms her weekly. A bond between them starts to form. Navy adores him, and for all his faults, Hunter seems to adore her too. A few phone calls in, he begins telling her how much he loves her before hanging up the phone. Maybe I wasn't lying when I said he had kept her in his heart.

The calls are the highlight of Navy's weeks, and Hunter does a remarkably good job of making them happen, even when his life must feel out of control.

On one Wednesday afternoon her iPad lights up. Navy answers; she's been waiting for her dad. But something is very different this time. Instead of being alone on the screen at his home or in his art studio, Hunter is in an office setting, flanked by his team of attorneys in the background.

Navy's eyes get sort of big and her face looks like a turtle pulling back into its shell. "Uh Daddy, who are those people?" she says, looking at me, then looking back at him.

In his kind voice Hunter replies, "Oh, well uh, honey those are my friends."

I laugh as I walk around to look at the screen. Hunter gets up and leaves the office, phone in hand to find a more private place to have a better conversation with Navy.

It takes her a moment to consider, then in a not-so-quiet child's whisper she says to me, "Uh Mama, is that really who Daddy hangs out with?"

"Yep," I laugh. "Right now he hangs out with them a lot more than he would like to."

It's the day before he's indicted on tax charges, and he's swarmed with legal obligations. But give the devil his due—as busy as he is, Hunter comes through and takes a few minutes out just to see Navy and tell her he loves her. She walks away from the iPad on cloud nine.

I'm thrilled that he made the effort. But not all calls end so happy.

One day they're talking when Navy notices a guitar hanging on the wall in the background of Hunter's art studio.

"Daddy, is that your guitar?" she asks with her usual interest.

"It is honey. I wish I could say I play, but it was actually just a gift. Do you like music?"

"Uh huh, I do."

"What kind of music do you like?" he asks. I'm expecting her to tell him all about her love for Morgan Wallen and the phase of music she's going through, but she surprises me and him with her response.

"I play the piano."

How's that for a curveball? We don't have a piano, and she's never taken a lesson a day in her life.

"You can play the piano? Wow! That's great!"

She beams.

After the call ends, I ask, "Navy, why did you make that up?" I'm ready to remind her that we are always respectful, kind, and honest. Lies aren't taken lightly.

"I just want him to like me so much," she says in earnest.

The pain rips through me again, and I spend the rest of the day telling her just how much she is loved.

Their first calls all happen at the kitchen counter. Navy watches the "Waiting for host to join the meeting" message until Hunter arrives. No matter what bow she has in her hair, he tells her how much he likes it, then she beams and talks away. But pretty soon she wants to show him her favorite things, and is running back and forth from her room to get them.

"Honey," he says one day, "you can take me with you." It's a revelation for Navy that she can bring her dad with her throughout the house.

Once she knows she's free from the counter, she takes him all over. I find them one day talking down under an end table. All I can think about is how much I hope I dusted down there and he isn't having to stare through cobwebs to see her. But she wants to feel like he's there with her, and he's her family. If my parents stopped by when the house wasn't clean, they wouldn't care. And Hunter won't either; he's her dad.

On another call, Navy wants to show Hunter our baby bunnies. Our French Bulldog, Kobe found them abandoned. They were out in the yard, couldn't be older than a few days, and I can't let them suffer. So we've been bottle-feeding two wild rabbits, and they're living in a box in our garage.

I bring in the box as Navy tells her dad about Kobe bringing one up on the porch and laying it by his water bowl, and barking until we got the other one out from under Navy's Barbie RV. Hunter is amazed we were able to keep them alive, since baby bunnies are apparently some of the least likely wild animals to survive if abandoned. They're getting to hopping age, and decide now is a good time to jump out of the box and start hopping around my kitchen. Navy screams and giggles, but not as much as Hunter, and both yell out instructions for me to follow.

"I got this," I insist, as I chase wild rabbits in circles around the island.

Navy is building a relationship with her dad, and that means that he sees the chaos of my life. I know he's got chaos in his life too, but there's nothing quite like the chaos of being a mom, taking care of a little girl, and chasing bunnies around your house.

No family has it all together and we're just one of those families. It's not perfect, but nothing ever is. We don't do it all right, or go by the book on everything, but that's just part of being a family. And that's what Navy needs.

Chapter 24

Out of the Shadows

"Daddy, look what Yaya lets me have at her house," Navy bursts with excitement while showing the man on the iPad screen her hand full of slime. He squints, trying to get a clearer look at what she's holding out to him.

"What? Is that slime? Oh my goodness, be careful with that," Hunter laughs.

"Yes, listen to your dad. Do not get that in your hair," I yell, while we both laugh at the silly face she gives her father, letting it be known that there are no rules at Pappy and Yaya's. It's nothing Hunter doesn't already know.

Times are changing for the better. Navy and her father are building a bond that fills the void that once existed. She's become so comfortable talking to him that most times I have to tell her to calm down and act right. And sometimes he even has to tell her that giving me a hard time just to make him laugh is never okay.

Navy is a lover, that's a given. But there is nothing she loves more than her family. The light in her eyes gets brighter every time her father pops on the screen. And having that happen while we visit her Pappy and Yaya triggers her to be even more alive, having all her worlds come together.

"Did you show your daddy some of your art?" Yaya asks Navy while hiding on the other side of the iPad due to her "bad hair day." Navy has already told her father about Yaya's situation, and of course, he laughs at Navy's need to be "too honest" sometimes.

She hands Navy a small wooden statue painted purple and pink.

Hunter's face lights up. "Oh wow, Navy that is so good! You did that?" he asks.

"I did, Dad! I want to be an artist like you!" This comes as no surprise. She's been telling him that just about every time they talk, and painting, sculptures, and doing any other artsy things she can get her hands on.

"Well, I think that's great," Hunter tells her with a smile the size of Texas across his face.

"Then I'll be busy and have lots of meetings like you, won't I, Dad?" she asks, never missing an opportunity to say the word "dad."

"Honey, I hope you never have to have all the meetings I do." Hunter grins.

A small familiar sting pings through my chest but is immediately lifted. I hate what he's going through and I know it takes a huge toll on him. It would on anyone, and I would have that same empathy for anyone who has fought so hard to live a life in recovery while also having a political target on his back that has to be dealt with every day. But he makes it seem effortless, showing up for Navy and juggling the world around him. His fight and resilience are admirable.

"Howdy! Howdy!" Pappy says as he enters the room, waving at the screen to Hunter.

Hunter waves back. "Hi! How are you?" he asks in his oh-so-Hunter way.

"I'm good! You? Sorry, I didn't mean to interrupt y'all," Pappy says, wrapping Navy in his infamous bear hug.

"I'm well . . . oh, no worries! Glad to hear your voice!"

In a world where everyone would rather see the *New York Times* article "A Tale of Two Families" in which the differences divide, our story rises above. We love Navy, and that love conquers all.

"Daddy, look at my glasses, I'm gonna wear these for the solar eclipse," Navy shouts, holding up a pair of dark lenses.

"Oh, does the eclipse come through that way? That's so neat! You'll have to Zoom me so I can see." He sounds excited too.

Our little part of Arkansas is at nearly the epicenter of the solar eclipse. Media is descending on our town, and this time for something more than my baby mama drama. People are coming from everywhere to witness it. Hotels are sold out and campsites have been booked for months. It's a lot for a state that doesn't have many tourists to now be flooded with millions of people from all over the world.

"Lunden, is that okay? Can we Zoom for the eclipse?" Hunter asks. "Or if nothing else, can you video it so I can look at it with Navy later?"

"Yeah, of course." I've never denied them a time to talk, and I never will. The mere fact that he looks forward to the calls as much as Navy does makes me so happy for the both of them. We have come such a long way, and there is nothing in this world that can stand between where we have been and where we are going.

My mother chops apples and carrots while Navy continues on in conversation with her father. The smile on her face is a mirror of the one on her granddaughter's. It's the same one I feel creeping across my own. This is happiness. This is moving forward.

"We have to feed the horses," Navy bursts out when the chopping is done.

"What do you feed them?" Hunter asks, smiling at her excitement.

"Apples and carrots," Navy tells him, lifting the plate for him to see.

"Which ones do the horses like more? Carrots or apples?" Hunter asks.

"Well, I don't know," Navy says.

"You'll have to ask them," he laughs.

"Daaaadd! Horses don't talk." She rolls her eyes.

We all join in the laughter. Our new normal is one I wouldn't trade for the world.

The hate mail that at one time kept my phone lighting up has slowed to a trickle. In a world full of opinionated people, it's expected. But as the dark shadows in my life begin to lift, light breaks through in my messages too. Women, mothers, especially single mothers doing their best on their own, reach out with their support.

"Those beautiful blue Biden eyes," one says in a social media comment. "You and your beautiful daughter deserve the world!"

Another one comes during a trip to Walmart. "Your sweet family is in my prayers. I actually live in AR and saw you this evening with your daughter. I decided not to speak for the sake of your privacy, but watching you brought tears to my eyes. You're such an amazing person, it's evident, setting such an amazing example for your daughter. She will be a strong brave, fighter like the mama who's raising her."

Sometimes they're messages that stir my heart. "Your public debacle with the father of your child has given me hope. I too have a child out of wedlock. The paternal side doesn't have much to do with her, but watching the strength and courage you've held against the world has been such an inspiration in the weakest times for me."

And other times they're messages that make me cry. "So I know this is random, and I don't follow politics much but somehow I've come across your story and I've been sitting here crying my eyes out. My daughter's father and family have never met her . . . she just turned three and my heart breaks every day thinking about how I'm going to somehow have to have that convo with her. I've spent two years in therapy trying to work through this and have nightmares frequently. Sending you so much love. You are an inspiration to us mamas!"

If I can help anyone in any time of their life with my testimony, then anything I've gone through is worth it. If I can be a voice for the mothers out there who love their children out loud, despite any hardships we may face on the side, then I've added to my purpose. There is always light on the other side of any hardship and being a voice for my child while giving hope to mothers around the world has created the cracks in the shadows where the light pierces through.

On a cool, spring night, walking down the dark drive to check the mail, I feel my phone vibrate from my back pocket. It's a friend from D.C. who I haven't heard from since before Navy was born. Wondering what she could possibly be up to that made her reach after not having talked for years, I slide my finger across the bottom of the screen. "Hello?"

"Hey, Lunden?"

Her voice is hesitant. It's been so long that she's questioning if it's me and my number anymore.

"Yes, how are you?" I ask.

"I'm okay, I guess. I didn't know who to call, but you came to mind."

"What's wrong?" Here it is—the need to help—and I can tell she called me out of desperation.

"I . . . um, found out a few weeks ago that I was pregnant," she says, and I can hear the emotion in her voice.

"Oh! Congratulations!"

"I think I'm going to have an abortion . . ." she tells me, unable to hold back the sobs.

"Oh . . . are you okay?" I ask, unsure exactly what to say.

"I don't know. I think about you and everything you've gone through. I'm not strong like you," she says.

"If I can do it, anyone can. There is absolutely nothing more reward-ing. I won't tell you what you should do; it's your life to live. However, considering you called me lets me know you have a tiny ounce of doubt in you," I say.

"I do." She sobs again.

"Listen, I really think you would be a great mom. If you have a tiny ounce of doubt, you will have a huge load of regret going through with an abortion."

I try to talk to her and let her know she is not alone. So many women have been in that dark place. Pregnancy isn't supposed to be a stage in your life where you feel alone, in fact, it's the only phase of one's life where you're never alone. A tiny human is inside you, growing and learning to love your voice before they're ever able to form one of their own.

Sometimes we become pregnant under not the best circumstances, and it can be hard mentally and emotionally to accept. But the reward that awaits you in motherhood outweighs any of those circumstances.

We talk for a few more minutes and she seems to get off the phone sounding like the strong woman I knew she could be. If my journey can encourage just one person, then every bit of it was worth the struggle.

At a birthday party for Brandi's little boy, I notice Brandi's grandmother watching Navy. "I know someone who would have loved that little girl," she muses, her eyes never leaving the little spitfire darting around the room. Brandi's grandma and my grandma Tomi used to run around, and I'm sure she saw her through her darkest times. I smile, knowing she's right, and knowing the brightness and healing Navy's life has brought to us all.

When I found myself in my darkest times, I wrote letters to the people who mattered in my life. Letters asking for forgiveness and letters giving it. But there was one letter I didn't write while my heart was so heavy. One that it's time for me to write now.

Hunter,

Without you I would not have been blessed with the greatest role of my entire life, a mother—for that I am eternally grateful. Our daughter brings the goodness into the world that it so needed, that I needed. And a lot of her best traits, although I wish I could take credit for, are inherited from you.

However, as you know, motherhood for me looks a lot different than your American tradition. Many feelings of desperation and helplessness have surfaced as I've reflected on my story. But they have been outshined by feelings of pride and relief, and the awareness of how I've protected and provided for Navy Joan mostly on my own. The stockings at the White House, the years of un-acknowledgment, and the excluding of our daughter will raise questions for her someday. Those will be conversations for you to have with her and opportunities to make it right.

For a long time I have held resentment and given you the blame for the darkest times in my life, but those aren't yours to hold onto, those are my own. I know you have had your own dark moments in this life. Mental health is something that we as individuals have to take accountability for and seek help with. We have to dig ourselves out of the deep, dark hole our minds allow us to crawl into. I take responsibility for my own. You were never to blame. The reins to my life, my actions, and my consequences are in my own hands. The burden of those times is not yours to bear; in fact, you gave me my purpose and a love I've never known; a mother's love for her daughter.

My one regret through it all is wishing I could go back in time and give you your request in the last opportunity offered from Mr. Mesires to make things right off the record. There are things that I've gotten wrong, and this just may have been one of them. I was wrong. I understand the reservations you and your family may have. Had we communicated sooner, maybe we could have gotten on the same page and you wouldn't have missed some of the most precious years of our daughter's life, then she would have had your constant presence since she could remember.

I admire your ability to bounce back from all life's tragedies and mistakes. You could've given up and found a way to just walk away from everything, including our daughter, but you haven't. Keeping the genuine side of you while having to be strong is commendable to say the least.

You go above and beyond for Navy to know she is loved by her father and making up for lost time. The countless Zoom calls that make her day in the midst of congressional hearings, meetings with attorneys, and the weight of the world on your shoulders prove the type of father and person you can be.

The two of us have both been blessed with fathers who have been incredibly strong role models in our lives, molding us into the resilient individuals we are today, and I can see how you are becoming that for Navy. I can already see the fingerprints you are leaving on our little girl's heart, and I can't wait to see what your imprint on her life will be.

Sincerely,
Lunden

Epilogue

The solar eclipse is passing overhead, and we're standing in the center of the totality. The moon inches across the sun, and the world around us turns to night.

Navy sits on Pappy's lap, mesmerized by the sudden twilight and the chirping of confused cicadas. The darkness lasts for four minutes, until a sliver of sun breaks through, illuminating the sky. It's magical.

Hunter's been meeting with attorneys all day, and I can only hope it pays off and the investigations end once and for all for Navy's sake. She knows her daddy loves her and that he's super busy, and she understands that. It's our life, but she is thankful for every minute she spends with him.

My phone goes off and I hand it to Navy.

"Hey honey, did you see the eclipse?"

"Yes, Daddy! It got really dark, but it didn't last long, then the sun came out again."

"That's so neat. I love you, honey."

"I love you too, Daddy."

Times are changing for the better. The bond Navy is building with her dad is filling the void that once existed, and I'm learning to trust again that he will follow through. We're not entirely out of the shadows yet, but each day, I can see the sun growing brighter.

Life looks different for every individual who walks this earth. We all have demons that come in different shapes and sizes. I can't say I've fought off every demon on my back, but I've found the purpose in my life that's worth the fight every day.

For four minutes the moon covered the sun and blotted out the light, and in Navy's life the darkness lasted for four years. Every one of us faces the dark, and it takes everything we have to move through it. But darkness does not get the final say. Eventually the light will overcome.

Afterword

It's Monday afternoon as I'm writing the last lines of this story, marveling at how far things have come, and how the shadows are growing shorter in the brightening light. Then my phone buzzes. It's my attorney.

"Lunden, we've just been subpoenaed by the Department of Justice to testify on Hunter's tax dealings in the state of California. Get ready."

And here we go again. It's my life, but it isn't my first rodeo. After everything I've learned to this point, I've got this.

Acknowledgments

To my dad: Thank you for always being in my corner.

To my mom: Thank you for always pushing me.

It's by the love of you two that I'm able to exhibit the strength needed throughout my journey in life.

To the rest of my family, and my tribe (you know who you are): Thank you for always having my back and helping me build a solid foundation to raise my daughter upon.